The Practical Safety Guide To

Zero Harm

How to Effectively Manage Safety In The Workplace

Wayne G Herbertson, MSc.

www.practicalsafety.org

Published in Australia by The Value Organisation Pty Ltd,
PO Box 414, Salamander Bay, NSW, Australia, 2317.

Editors: J L Arnold, M Ravenhall, R Watson and P Smith.

Cover Photo: © jupiterimages 2008
Front Cover Design: Goulburn Valley Printing Services
Illustrations: Madelynne L Herbertson (13yrs old -Get Your Children
Involved in Safety)
Internal Graphic Design: A Pobie of Pobie Design

National Library of Australia Cataloguing-in-Publication Data

Author: Herbertson, Wayne, 1961-

Title: The Practical Safety Guide to Zero Harm: How to
               Effectively Manage Safety in The Workplace /
               Wayne G Herbertson.

ISBN: 9780980530209 (hbk.)
               9780980530216 (pbk)
               9780980530223 (pbk chinese)

Notes: Includes index.
               Bibliography.

Subjects: Industrial safety--Management
               Industrial hygiene—Management

Dewey Number: 363.11

E-mail queries to: cip@nla.gov.au
Telephone: (02) 6262 1458

DEDICATION

This book is dedicated to all those who have lost their lives in the course of their work.

To Neville Handreck a buddy who tragically lost his life in 2007, and whose death inspired me to complete this book. He was an exemplary engineer, an inspiration to all, a loyal friend, husband and father to 3 beautiful children.

To my father and mother who afforded me the opportunity to learn, and to my family, without whose support, I would not have completed this book.

To my work colleagues, I trust that the management of Safety becomes your passion to ensure no person ever suffers harm in the course of their work.

To all employees, look after your mates.

www.practicalsafety.org

Contents

FOREWORD v
ACKNOWLEDGEMENTS vii
PREFACE ix

1. ORGANIZATIONAL DESIGN 11

1.1 Introduction 11
1.2 External Environment 12
1.3 Outcomes 16
1.4 People 17
1.5 System Choices 21
    1.5.1 Unifying System Choices 23
    1.5.2 Differentiating System Choices 25
    1.5.3 Renewal System Choices 28
        1.5.3.1 Balanced Scorecard 28
        1.5.3.2 Linking Safety and Financial Benefits 34
        1.5.3.3 Transition Change Management 36
1.6 Conclusion 38

2. THE PRACTICAL SAFETY PROCESS® 39

2.1 Setting a Target and Ensuring Commitment and Involvement 42
    2.1.1 The Importance Active Involvement of Management 42
    2.1.2 Ensuring Commitment and Involvement 46
        2.1.2.1 Visioning Process 46
        2.1.2.2 Safety Values and Principles 49
        2.1.2.3 Safety Planning 51
        2.1.2.4 Allocation of Responsibility and Authority 52
        2.1.2.5 Consultative Process 56
        2.1.2.6 Communication Process 57
        2.1.2.7 Safety Goals and Objectives 61
2.2 Conclusion 61
2.3 Check Your Progress 63

3. STEP1-IDENTIFY HAZARDS AND ASSESS RISKS   64

    3.1 Practical Safety Approach to Hazard Identification   64
        and Risk Assessment
        3.1.1 Hazard Identification   64
        3.1.2 Risk Assessment   67
    3.2 Hazard and Risk Management Assessment   69
        Processes
    3.3 Conclusion   77
    3.4 Check Your Progress   78

4. STEP 2 - IDENTIFY DESIRED PEOPLE   79
REQUIREMENTS BSAFA®
    4.1 Conclusion   82
    4.2 Check Your Progress   83

5. STEP 3 - IDENTIFY COMPLIANCE   84
REQUIREMENTS
    5.1 Conclusion   86
    5.2 Check Your Progress   87

6. STEP 4 - ENSURE SAFE PHYSICAL WORK   92
ENVIRONMENT
    6.1 Conclusion   94
    6.2 Check Your Progress   95

7. STEP 5 - DEVELOP SAFE SYSTEMS OF WORK   98
    7.1 Safety Processes   98
    7.2 Writing Procedures   100
    7.3 Conclusion   103
    7.4 Check Your Progress   106

8. STEP 6 - ASSESS COMPETENCY   111
    8.1 Conclusion   121
    8.2 Check Your Progress   122

9. STEP 7 - MONITOR AND REVIEW   123
   PERFORMANCE

   9.1 Measuring and Reporting   123
   9.2 Auditing   128
   9.3 Observations   132
   9.4 Workplace Inspections   134
   9.5 Health Assessment   136
   9.6 Rehabilitation   137
   9.7 Incident Investigation   142
   9.8 Corrective Action   144
   9.9 Recognition   146
   9.10 Change Management   147
   9.11 Records Management   153
   9.12 Conclusion   154
   9.13 Check Your Progress   155

10. ESSENTIAL QUALITIES OF A SAFETY   157
   PROFESSIONAL

11. APPENDICES   160

12. REFERENCES   193

13. INDEX   195

14. RESOURCE CENTRE   201

www.practicalsafety.org

FOREWORD

In contemplating the contents of this book, one realizes the potential it contains to contribute to the reformation of attitudes on the job toward an environment of limiting if not eliminating physical harm in the workplace.

Through the proposition of marrying behavior to attitude, feelings and skills in the workforce, safety in the organisation can be lifted to its rightful place against the demanded outcomes of operational entities usually considered to be only financial success.

This publication lifts the consideration of zero harm in the workplace to be not only of equal importance, but in fact to be the driver of success for the enterprise, not only economically but also of good corporate behavior.

By patient demonstration this volume will assist management to arrive at and set values compatible with the installation of processes to build skills, set attitudes, and encourage pride across the workforce to deliver superior outcomes with respect to safety.

As demonstrated, a leadership focus extending from management through to individual team, and ultimately to total company commitment, can be put into practice to enable continuous improvement to occur through safety as a core value.

Regulation and risk control is becoming a subject of heightened focus by government authorities, and management obligations continue to be raised with appropriate penalties extracted for non compliance.

Procedures and processes to help the practitioner "continuously improve" his performance are laid out with clarity in this volume, having been developed and tested thoroughly by professionals having had many years experience in building up procedures to ensure compliance with the regulatory framework at the highest levels.

This volume is a must as a handbook and ready reference for all management seeking continuous improvement in safety maturity and leadership.

Dr Ian F Burston, AM

Fellow of Australian Institute of Company Directors
Fellow of Institution of Engineers, Australia
Fellow of Australian Institute of Mining & Metallurgy

ACKNOWLEDGEMENTS

This book would not have been possible without the organizational design teaching from P Gustavson of Organizational Planning and Design Inc. and the support and input from J Arnold of Emergency Management Planning Pty. Ltd.

www.practicalsafety.org

PREFACE

Safety influences every aspect of our lives. This book is designed to give practical safety guidance with respect to the what, and how questions that are often asked with regard to safety.

The book also contains anecdotes and examples about what has been successful and what has not from my own personal experiences. It is designed to give practical knowledge gained from working in the field of safety to support those people entrusted with safety management. It will particularly help those who are students of safety or who are new to safety as a profession and will also be a valuable guide to those who need basic safety knowledge as part of their supervisory or management role.

The management of safety is reviewed in both an organizational and situational landscape to provide the reader with a sense of how safety should be managed at senior management levels and in the workplace. There are various process flow diagrams and other illustrative media given throughout the book to describe what needs to be considered. These will direct the reader to important elements to consider from a practical safety point of view. The book is a product of experience across many jurisdictions however the reader should always consult the relevant local legislation and standards before any system implementation.

The writing style is more conversational than academic and technical. This means that all those who read the book will have little difficulty in interpreting the information it contains.

www.practicalsafety.org

1. ORGANIZATIONAL DESIGN

1.1 Introduction

It is important that the Safety Management System is integrated into the organization as a whole. It is impossible to be successful in improving safety if the Safety Management System is designed and developed in isolation from other parts of the organizations management system. To this end the safety professional must have a base understanding of other organizational systems and their points of integration. To help understand this it is often helpful to have a framework through which the organization can be examined. A simple framework is shown below in Fig 1.

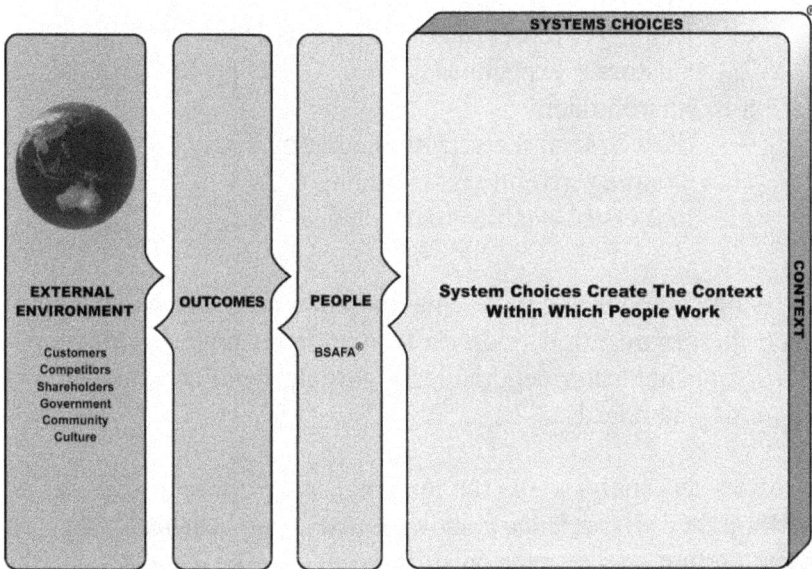

Fig 1 Organizational Framework.[7,8]

This framework can be used to help guide the organizational design and hence the Safety Management System design. Organizational design as a process will be discussed in some detail as its application is often little understood by safety professionals. Let's begin with an examination of the external environment.

1.2 External Environment

In any organizational design methodology it is essential to begin with an analysis of the external environment. This analysis is crucial in gaining an understanding of the:

1. Prevailing culture
2. Community where the organization/project is to be or is established
3. Local regulatory requirements
4. Regulators
5. Employee representative organizations
6. Employer representative organizations
7. Customer expectations
8. Shareholders
9. Skill base in the surrounding community
10. Training institutions including technical, trade and university establishments and so on..........

It is as much about understanding and embracing the world within which the organization finds itself in as it is about establishing a clear insight into non-negotiables regarding legal compliance and community standards.

So often an analysis of the external environment can be an afterthought. Experience shows that the earlier that an understanding of the external influences can be established, the better the organization can be prepared for deciding on the most appropriate strategies. Such strategies might vary from proactively trying to influence the external world to merely coping or reacting as it changes.

From a safety perspective it is of utmost importance to have an intimate understanding of the local legislation, acts and regulations, codes of practice, technical and other standards, industry guidelines and the expectations of the regulators. Legislation is particularly important as it establishes the minimum community expectations. The relevancy to the organization of such legislation must be known as early as possible to avoid unnecessary problems and costs. As a company there is no choice but to embrace these. However as stated earlier there is a choice about whether you wish to proactively influence future legislation by getting involved in standard committees, industry groups and like. Traditionally industry has not been very good at doing this but finds itself whining about the consequences of what evolves. There is a moral here, get involved.

Governments also must understand the impost that legislation can sometimes bring where within a single nation industry often finds different states, territory's, provinces, and local governments with different laws. This is a significant and unnecessary impost on industry and we need governments to minimize this unnecessary complexity and let industry get on with implementation of safety systems within a harmonized regulatory framework and a single regulatory body.

Benchmarking best practice also provides valuable insights for the organization. I've gleaned a lot of great ideas from many different industries just by asking to visit. I found this particularly useful in the early part of my career where I would set aside a day a month to visit another factory, mine or office. It's not all that hard to pick up the phone and organize something, and the rewards can be great. I found most people are willing to share information, especially when it comes to safety. When sitting down to decide what a safety management system should contain there are several standards available that can set you on the right path.

It is important to have a base understanding of the various company and proprietary safety management system elements. See Table 1. This evaluation provides an important input into the design of your own organizational system elements. It is important that your system design choices are aligned to your desired outcomes and culture. A common mistake by many organizations is to buy an off the shelf system and implement it without any due process or thought. This is often costly and often does not yield the desired results.

I see these systems as external benchmarks that can be used when designing the individual systems to be employed within your own organization and perhaps prompt your thinking. However it is very difficult to establish any form of ownership if the system is clearly someone else's. The system elements need to developed more from the individual organizational needs and the nature of the hazards involved.

Table 1. Safety Systems Element Comparisons

AS4801¹ — 24 Elements	BS18001² — 20 Elements	SafetyMAP³ — 12 Elements
4.2 OHS Policy	4.2 OHS Policy	1. Building and Sustaining Commitment
4.3.1 Planning Identification of hazards, risk assessment & control of risks	4.3 Planning	2. Documenting Strategy
	4.3.1 Planning for Hazard Identification risk assessment and risk control	3. Design and Contract Review
4.3.2 Legal and other requirements	4.3.2 Legal and other requirements	4. Document Control
4.4.3 Objectives and targets	4.4.3 Objectives	5. Purchasing
4.3.4 OHS management plans	4.3.4 OHS management programs	6. Working Safely By System
4.4.1 Structure and responsibility	4.4 Implementation and operation	7. Monitoring Standards
4.4.1.1 Resources	4.4.1 Structure and responsibility	8. Reporting and Correcting Deficiencies
4.4.1.2 Responsibility and accountability		
4.4.2 Training and competency	4.4.2 Training awareness and competence	9. Managing Movement and Materials
4.4.3 Consultation, communication and reporting	4.4.3 Consultation and communication	10. Collecting and Using Data
4.4.3.1 Consultation	4.4.4 Documentation	11. Auditing and Management Systems
4.4.3.2 Communication	4.4.5 Document and data control	12. Developing Skills and Competencies
4.4.3.3 Reporting	4.4.6 Operational control	
4.4.4 Documentation	4.4.7 Emergency preparedness and response	
4.4.5 Document and data control	4.5 Checking and corrective action	
4.4.6 Hazard Identification risk assessment and control of risks	4.5.1 Performance measurement and monitoring	
4.4.7 Emergency preparedness and response	4.5.2 Accidents, Incidents, non-conformances and corrective and preventive action	
4.5.1 Monitoring and measurement	4.5.3 Records and records management	
4.5.1.1 General	4.5.4 Audit	
4.5.1.2 Health surveillance	4.6 Management Review	
4.5.2 Incident investigation, corrective and preventive action.		
4.5.3 Records and records management		
4.5.4 OHSMS Audit		
4.6 Management Review		

1.3 Outcomes

Company outcomes for many years have been described more in terms of financial performance. Our understanding of business has now evolved to the point where this is no longer the case with environmental and community now seen as being important with the advent of triple bottom line reporting. The financial stock markets have embraced this emerging trend through the establishment of the Dow Jones Sustainability Index. Interestingly this new metric has financially outperformed the traditional Dow Jones Index illustrating that companies with financial, environmental and community emphasis can be better businesses overall. Business ethics is also another emerging issue with the failures of major corporations to protect people, property and the environment attracting major attention. This then leads to the question of where does safety fit into business outcomes?

Business outcomes determine the very essence of the organization, its purpose and hence its reason for being. If safety is not part of the desired outcomes for the organization then this presents a real problem for the safety professional and for the business. I often have used the principle that an organization must "Safely do what it says when it says". For me this encapsulates what we are all striving to achieve, "Zero Harm".

These outcomes go beyond the old goals of reducing lost time injuries. It describes a desired culture for the organization. It means that this organization wants a zero harm culture as an outcome. It's an embodiment of a will and desire at all levels of an organization to not adversely impact the individual, the community or the world within which we live.

For the safety profession this means that there is a need to understand how an organizational culture can be influenced and created. It begins with an understanding of people.

1.4 People

Every organizational outcome that is achieved must go through people. Without people an organization is merely an empty shell of equipment and buildings. The interactions of people together with their surroundings determine the culture within which work is done.

The importance of desired behaviors being defined has been researched by many organizations including Dupont and most notably by Thomas Krause[4, 5] and Scott Geller[6] in recent years. This has resulted in a "behavioral safety movement". In practice I have found that behavior alone is not the answer. Care needs to be taken not to over emphasize one aspect of safety at the expense of the other. A balanced and measured approach is required.

The way people behave, feel, and use their skills will determine whether outcomes are achieved, and how well or easily they are achieved. For example it is unlikely that an outcome will be achieved if a person comes to work disliking everything about their work even if they have the skills or physical attributes to do the job. Therefore in evaluating desired outcomes there needs to be a link made to people in terms of their:

1. **Behaviors** - What desired behaviors are required to deliver the outcomes

2. **Skills** - What qualifications, competencies and knowledge are required to deliver the outcomes

3. **Attitude** - A person's thoughts and motivations

4. **Feelings** - What general feelings will enhance the achievement of outcomes

5. **Attributes** - What are the physical attributes required (if any) to do the work

I define these as the "BSAFA®" requirements for people to deliver outcomes. These need to be determined carefully for each desired outcome. For example if the desired outcome is Zero Harm then the desired BSAFA®s need to be determined to achieve this. These might include such things as those shown in Table 2.

Table 2: Example Determining BSAFA®s

BSAFA®s	
B (Behavior)	Able to confront colleagues Follows procedures Looks to improve Care for each other
S (Skills)	Able to identify hazards Can assess risks in terms of likelihood and consequence Can apply the risk control hierarchy Knows escalation procedure Understand laws and standards relating to job Knows where to find information
A (Attitude)	Safety is core value Goals aligned
F (Feelings)	Proud to work here Contented Motivated, etc
A (Attributes)	Average fitness Has 20/20 vision Not color blind Caring for disabled

This is by no means an exhaustive list but merely an example of the process. At the macro organizational level the requirements can be quite broadly defined. In determining the BSAFA®s it is important to have the right people involved to arrive at the best outcome. This normally includes the whole management team as a minimum requirement. It also means that the current state of the organization needs to be put aside. This exercise is about looking at a future state with a totally open mind. The transition to this future state will be dealt with later.

At the workplace level the BSAFA®s should be determined specifically for the task. Unlike the macro determination these task specific BSAFA® requirements need to be carefully evaluated and researched to achieve the desired result. This will be discussed in chapter 4 in more detail. For now I want to concentrate on the macro organizational level so that you gain an understanding of the basic design process.

Once the BSAFA®s have been determined for each of the desired outcomes the design process can begin by developing Design Principles from the BSAFA®s. The easiest way to do this is by asking the question, "My people will ….. (insert BSAFA®)…… when what?" Taking "able to identify hazards" from the Table 2 above, the question would be written as, "my people will be able to identify hazards when what……?" The answers might be when:

a. They know what a hazard is,
b. They are involved in the hazard identification, risk assessment, and control of risk process,
c. They are recognized for doing so,
d. It's acceptable to do so,
e. There is a process for reporting hazards etc.

The answers to these questions provide the organization with a comprehensive checklist of Design Principles that can aid in determining organizational design choices. However before they can be used these Design Principles must be checked for alignment. i.e. do they all support one another? If the fundamental

Design Principles are not aligned at this stage then there is no point in using them for making important design choices. It is often beneficial to use an "Alignment Choice Table" to facilitate this process. See Table 3

Table 3: Example Alignment Choice Table

Desired Outcome	BSAFA®	Design Principle (My people will …insert BSAFA®…. when what?)	? Conflict
Zero Harm	1. Able to identify hazards	a. They know what a hazard is, b. Are involved in the hazard identification, risk assessments and control of risk process, c. They are recognized for doing so, d. When it's acceptable to do so, e. When there is a process for reporting hazards f. There is money to spend on controls .	2 c.
Maximize Profit	2. Minimize Costs	a. Approved budgets b. Transparent reporting c. Rewarded for meeting budget	1f.

From the example in Table 3 it shows a potential conflict between the desire to spend money on safety controls and rewarding people individually for meeting budgets. This conflict will require a shift in the design principle in either or both outcome areas to ensure no misalignment. It might also lead to a new Design Principle being created.

It is important to remember that the Design Principle list is not exhaustive and that it can be revisited, especially if the desired results are not being achieved. A realignment exercise must be actioned as this occurs.

What does become apparent is that a clear set of Design Principles have now been created for the management team to consider when making design choices. These design choices need to support the desired BSAFA®s in people which are linked to achieving the desired business outcomes.

By undertaking this exercise the organization has defined a set of Design Principles for the desired future state. Also by reviewing the Design Principle list created it is also possible to distill out some core Design Principles and even distill some Core Values for the organization.

1.5 System Choices

The role of management is to make choices that deliver the desired business outcomes. Some of these choices relate to the design of the organizational systems that create the context within which work is done. These choices are critical in determining not only what systems will be deployed but also what culture will develop as a result of these choices. So often people are constrained with systems that are either outdated, or systems that actually make outcome achievement more difficult.

In the previous section we reviewed the need for Design Principles and how they are determined. It's now time to make some organizational Design Choices using these Design Principles as a guide. Let's review the example that we have been using. Table 4 shows the desired outcome, the BSAFA® and the resulting Design Principle that will aid in the Design Choice.

Table 4: BSAFA® Design Choice Table

Desired Outcome	BSAFA®	Design Principle (My people will ...insert BSAFA®.... when what?)	Design Choices
Zero Harm	1.Able to identify hazards etc	a. They know what a hazard is,	i. Hazard identification and risk control training for all personnel. ii. Areas clearly marked and signposted
		b. They are involved in the hazard identification process,	iii. Common hazard identification process involving consultation at all levels.
		c. They are recognized for doing so,	iv. Hazard Identification and Risk control is part of bonus scheme.
		d. When it's acceptable to do so,	v. Hazard Identification and risk control suggestion scheme
		e. When there is a process for reporting hazards	vi. Standard hazard reporting system/form
		f. There is a safety budget	vii. Safety included in general ledger to provide for budgeting and tracking costs

In making the Design Choices the right people must be involved. This should include the management team, required specialists and any other appropriate personnel. These design teams may vary in size and composition depending on what choices are being made. It is important to remain flexible and open to suggestions. In the example the Design Choices relate to the one outcome, zero harm. It is important to recognize that in an organizational context that there will be many Design Choices made, and that there may be more than one Design Choice made against a Design Principle. Again an alignment exercise needs to be carried out on all the proposed choices to ensure that no potential conflict exists.

Once all the choices have been determined attention now turns to the organizational systems that are impacted. An organizational model is often useful when conducting this exercise. The model depicted in Fig 2. is one that I have adapted from various sources over the years.[7,8] The important thing to note is that the Design Choices made by management create the context within which work is to be carried out. Safety is an integral part of the organization and therefore cannot be seen in isolation but as part of the whole organizational system.

In this model there are 3 major systems choices shown, Unifying, Differentiating, and Renewal Systems choices. These will be examined in more detail in the following chapters.

1.5.1 Unifying System Choices

Unifying systems are those things that bind an organization together, define its distinctive competency and set its direction. The Unifying System has 3 elements:

1. Vision
2. Values and Principles
3. Mission

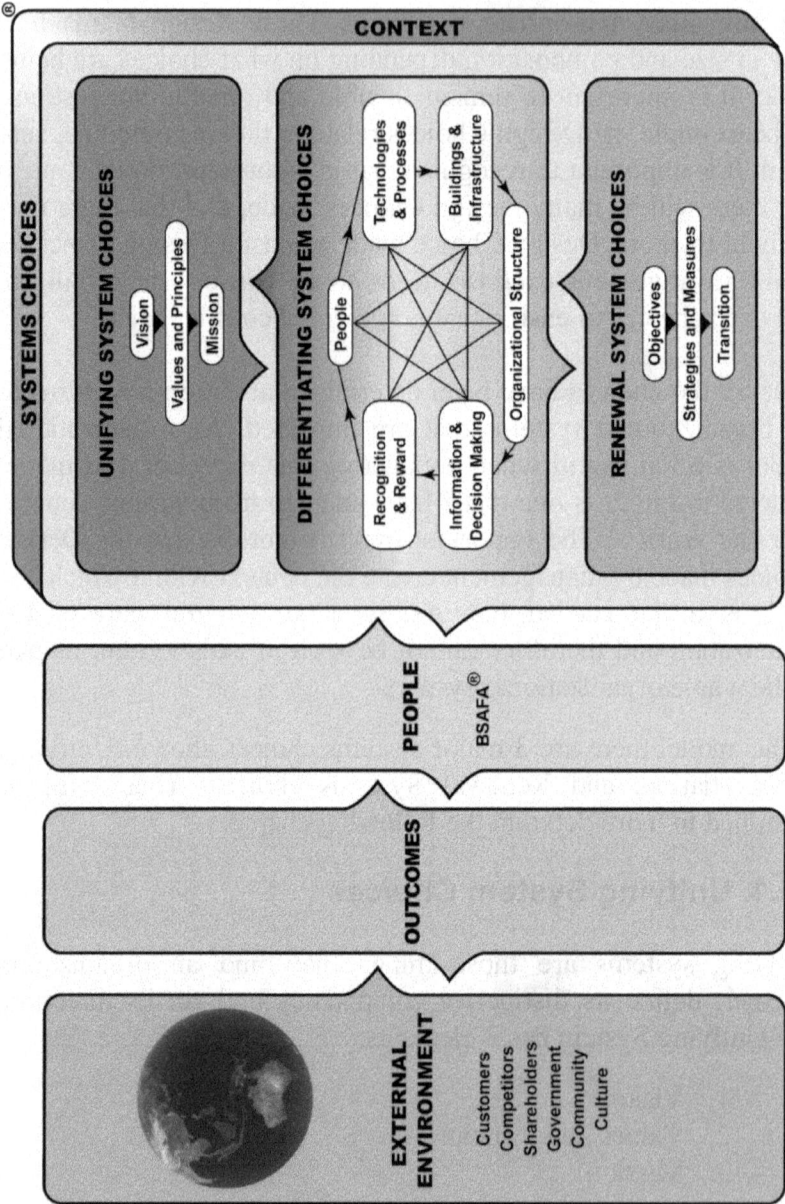

Fig 2 Organizational Model Showing Systems

The Vision describes the organizations ultimate reason for being and the Mission describes how the organization expects to get there. These elements are normally set at executive level and the safety professional may have limited input. However this does not stop the safety professional from developing a safety vision and mission in consultation with the executive team. Far too often safety professionals have no idea what they are striving to achieve, or worse still do not have the support of the executive team for their safety vision. An Organization without a Vision and Mission is like having a ship without a destination or rudder! There is a need to have a desired future state otherwise the transition to get there cannot be mapped.

The Organizational Values and Principles are essential in describing the desired culture of an organization. They can be derived from the earlier work described in establishing the BSAFA®s, but more often than not, they have evolved over time in many organization. They are often proudly posted on walls but really have no link to the desired outcomes. A Value and Principle led organization is one where the management and employees have embodied the Values and Principles to such an extent that they use them in every day decision making and conversation. They are not merely written and placed on a wall but embody the organizational culture. These are discussed further in chapter 2.4

1.5.2 Differentiating System Choices

Having completed the background work of establishing the BSAFA®s, the unifying system and the design choices resulting from this preliminary work, it is important to map these choices into the differentiating systems that are core to the organization. In this system there are 6 important components.

1. People System – This system deals with examining the BSAFA® requirements and how people are recruited, inducted, assimilated and trained

2. Technologies and Processes – This system describes the technologies to be employed along with the required business processes to support the BSAFA® and desired business outcomes...

3. Buildings and Infrastructure – In this system the required facilities are examined.

4. Organizational Structure – This system defines how people are organised to achieve outcomes.

5. Information and Decision Making System – This system defines how and what decisions are made, what information is needed to make them and how this information is captured stored and distributed.

6. Recognition and Reward – This system examines how personnel are formally and informally rewarded.

If we take the design choices made from Table 4 on page 22 it is important to know what organizational systems might be impacted. In this way we can map choices against the system design elements. This can be done as shown in Table 5.

The result is that systems have been designed to support the BSAFA®. In completing the action table it clearly shows the system impacts from the decisions that have been made. It also demonstrates that in the area of safety a Safety Professional cannot work in isolation. It's as much about cultural integration as it is about applying processes.

Table 5. Design Choice Action Summary Table

Differentiating System Impacted	Design Choices	Responsibility	Due Date
People	Hazard identification, Risk assessments and control training for all personnel	Joe	10/06/08
Technologies and Processes	Common hazard identification and hazard reporting system/form	Fred	12/09/08
Buildings and Infrastructure	Areas clearly marked and signposted	Harry	04/04/08
Organizational Structure	Safety consultation at all levels	Christine	05/06/08
Information and Decision Making	Safety included in general ledger to provide for budgeting and tracking costs. System in place to track training planned versus delivered	Henry Henry	13/02/08 15/12/08
Recognition and Reward	Hazard identification and risk control is part of bonus scheme. Hazard identification and risk control suggestion scheme	Sue Sue	01/02/08 04/04/08

1.5.3 Renewal System Choices

The renewal system looks at the systems required to develop strategies, set objectives and measure the transition to the future desired state. Whilst organizational strategic development is the work of the senior management group all parts of the organization are involved in developing strategies and examining performance at some level. The safety professional must be able to link their strategies to that of the organization. To do this it is important that safety is part of the strategic planning cycle of the organization. See Fig 3.

In this example the safety and environmental audits and statistical reports form part of the strategic planning cycle inputs. Without this and other inputs the annual renewal and planning cycle within the business can turn into an annual budget process. Who would board a plane that flew with only a single measuring instrument? Sounds like an absurd question, but why do so many companies still operate with finance as the only or primary input to their renewal and strategic planning.

1.5.3.1 Balanced Scorecard

A tool often helpful in ensuring that safety is discussed as part of strategic planning is the "Balanced Scorecard". [9, 10] This can be very effective in ensuring that "people" are considered in the strategic planning process.

Whilst there are different forms of its application they all generally have a people component. See Fig 4. As a guide there are normally four components to a scorecard:

1. Customers
2. Financial
3. People
4. Business processes

Planning Cycle Objectives		Jun	Jul	Aug	Sep	Oct	Nov	Dec	Jan	Feb	Mar	Apr	May
Where are we now? Where do we want to be?	Strategic Planning Cycle			**Gather Information** Budget Performance Data / External Customer Survey / Internal Customer Survey / Employee Attitude Survey / Company safety Audit / Company Environmental Audit / Safety Statistics / Environmental Statistics / Organizational Self Assessment			Analyze Survey Information and Define Improvement Projects		**Corporate Planning** Senior Management Seminar		Information Presented To Board	Operating Budgets and Target Figures Summarized	Communicate Strategies and Budgets to Employees
How will we get there? Who will do that?	Business Planning and Annual Budget Process	Individual Employee Scorecards Developed Through Employee Dialogue	New Incentive Plans Effective					Input From Board Prior to Preparing New Year Business Plan	Corporate Scorecard Effective	Business Scorecards; These are prepared for business units as detailed functional action plans to achieve strategy			
How are we going?	Quarterly Business Reviews		Year End Review			Business Quarterly Review			Business Quarterly Review			Business Quarterly Review	

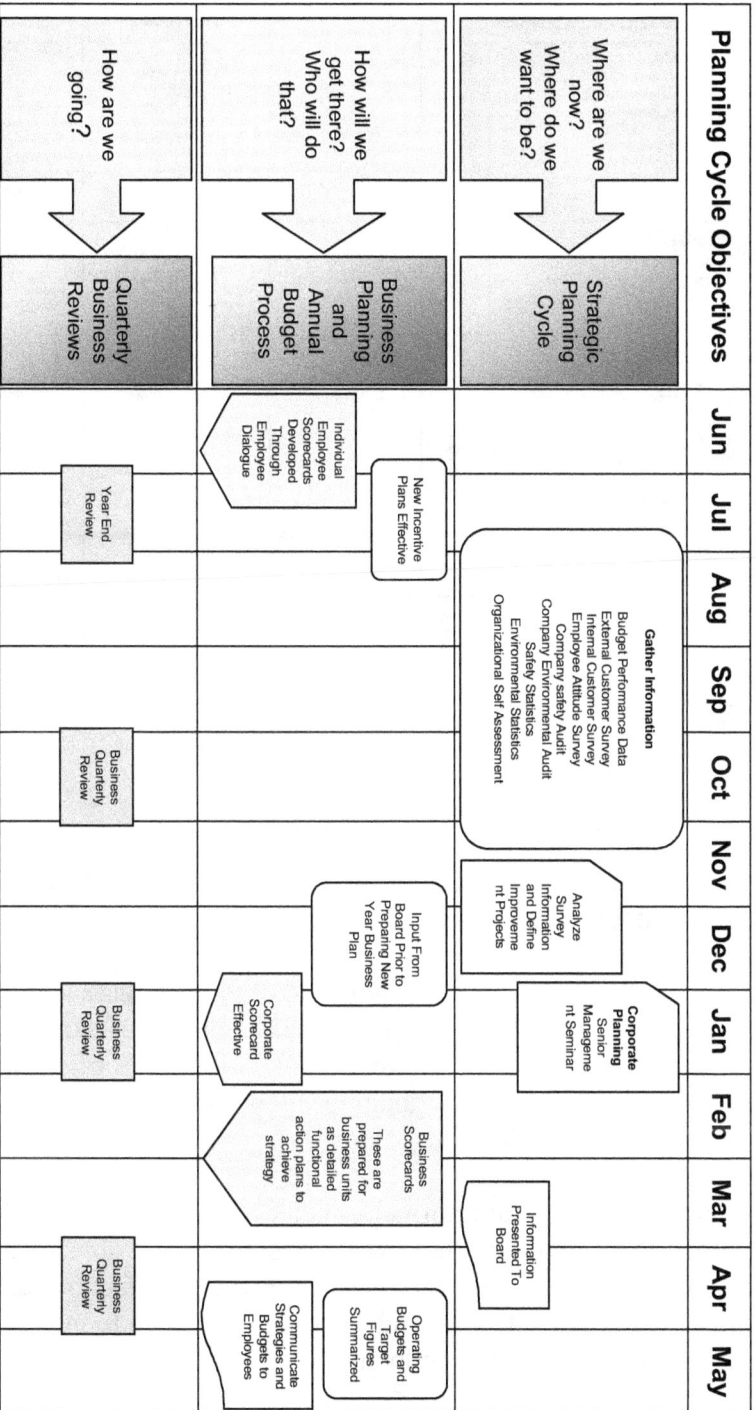

Note: This chart is based on a June ending financial year

Fig. 3. Example Strategic Planning Calendar With Safety Components Included

SCORECARD 2008-09		BUSINESS OBJECTIVES	STRATEGIES	MEASUREMENTS
VISION To be the best of the best in our chosen markets	**FINANCIAL**	15% EBITDA improvement	Decrease business assets Increase productivity and business volume to improve NOPAT Add to product and service portfolio Increase local value add Make acquisitions as appropriate	EBITDA increase 15%
MISSION To deliver shareholder and customer value through our people and safe work processes.	**CUSTOMERS**	Add value to our customer's business	Develop integrated solutions in line with customers needs through focused account management and strategic partnerships	Customer satisfaction index improved by 10%
		Improve customer contact to the business	Implement centralized hotline service Improve customer data acquisition and storage	Hotline in place CRM system in place
		Utilize regional resources	Empower regional managers to deploy resources to implement strategies Leverage knowledge capital of the group through share portal	Regional sales volumes increased by 15% Share portal utilized
VALUES Zero harm to anything anywhere anytime Ethical behavior Loyalty Courage Initiative and drive Focus Learning and Improvement Respect Sustainability	**PEOPLE**	Assure the commitment of employees to business objectives	Enhance internal objective communication Develop business unit and	Communicates held quarterly Scorecards in place at all levels 10% Employee survey satisfaction
		Improve employee satisfaction	**Protect employee safety and wellbeing through:** • **Management commitment** • **Employee involvement**	**a. 4% management time spent doing observations** **b. % Employees involved in risk assessment** **% Improvement in safety statistics**
		Improve employee capability	Review flexible work and benefit arrangements Enhance management and employee competence and performance	HR development plans in place Training in place Performance reviews show enhanced performance
	BUSINESS PROCESSES	Improve productivity	Implement model for Business Excellence by applying AQC methodology throughout the organization	Organizational assessment to show continuous improvement towards the business excellence award level

Fig 4 Example Scorecard

The scorecard requires that all four areas be discussed as part of the strategic planning process of the organization[8].

For each of the four components described there are business objectives, strategies and measurements required. The organizational vision, mission and values are often included. Some scorecards also include other components such as a responsibility or due date column.

Safety objectives are normally included in the people or business processes areas. In the example shown the objective of the organization was to improve employee satisfaction under the people component. The strategy to be employed to achieve this is to improve safety and wellbeing.

It is important to realize that one scorecard does not exist in isolation. To implement this method of objective setting there are normally at least 3 levels.

1. Company Scorecard (as in the example)
2. Divisional/Business Unit Scorecard
3. Individual Employee Scorecards

These 3 scorecards are interrelated and alignment of objectives is crucial for successful implementation.

At its very simplest, alignment can be achieved as shown in Fig. 5[11] following. The alignment is demonstrated by the linkage of strategy to objectives at the various levels of scorecards. i.e. Strategies from the corporate scorecard become the objectives of the business unit scorecards and the strategies of the business unit scorecards become the objectives for the individual employee. This ensures that all objectives are aligned to overall company objectives. This methodology is very powerful in achieving objective alignment and traceability as the cascade of objectives multiplies as move down through the various levels of the organization.

The safety professional must therefore ensure that safety data is provided to the strategic planning group to ensure that safety objectives and strategies are adequately addressed at the company level. Failure to do so will mean that there will be no safety objectives to cascade, and therefore safety will not be on the planning agendas of any level of the organization. This will result in safety not being seen as important and hence it will not receive the attention required to achieve the desired outcomes. When the system is applied correctly the company scorecard will lead to business units and individuals having corresponding objectives that relate to safety. See example in Fig.6[12]. This methodology is very effective in ensuring alignment of strategies and objectives. Used correctly it can be a very useful ally to the safety professional.

Corporate Scorecard			
	Objectives	Strategies	Measures
Financial			
Customers			
People			
Business Processes			

Business Unit Scorecard			
	Objectives	Strategies	Measures
Financial			
Customers	Corporate Strategy Leads To Business		
People			
Business Processes			

Individual Employee Scorecard			
	Objectives	Strategies	Measures
Financial			
Customers	Business Unit Strategy Leads To Individuals		
People			
Business Processes			

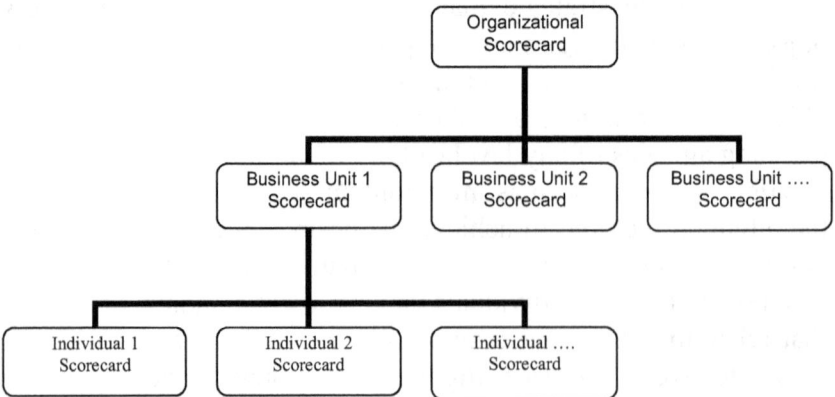

Organizational Scorecard

Business Unit 1 Scorecard

Business Unit 2 Scorecard

Business Unit .... Scorecard

Individual 1 Scorecard

Individual 2 Scorecard

Individual .... Scorecard

Fig 5 Strategy Alignment through Multiple Organizational Layers

Corporate Scorecard

	Objectives	Strategies	Measures
People	Zero Harm	Provide safeguards and training	Safety Scorecard = Zero Harm

Business Unit Scorecard

	Objectives	Strategies	Measures
People	Provide safeguards and training	a. Conduct training needs analysis and develop and implement safety training course b. Conduct Risk assessments c. Prioritise actions	a. Training plan versus training delivered b. % risk assessments completed c. % Actions completed

Individual Scorecard

	Objectives	Strategies	Measures
People	a. Conduct training needs analysis and develop and implement safety training course b. Conduct Risk assessments c. Prioritise actions	a. Engage contractor to conduct needs analysis and provide training b. develop risk assessment methods c. Develop and schedule risk assessment training d. Schedule assessments e. Actions prioritized and monitored at management meetings	a. Training contract signed June 09 b. Method available Jan 09 c. Training completed Feb 09 d. Assessments completed Dec 09 e. Agenda item included in management meetings Mar 09

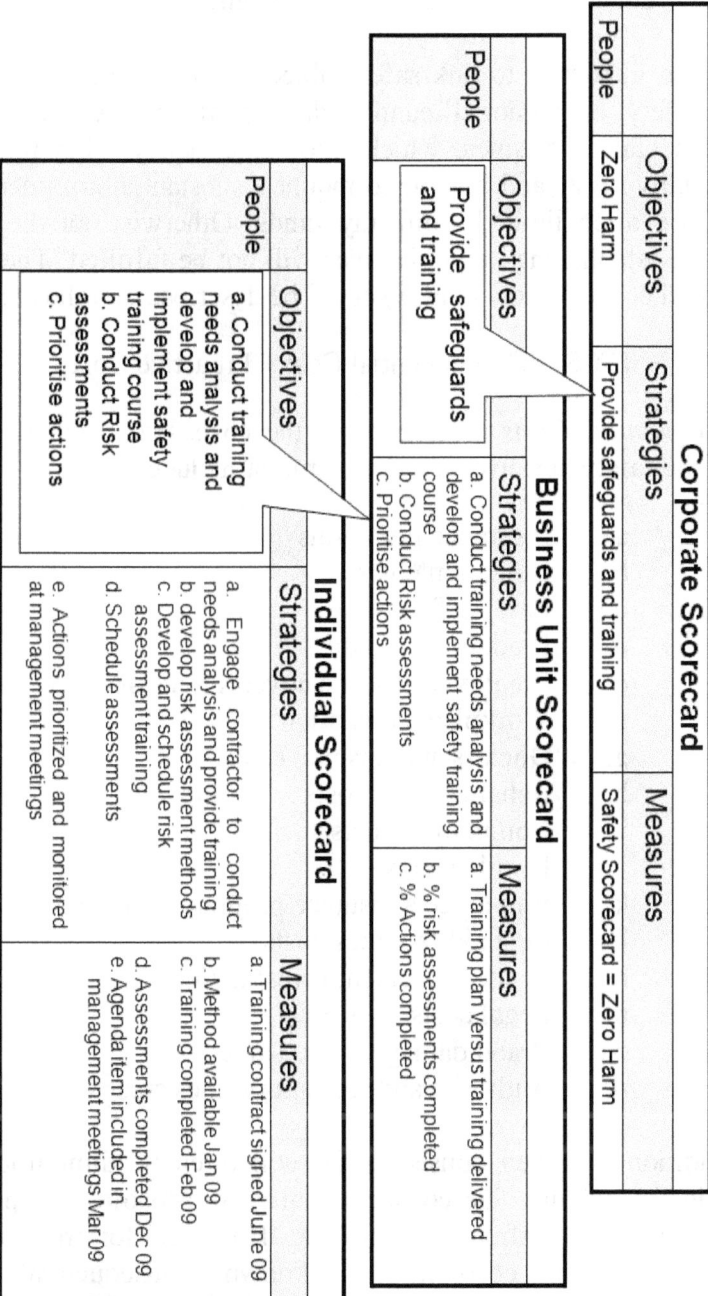

Fig 6 Example Scorecard Strategy Cascade

1.5.3.2 Linking Safety and Financial Benefits

It is also important to link safety objectives to financial benefits. The safety professional cannot divorce themselves from the fundamentals of business which is to make money. They must be financially savvy and be able to mount a substantial argument for what are often limited Company funds. Otherwise all the hard work in establishing key objectives will not be fulfilled. The total financial cost of safety (TFCS) could be described as follows:

$$TFCS = Consequential\ Cost + Proactive\ Cost$$

Consequential Costs – These are the costs that result directly from the safety performance. These might include:

a. Insurance premiums
b. Litigation costs
c. Lawyer fees
d. Productivity losses
e. Employee absence coverage costs
f. Workplace disruption costs
g. Doctors and hospital costs
h. Rehabilitation costs
i. Community costs
j. Family Costs
k. Employee assistance program costs
l. First aid facilities costs
m. Incident accident investigations costs
n. Legal costs
o. Brand damage – loss sales
p. Authority and regulatory fines etc.

In addition a hidden consequential will often be diminution of morale throughout. The consequential costs can often be poorly quantified and difficult to collate. However for the safety professional these costs must be known. Consequential costs should reduce as safety performance improves. This linkage is vital to establish with management when arguing for funds for proactive measures. There should also be some accountability to ensure that these savings are realized.

Proactive Costs – These are the costs associated with implementing proactive safety. These costs include:

   a. Safety training costs
   b. Competency assessment costs
   c. Risk assessment time
   d. Work instruction costs
   e. Expenditure on risk controls such as guarding, PPE
   f. Medical testing costs
   g. Environmental testing costs
   h. Recruitment testing costs etc.

Interestingly I have not seen any studies that make a correlation between consequential and proactive costs and safety performance. From my experience in business the consequential costs are generally much higher than proactive costs.

In mounting an argument for funding the safety professional must be prepared to argue a budget for proactive cost increases and improved safety performance versus a lowering of consequential costs as a benefit. Hence there is no net change to the TFCS, just a change in emphasis on where the funds are to be spent. This makes decision making much easier. It's often a case of arguing whether to put the money that you would have normally spent on dealing with consequences, (some of which can be very high indeed) to actually doing something much more proactive which will positively affect safety and ultimately productivity. The securing of this commitment to the zero harm objective and the funding to achieve it is fundamental to the safety professionals peer position within the management structure.

1.5.3.3 Transition – Change Management

A management of change system demands a disciplined process to strictly control additions, modifications and deletions within the organization. This is the area where most organizations fail. This failure is not normally through lack of ideas but rather through lack of consultation, planning and execution. It's action that counts, and thus to be effective in change management requires strong accountability combined with effective and disciplined monitoring. The balanced scorecard described previously can help in this regard.

The planning and execution of change also requires commitment at all levels with respect to consultation, training and instruction to all who will be affected by any change. With respect to safety this consultation and communication is of paramount importance and is integral to compliance with performance based health and safety legislation. Input by operational, maintenance and other personnel will have a positive effect on the outcomes of change. These outcomes should result in improvement and hence change also needs to be evaluated for effectiveness.

Industry is littered with poorly planned changes to the work environment that have had an adverse effect on safety. Expediency for the quick solution pressured by operational and financial considerations often negates the opportunity for consultation and planning which ultimately yields a poor result.

Fig 7 Valve Adjustment in walkway[13]

The illustration in Fig 7. shows a shut off valve handle that has been added after initial installation of the walkway. It demonstrates all the things that have been spoken about. The installation demonstrates the failure to perform hazard identification and risk assessment at all levels including designer, installer, supplier and employer. It's added the hazards of tripping, slipping, falling and striking and also demonstrates lack of planning and consultation and compliance considerations. Not only could this result in harm to an employee but also the employer has no longer provided a work environment that is safe and without risk to health as required by legislation.

Change management processes are crucial for success. The practical safety approach to this is to analyze proposed changes thoroughly through consultative processes and summarize observations, recommendations and actions utilizing a standard observation, recommendation and action (ORA) form. See Fig 8

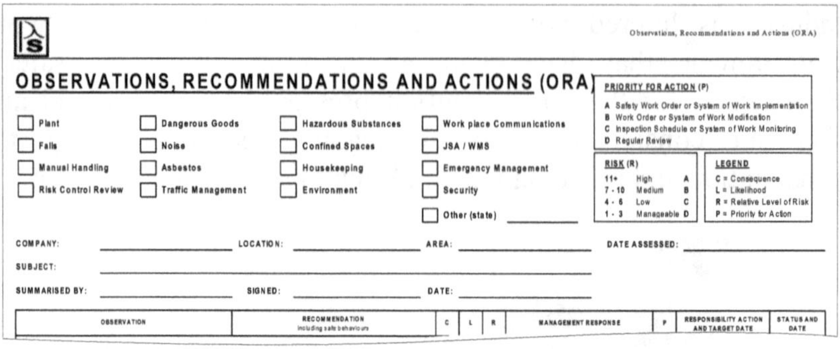

Observations, Recommendations and Actions (ORA)

OBSERVATIONS, RECOMMENDATIONS AND ACTIONS (ORA)

PRIORITY FOR ACTION (P)
A Safety Work Order or System of Work Implementation
B Work Order or System of Work Modification
C Inspection Schedule or System of Work Monitoring
D Regular Review

☐ Plant ☐ Dangerous Goods ☐ Hazardous Substances ☐ Work place Communications
☐ Falls ☐ Noise ☐ Confined Spaces ☐ JSA / WMS
☐ Manual Handling ☐ Asbestos ☐ Housekeeping ☐ Emergency Management
☐ Risk Control Review ☐ Traffic Management ☐ Environment ☐ Security
☐ Other (state) ________

RISK (R)
11+ High A
7 - 10 Medium B
4 - 6 Low C
1 - 3 Manageable D

LEGEND
C = Consequence
L = Likelihood
R = Relative Level of Risk
P = Priority for Action

COMPANY: ________ LOCATION: ________ AREA: ________ DATE ASSESSED: ________
SUBJECT: ________
SUMMARISED BY: ________ SIGNED: ________ DATE: ________

OBSERVATION	RECOMMENDATION including safe behaviours	C	L	R	MANAGEMENT RESPONSE	P	RESPONSIBILITY ACTION AND TARGET DATE	STATUS AND DATE

Fig 8 ORA Form

This form is used throughout the Practical Safety Process to manage the change process in a very simple way. It asks the user to note the observation made and the associated relative level of risk in a disciplined identification process. Recommendations are then made based on the risk control hierarchy (see Table 7 pg 102) and priorities are assigned for action. Management is then able to respond to these recommendations to ensure support is forthcoming, responsibilities are defined and completion dates assigned.

The system that you use needs to be accessible to all and simple enough for all levels of the organization to use. To achieve credibility it must be monitored to ensure commitments are being met in terms of completion dates.

1.6 Conclusion

Organizational design is critical to the success of the safety effort. Design Choices must be aligned to the desired objectives and be supported through the allocation of responsibility for achievement throughout the organization. As Design Choices are changed these need to be communicated effectively through a robust change management process. This is fundamental to the successful implementation of the Practical Safety Process.

2. THE PRACTICAL SAFETY PROCESS

From the previous chapter it is clear that without management commitment then very little can be achieved in the practical application of safety. This commitment is more than just a policy statement but is embodied in the very culture of the organization and the organizational processes that support it.

Therefore it is also important to gain an understanding of what the core safety process is. The management systems fraternity saw the importance of defining organizational processes with the advent of the ISO9000-2000 Quality Management Systems Standard[14] where processes became the core issue for definition rather than prescribing management system elements. The advantage was described as, "providing ongoing control over the linkage between individual processes within the system of processes". But what does this mean for safety? Firstly there is a need to understand the core safety process and, secondly having understood this, how does this process fit within the overall management systems of the organization.

From a practical safety point of view this brings us to the point where we must understand the fundamental process steps that need to be in place to accomplish zero harm. This I have defined as the "Practical Safety Process." This process is represented in the Practical Safety Process Model shown in fig.9.

THE PRACTICAL SAFETY PROCESS®

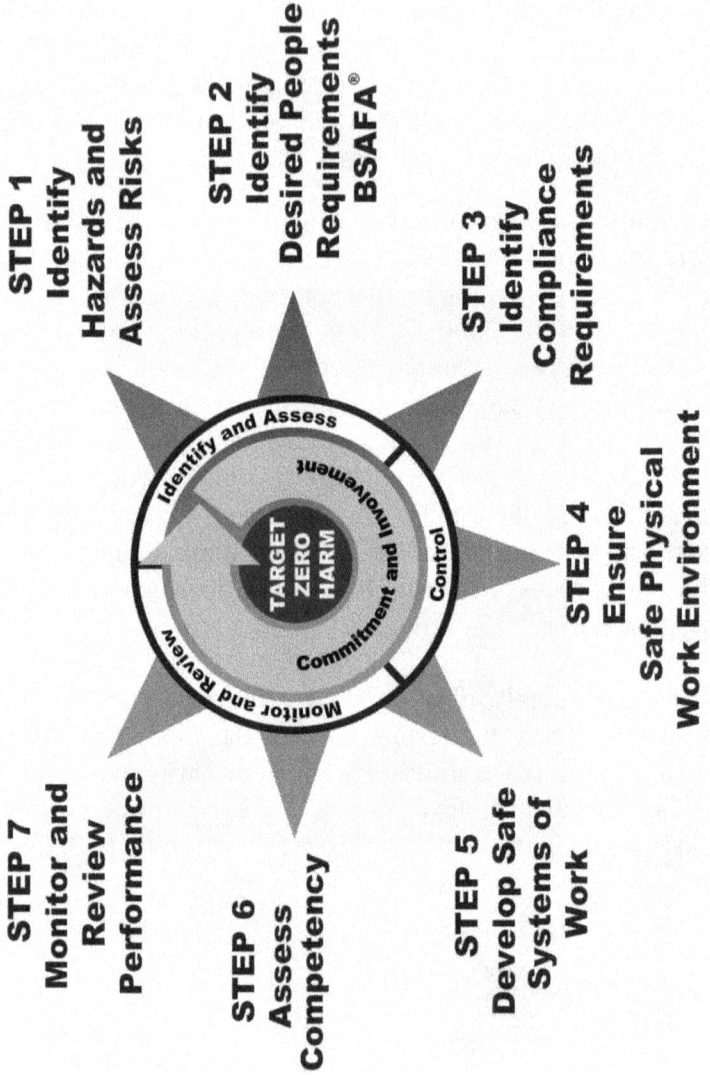

STEP 1
Identify
Hazards and
Assess Risks

STEP 2
Identify
Desired People
Requirements
BSAFA®

STEP 3
Identify
Compliance
Requirements

STEP 4
Ensure
Safe Physical
Work Environment

STEP 5
Develop Safe
Systems of
Work

STEP 6
Assess
Competency

STEP 7
Monitor and
Review
Performance

Identify and Assess

Commitment and Involvement

Control

Monitor and Review

TARGET
ZERO
HARM

Fig 9 Practical Safety Process Model®

As shown there are 2 Fundamentals represented by the inner circles:

1. A Target Zero Harm and,
2. Commitment and Involvement

These are deemed to be the fundamentals because they lie at the core of the cultural requirements for effective safety management. Without a target, commitment or involvement by all, effort will be wasted and the target will be unattainable. In addition a willingness and desire to embrace change will be key cultural attributes.

The outside circles represent seven process steps:

Step 1. Identify Hazards and Assess Risks

Step 2. Identify The Desired People Requirements BSAFA®

Step 3. Identify Compliance Requirements

Step 4. Ensure Safe Physical Work Environment

Step 5. Develop Safe Systems of Work

Step 6. Assess Competency

Step 7. Monitor and Review Performance

The Practical Safety Process will be discussed in detail in the following chapters.

2.1   Setting a Target and Ensuring Commitment and Involvement

2.1.1 The Importance of Active Involvement of Management

The two fundamentals are described by the core of the model as a target of zero harm, and commitment and involvement. These fundamentals are the hardest issues to address because they go to the essence of the culture of the organization, and the willingness of all personnel to address safety issues. In chapter one the importance of organizational design was discussed in detail. Organizationally the process starts with the senior management group establishing a target. This target underpins all subsequent choices. As I have never met anyone who has a desire to be injured, I believe there can only be one target and that is Zero Harm. As a philosophical target this can be extended beyond safety to include community and environment.

The commitment of management and the involvement of all employees in a sustained effort to achieve this target are the foundation stones of a company culture that has safety as an underlying value. It also means that the management behavior demonstrates commitment, and that all personnel at all levels are involved. Having a clear target and demonstrated commitment at all levels must underpin all steps in the safety process. Applying the principles of organizational design to the safety process is a valuable exercise in defining the essential design choices required for support. These choices result in controls or barriers to harm being advocated and implemented. See chapter 1.

I strongly support measuring management commitment. It can be measured in various ways, often reluctantly I might add. However over the years I have seen strong correlations with safety performance and commitment. One of the easiest ways of doing this is to observe and record the amount of quality time management spend in safety related tasks and ratio this over the total time available.

In major engineering projects I correlated this time spent and found that unless supervision and management were spending at least 4% of their time in safety related activity then a lost time injury would result. This is not just any time, but quality time as measured by involvement in tangible safety activities including audits, observations, safety committees, toolboxes and other methods of workplace safety communication. The largest correlation appeared to be with observation time spent. The old saying of "management by walking around," or "you get what you inspect, not what expect" seems to ring especially true when it comes to safety. Why? Because demonstrated commitment by management is essential. Their behavior sets the tone for the whole organizational culture and demonstrates their commitment to the safety target, the systems, each other, and the behavior necessary to achieve zero harm. In safety circles we often use the phrase, "you get the level of safety that you are prepared to walk past."

A few years ago I remember seeing a cultural journey map that showed the essential steps required to transition to a more mature safety culture. Whilst I am unclear of the source I have adapted the original journey map as shown in Fig. 10, as I believe it gives some valuable insights. To have nothing in place means that we are reliant on natural instincts and the expectation is that injury rates will be high. As management demonstrates their commitment then individuals and eventually teams will follow as peer pressure builds and the culture matures. However any inconsistency by management in the early stages will halt progress as a culture of disbelief and disinterest will reign amongst employees.

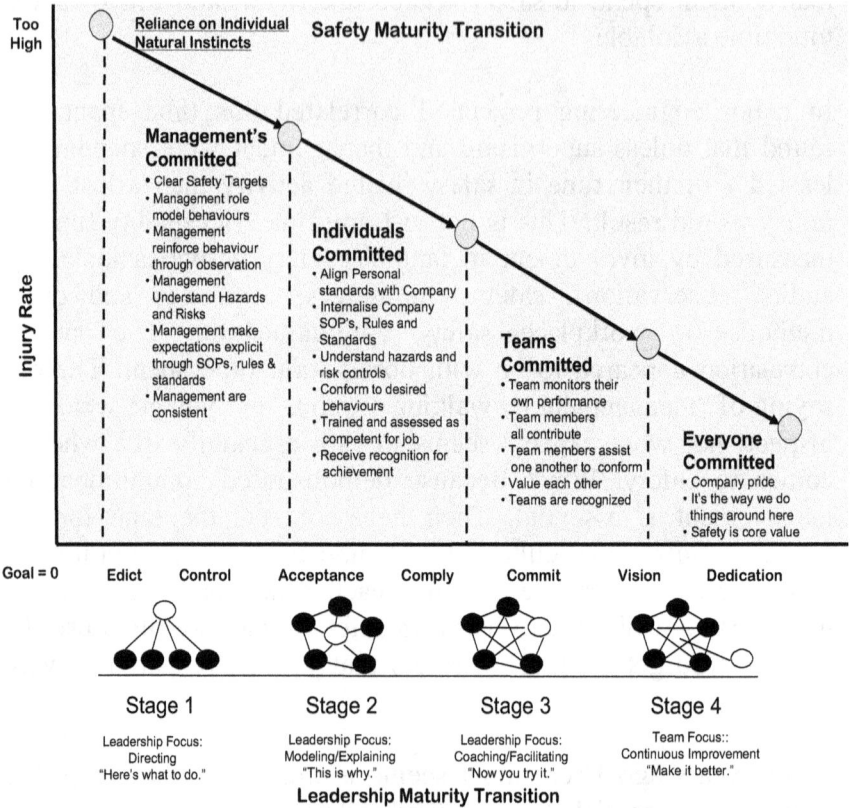

Fig 10 Safety Maturity and Leadership Transitions

Also shown in Fig. 10. is the leadership journey[15] which needs to transition from directing to letting employees have more input into daily safety management. This is illustrated with the managers being the white circle starting out in a traditional hierarchy at Stage 1 and progressing through to be part of the team and then to become the team mentor at Stage 4. At Stage 1 there is no consultation but rather a directing management style. However as the teams mature more consultation ensues with more team interaction and involvement.

This requires managers to develop a coaching and mentoring style over time. Some managers/supervisors will stifle this by wanting to hold on to control because that is where they are comfortable themselves. These managers become very obvious as the culture matures. Their inadequacies will need to be addressed if the safety journey to full maturity is to continue.

Interestingly whilst overseeing some power station projects I started measuring observation time spent and the types of issues being reported over time. See Fig 11.

Observations Made	Attitude	PPE	Heights	Electricity	Positions People	Equipment	Housekeeping	Work Practices	Observation Time hrs	At Risk Behaviours/ hr	Total Work Hours	% Time Observations
Jan	22	250	59	30	310	291	461	270	60	28.2	998	6
Feb	22	263	67	30	308	198	263	183	58	23.0	2993	2
Mar	22	191	90	20	261	177	230	166	62	18.7	3898	2
Apr	15	90	142	30	234	118	194	97	80	11.5	3912	2
May	6	21	243	30	155	128	90	42	60	11.9	1997	3
Jun	15	130	150	120	172	218	254	183	65	19.1	2106	3
Jul	23	125	43	150	251	192	237	134	65	17.8	3605	2
Aug	23	90	20	160	127	108	191	92	60	13.5	2402	2
Sep	10	45	15	120	89	88	131	83	40	14.5	1800	2
Oct	7	21	10	90	67	78	121	23	30	13.9	1318	2
Nov	5	24	5	70	39	18	94	15	27	10.0	1008	3
Dec	1	15	6	50	19	5	46	5	20	7.4	657	3
Summary No	171	1265	850	900	2032	1619	2312	1293	627	16.7	26694	2
Summary %	1.6%	12.1%	8.1%	8.6%	19.5%	15.5%	22.1%	12.4%				

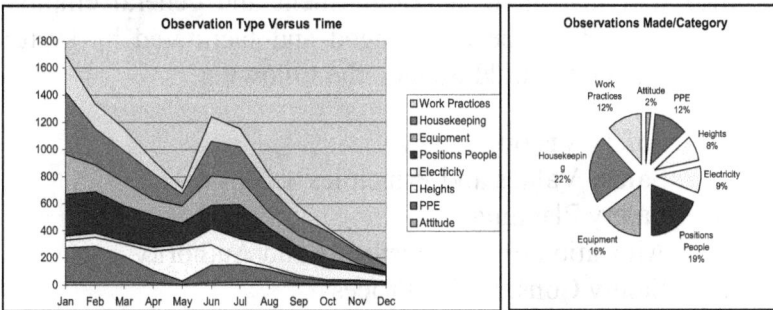

Fig 11 Project Observations Analysis

The management commitment to observations averaged out at 2% of their total time available. By plotting the observations over time on the project there is an obvious measure of maturity as the At Risk behaviors declined at least until May. For me this is the most interesting point as in May the entire workforce changed from civil to mechanical and electrical contractors. The At Risk behaviors rose, but not to the original levels at the start of the project, but to two thirds that level. I have seen this on many construction sites and I have come to the conclusion that the residual culture left from the first contracting group does impact subsequent parties entering the site. The rates of improvement as indicated by the slope of the curve are effectively the same even though the types of observations are different due to the nature of the work changing. Although this site achieved zero lost time injuries there is more work to be done to establish observation time correlations to optimize the time spent by management. i.e. how much time is enough? and at what point is there a diminishing rate of return? Similar results can be seen in manufacturing where a significant change has occurred. The objective must be to determine what strategies combined will yield Zero Harm.

2.1.2   Ensuring Commitment and Involvement

The impact of management commitment and general employee involvement needs to be encouraged and facilitated by systems that support it. This should include the following:

1. Safety Vision
2. Safety Values and Principles
3. Safety Planning
4. Allocation of Responsibility and Authority
5. Safety Consultative Process
6. Communication Process
7. Safety Goals and Objectives

2.1.2.1 Visioning Process

Establishing a vision for safety is critical in securing commitment. The organization must understand where it is going if it is to ever have a chance of formulating a plan to get there. This future desired state is determined through consultation and involvement of all levels of the organization. A vision is something that is peculiar to an organization. Resist the temptation to copy someone else's vision and adopt it as your own. It won't be culturally sensitive or have ownership in your organization if it is not developed from within. Ultimately the approval rests with the Chief Executive Officer, but every person must embody the vision. This will only happen if the processes employed support the achievement of the desired outcomes. This includes actual processes designed to produce, and those processes designed to create the desired culture. An example process flowchart is shown for reference purposes. See 2.1.2.1 process flowchart.

2.1.2.1 Vision Process

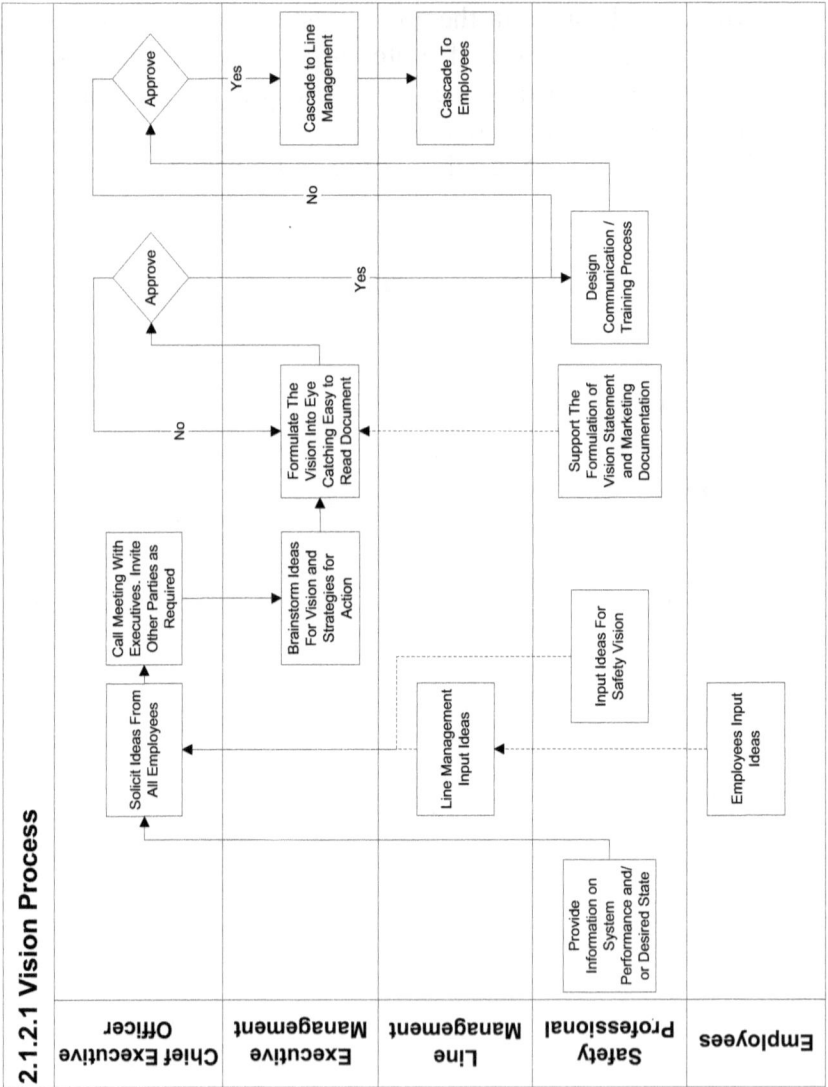

2.1.2.2   Safety Values and Principles Process

We have already spent some time looking at how principles and values can be derived from desired business outcomes in chapter 1. However it is also important to review general safety principles and values, particularly those that support the vision. See 2.1.2.2 process flowchart. These are important because they can be used to train and coach employees at all levels and help to guide decision making. Some examples might include:

- To safely do what we said when we said
- All injuries and accidents can be prevented;
- We demonstrate the level of safety that we want
- Zero harm anywhere, anytime to anyone.
- We look after our mates
- If it cannot be done safely then don't do it
- We get the level of safety that we are prepared to walk past
- We confront At Risk behavior
- We involve employees in decision making
- Training is not to be compromised
- A safe business is a good business
- All operating exposures can be safeguarded
- Management is accountable but everyone is responsible for safety
- Compliance with the law is a minimum requirement
- Risk assessment is to be based on facts and data
- A healthy workforce is a more productive workforce

This is by no means an exhaustive list but gives some insight into what has worked in some organizations. For values and principles to be effective these statements need to visible and internalized by all employees.

2.1.2.2 Determining Safety Values and Principles Process

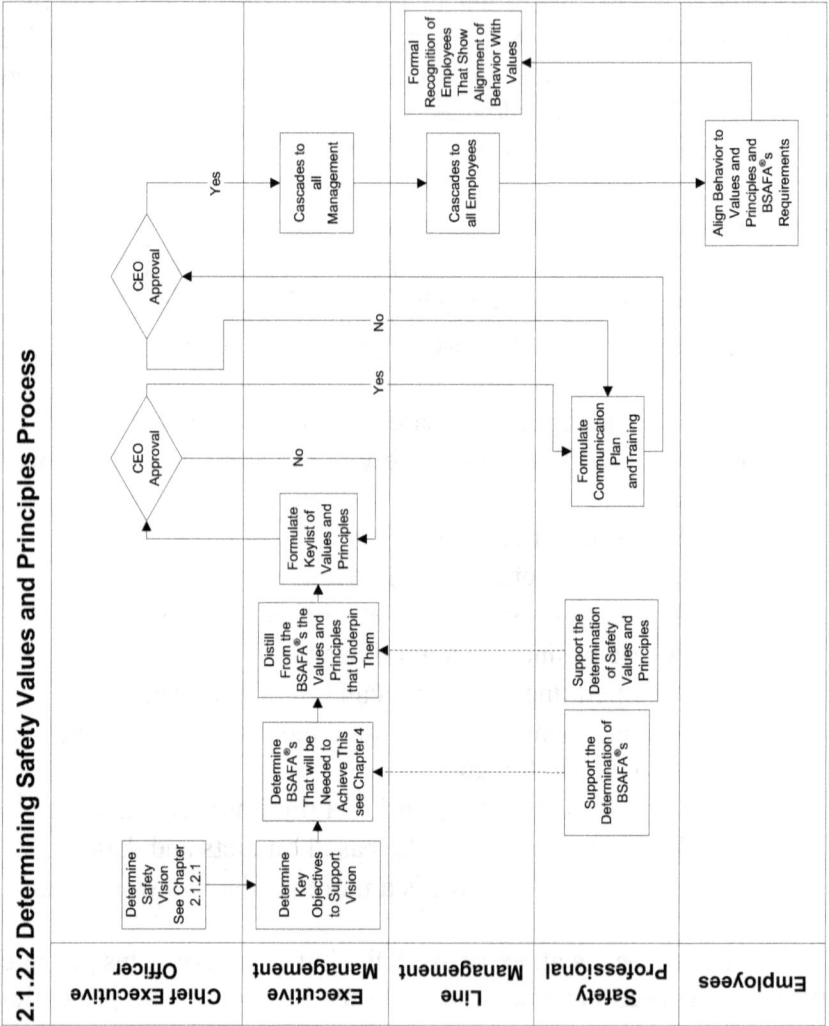

Chief Executive Officer	Executive Management	Line Management	Safety Professional	Employees
Determine Safety Vision See Chapter 2.1.2.1	Determine Key Objectives to Support Vision			
	Determine BSAFA®'s That will be Needed to Achieve This see Chapter 4		Support the Determination of BSAFA®'s	
	Distill From the BSAFA®'s the Values and Principles that Underpin Them		Support the Determination of Safety Values and Principles	
	Formulate Keylist of Values and Principles			
CEO Approval — No / Yes				
CEO Approval — Yes		Formulate Communication Plan and Training		
	Cascades to all Management			
	Cascades to all Employees			
Formal Recognition of Employees That Show Alignment of Behavior With Values				Align Behavior to Values and Principles and BSAFA®'s Requirements

The clue to success will be when the principles are used in every day conversation and particularly by management in their interaction with employees. The defining of these principles is crucial in establishing safety as a core value. They need to be reinforced at every opportunity and this will go a long way towards describing the desired culture of the organization.

Some companies have used recognition schemes and annual awards nights that recognize personnel who exemplify the desired values and principles. This can be extremely beneficial and uplifting to see the values being recognized in a formal way. It brings them to life rather than just seeing them on a poster in a foyer somewhere.

2.1.2.3 Safety Planning Process

The best advice that can be given here is to not have a safety planning process but rather to have a business planning process that has a safety component. All too often safety is seen as something separate to the rest of the business activities. This is a cultural mistake and unless safety is embodied within the normal business activities then rarely can success be achieved. This means that safety must be an important component of:

1. Strategic Planning

2. Business Planning and Meetings

3. Individual Employee plans

The decisions arising from some of these processes are typically beyond the safety professional to make and must come from, and be reinforced by the senior management group. This does not mean that the safety professional is without some responsibility. It is incumbent on them to ensure that safety is given due priority and that the relevant safety information is provided to the management teams to provide for inclusive decision making. Decisions can only be made where the facts and data are presented in a timely and concise way. For the safety professional this means providing information on:

1. Audit findings and recommendations

2. Safety observations and trends in behavior

3. Safety statistics

4. Budget projections for initiatives

There should also be some involvement in the business management planning sessions to ensure that safety matters are considered. Invites might not be forthcoming, (which is indicative of a cultural issue in itself) but that should not be seen as an excuse for non participation. See example process flowchart 2.1.2.3

2.1.2.4 Allocation of Responsibility and Authority Process

Company employees must be allocated the specific responsibility and authority for all activities that have the potential to affect the health and safety of individuals, plant and equipment and the environment. This responsibility and authority must be documented and communicated to all employees.

Due consideration should be given to local laws when allocating responsibility and authority. The law typically defines responsibilities for employers, safety representatives and employees. These are the minimum responsibilities that should be allocated. Often this is best done through a responsibility chart. See example in Fig.12. It is important to not only show what the responsibility is but also what authority there is with respect to the issue. The chart shows how this can be done. It remains that this must be communicated to the relevant people through position descriptions and appropriate training. See example process flowchart 2.1.2.4

2.1.2.3 Safety Planning Process

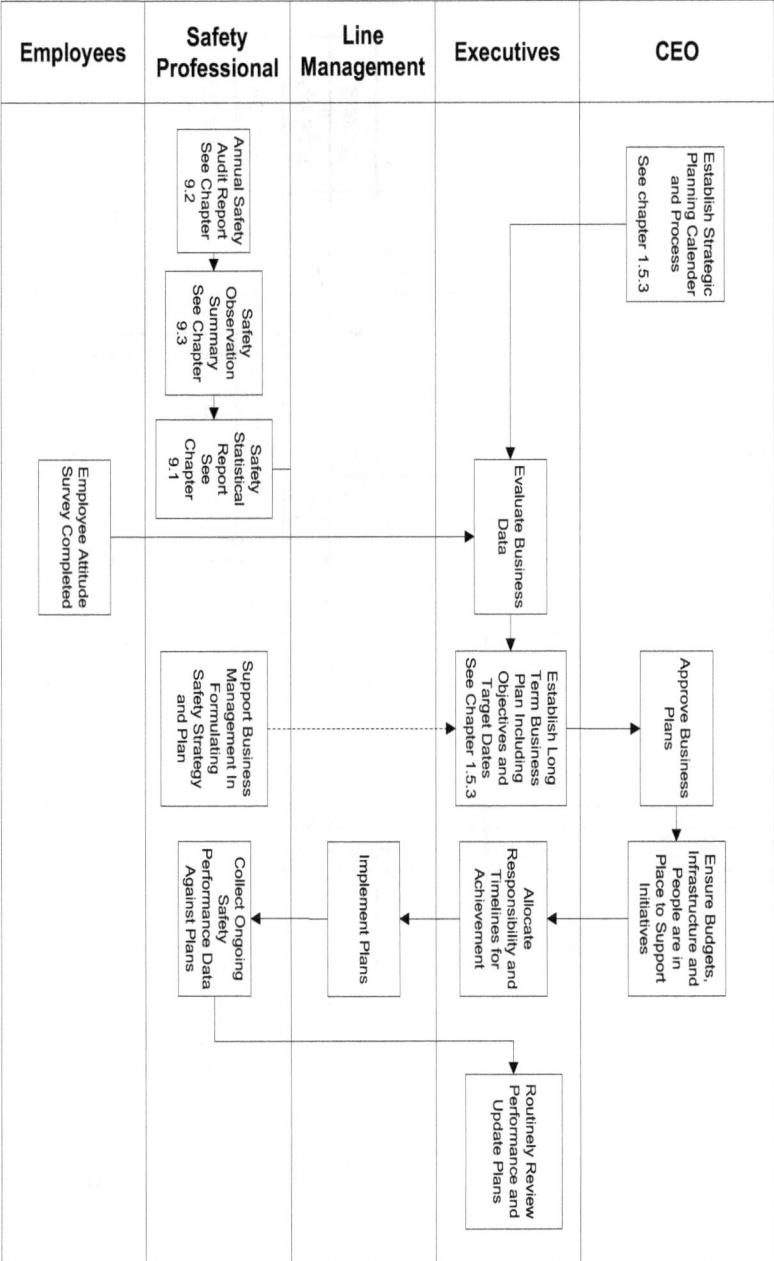

Employees	Safety Professional	Line Management	Executives	CEO
				Establish Strategic Planning Calender and Process — See chapter 1.5.3
	Annual Safety Audit Report See Chapter 9.2			
	Safety Observation Summary See Chapter 9.3			
	Safety Statistical Report See Chapter 9.1			
Employee Attitude Survey Completed			Evaluate Business Data	
		Support Business Management In Formulating Safety Strategy and Plan	Establish Long Term Business Plan Including Objectives and Target Dates See Chapter 1.5.3	Approve Business Plans
		Collect Ongoing Safety Performance Data Against Plans	Implement Plans	Allocate Responsibility and Timelines for Achievement
				Ensure Budgets, Infrastructure and People are in Place to Support Initiatives
				Routinely Review Performance and Update Plans

Area Of Responsibility	CEO	HR	GM'S	SITE MGR	Site OHS	SUPPLY	SUPER-VISORS	EMPLO-YEES
Corporate Responsibility								
OHS policies and objectives	A	D	S	I	I	I	I	F
OHS 21 Step Plan	A	D	S	I	I	I	I	F
OHS information system		D,I	S	S,F	S,F	S,F	S,F	F
Develop OHS intranet		D,I	S	S,F	S,F	S,F	S,F	F
OHS Responsibility and authority Charts	A	D	I	I	I	I	I	F
OHS Annual Assessments		G,S,P	S,P	S,P	S,P	S,P	S,P	P
Proactively influence legislators	S	I	S	S	S	S	S	
Report on OHS performance	S	G,S,I	S,I	S,I	S,I	I	I	F
Site Infrastructure Responsibility								
Maintain Site OHS Regulatory Requirements	S	G	S	D	G		I	F
Emergency systems	S	G	S	D	G		I	F
Maintain Essential Services	S	G	S	D	G		I	F
First aid	S	G	S	D	G		I	F
Hygiene management	S	G	S	D	G		I	F
Essential Service management	S	G	S	D	G		I	F
Maintenance Contractor Management	S	G	S	D	G		I	F
Maintenance Contractor Selection	S	G	S	D	G	S,G	I	F
Waste di~	S	G	S	D	G	S,G	I	F
				D	G		I	
Ergonomic office layout	S							
Dangerous Goods Mgt	S	G,S						
Management and Supervision								
OHS continuous improvement	P	P	P	P	P	P	P	P
OHS Competency assessment	S,P	G,S,P	S,P	S,P,I	G,S,I,P	S,I,P	S,I,P	P
OHS component in position descriptions	I	G,I	I	I	I	I	I	

LEGEND

A	Approve	CEO	Chief Executive Officer
D	Develop	GM's	Business General Managers
G	Provide Guidance	HR	HR Team
S	Support Implementation	Site OHS	Site Safety Personnel
I	Implement	Supply	Personnel in charge of purchasing
F	Follow Instructions		
P	Participate		

Fig 12 Example Responsibility Chart

2.1.2.4 Safety Responsibility and Authority Process

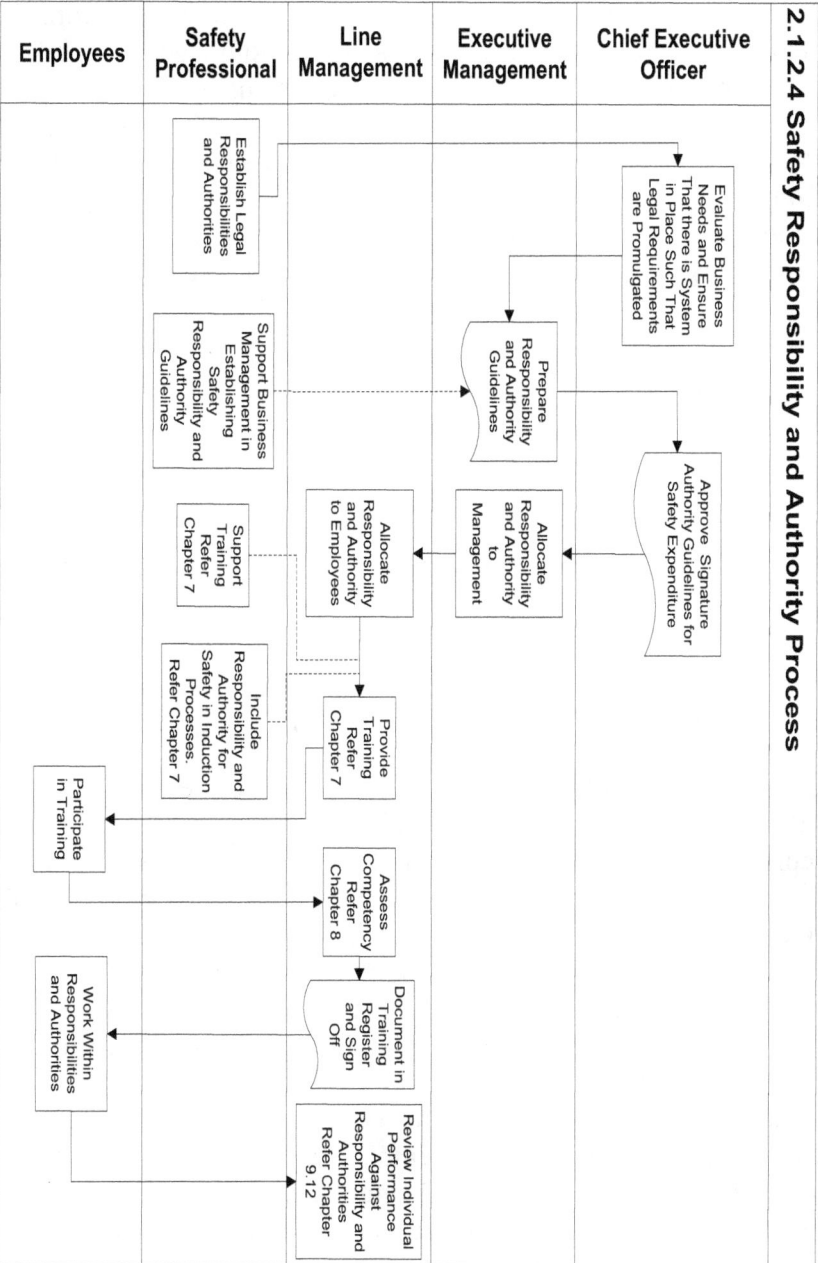

Employees	Safety Professional	Line Management	Executive Management	Chief Executive Officer
	Establish Legal Responsibilities and Authorities			Evaluate Business Needs and Ensure That there is System in Place Such That Legal Requirements are Promulgated
	Support Business Management in Establishing Safety Responsibility and Authority Guidelines		Prepare Responsibility and Authority Guidelines	
			Allocate Responsibility and Authority to Management	Approve Signature Authority Guidelines for Safety Expenditure
	Support Training Refer Chapter 7	Allocate Responsibility and Authority to Employees		
	Include Responsibility and Authority for Safety in Induction Processes. Refer Chapter 7	Provide Training Refer Chapter 7		
Participate in Training		Assess Competency Refer Chapter 8		
		Document in Training Register and Sign Off		
Work Within Responsibilities and Authorities				Review Individual Performance Against Responsibility and Authorities Refer Chapter 9.12

2.1.2.5 Consultative Processes

This is a critical component in gaining commitment from all employees and in many instances is also a requirement of the law. More importantly it also yields better end results.

Processes must be in place to solicit ideas/input and feedback from all employees at all stages of the safety process. Every opportunity should be taken to solicit, extract, and listen to all employees' views on how to improve safety. These might include:

a.   Consultative committees

b.   Toolbox meetings

c.   Shift changeover meetings

d.   Suggestion schemes

e.   Informal conversations

f.   Brainstorming sessions etc.

Consultation is often left at a relatively immature level where a safety committee is established and occupational health and safety representatives are nominated. I think it is unfortunate but I see it throughout industry where if asked the question, managers will refer to the safety committee as their consultative mechanism. In a truly mature safety culture the committee has a place but there is much more interaction between the individual manager and their employees. Safety becomes a routine topic where everyone is focussed on improvement. It becomes more one on one and face to face team consultation where results can be achieved quickly and efficiently. One thing with employees is that they are quick to learn whether consultation is being taken seriously. I'd like a dollar for every time I've heard an employee say, "They never listen." For management it's about using our ears and mouth in proportion. i.e. listen twice as much. Barriers to consultation often include:

a. Fear – both rational and irrational on both sides
b. Trust – the lack of
c. Politics – safety being used as leverage for other agendas

It is important to understand what these barriers are and how they can be overcome if consultation is to be successful. It often goes to the core of the company culture but can be changed through a committed management team.

In many instances the law requires employers to consult with their employees in a variety of ways including things such as:

1. identifying or assessing hazards and risk arising from the activities of the business
2. deciding measures to control these risks
3. deciding the adequacy of employee facilities
4. deciding on procedures for issue resolution
5. determining the membership of the safety committee
6. proposing changes that may affect health and safety

Consultation means that employers must share information with employees, give them reasonable opportunity to express their views and take those views into account. Consultation processes should be defined and known by all employees.

Increasingly management needs to be more inventive in the mechanisms they use to engage the workforce. The benefits far outweigh any possible negative issues.

2.1.2.6 Communication Process

The safety message must not only be communicated in words but also in actions, attitudes and the physical environment. All the senses should be used to convey the message. From my own experience I have walked into some places and felt safe, but then there were others that made me feel very uncomfortable. All our senses are at play as our bodies are tuned to avoid pain and suffering. Our experiences have taught us, and indeed our body is very well equipped, to sense danger. All these senses are also used by employees to sense commitment. It's just as much about what a manager walks past, as what they say that matters. Even the use of language including body language can be important in conveying the safety message. Psychologists describe "Soon certain negative" and "Soon certain positive" reinforcers in the use of language. For example if a supervisor says to an employee "I need you to get this truck loaded by 4pm this afternoon and make sure you do it safely" what has really been said? The positive reinforcement relates to getting the truck loaded by 4pm. The negative reinforcement is around safety. It will not be seen as important as the 4pm message relating to the truck loading. So often in the corridors of business this language is used. It destroys the safety culture and causes disbelief and mistrust in employees with respect to management commitment. i.e. production comes first.

The prevailing culture must be transformed to one of "safely doing what we said when we said". Safety must be communicated as a core value and then backed up by management and supervision role modelling behaviors and attitudes that are consistent with this. It is also about being inventive about creating forums for sharing. One of my former CEO's had what he called "communicakes", an informal morning tea where he would communicate a message and solicit questions from employees. Employees responded well to this open communication.

Induction and assimilation programs also play an important part as new employees may come with significant baggage from previous employers. Time must be spent on ensuring that company expectations are known and appropriately communicated.

The physical environment is another important way of communicating the safety message. I remember one instance where I was involved in a takeover of a business that was filled with old equipment, where the walls were black with dust and the safety record was appalling. After the aquisition was completed the decision was taken to initially stop production. In an attempt to change the culture a general clean up was started by removing all unbolted items out of the factory and several 44 gallon drums of white paint were purchased and applied to the walls and floors. Radical yes but in terms of communicating to the workforce that things needed to change it was very effective, and yes the safety improved. The working environment conveys a powerful message so utilise it. Things to consider are:

1. Wall Colours
2. Lighting
3. Meeting minute templates with safety as first agenda item
4. Meeting rooms with evacuation plans
5. Sign in book and induction for visitors
6. Noise suppression versus music
7. Signs
8. Posters
9. Banners including electronic
10. Machinery – guarding and well maintained
11. Demarcation – colour coded barriers, marked walkways, railing, floor areas etc
12. Process Mapping, video, pictures and words.
13. Air quality
14. Temperature
15. Housekeeping
16. Everything in its place and a place for everything
17. Rest and lunch room quality and cleanliness
18. Plants (preferably not plastic ones!)
19. Smell
20. Company bulletins
21. Staff newsletters
22. Shadow boards
23. Billboards
24. Performance Boards etc

All these things add to the safety message and hence the safety culture. I've found that visual stimuli can work very well at shop floor level. Things like shadow boards and highly visual procedures can be quite effective. See Fig 13

Fig 13 Everything in its place and a place for everything.[16]

When people ask how much communication is enough I refer to my karate days where the message/exercise would be repeated for as long as it took for it to become the normal way of doing things.

2.1.2.7   Safety Goals and Objective Process

So much has been written about this topic that it does not need a detailed review here. However if I may be somewhat provocative here, I really see no point setting goals around latent indicators like lost time injury, first aid injuries etc. If the target is zero harm then how do goals around such indicators help to achieve it? The answer is, they don't, but for many companies goals are set around these. Whilst I acknowledge they are important measures of safety performance, they do not form the basis for goals in achieving zero harm. So where do you go from here? Every safety goal and objective that is set must have a direct link to the zero harm target. In other words, how is this activity going to help achieve zero harm? This approach forces management to think quite differently. It's not about saying lets reduce lost time injuries by 20% this year. This objective accepts injury and defines a culture that is targeting to injure people in the coming year. If management truly believe that zero harm is the only acceptable target then careful planning must be carried out to examine what needs to be in place to achieve this. Refer to chapter 1 as organizational design has a significant part to play here. Its not just about saying lets use proactive safety objectives like audits planned versus delivered, % management time in observations, % people trained etc. What is crucial is that if the desired outcome is zero harm then management must understand the BSAFA® and the systems requirements that will support this desired culture. See chapter 1. This will give management the activities required and hence the goals and objectives required. See example flowchart. 2.1.2.7

2.2 Conclusion

The fundamental elements represented at the core of the Practical Safety Process® are essential for success. The successful application of the process relies so much on these elements being in place. To ignor them will yield substandard results. If you feel that you have a safety plan that is not being supported then you should have a careful review of this chapter.

2.1.2.7 Safety Goals and Objectives Process

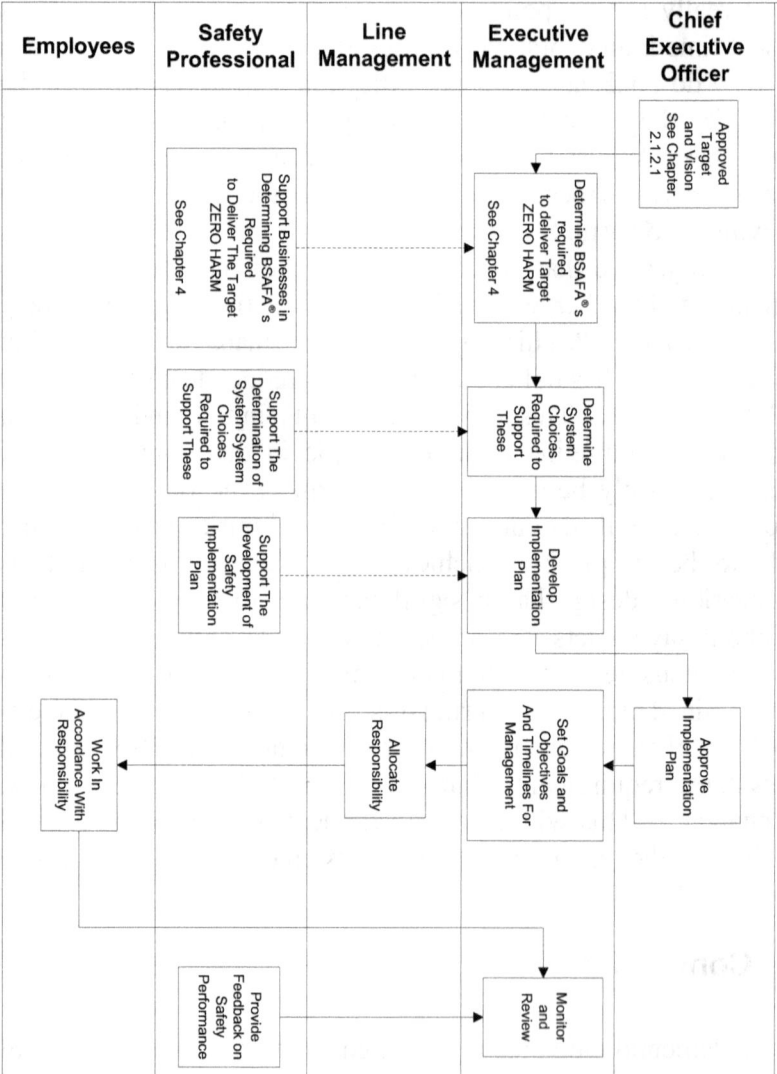

Employees	Safety Professional	Line Management	Executive Management	Chief Executive Officer
				Approved Target and Vision See Chapter 2.1.2.1
	Support Businesses in Determining BSAFA®'s Required to Deliver The Target ZERO HARM See Chapter 4		Determine BSAFA®'s required to deliver Target ZERO HARM See Chapter 4	
	Support The Determination of System System Choices Required to Support These		Determine System Choices Required to Support These	
	Support The Development of Safety Implementation Plan		Develop Implementation Plan	
				Approve Implementation Plan
			Set Goals and Objectives And Timelines For Management	
		Allocate Responsibility		
Work In Accordance With Responsibility				
	Provide Feedback on Safety Performance		Monitor and Review	

2.3 Check Your Progress

Practical Safety Process® Fundamentals Gap Analysis		
THE FUNDAMENTALS	**Y**	**N**
Do you have a safety vision?		
Are safety values and principles defined?		
Is there a planning system in place that includes safety?		
Are there systems for allocating responsibility and authority?		
Do you have a consultation system?		
Do you have a communication process for safety messages?		
Have you a system for setting safety goals and objectives?		
Have you mapped BSAFA®s to achieve this?		
Have you mapped your required design choices?		
Have you assigned personnel responsible for the transition?		
Are the deliverables measurable and do they have a set date?		
Have management set aside time to manage by walking around?		
Is this time measurable?		
Have you a good balance of proactive and reactive measures?		
Do you fully understand your safety costs? Proactive & consequential?		
Do you have a system for allocating budgets to safety?		
Do you have a document management system?		
Do you have a change management system?		
Do you have access to legislation and standards?		
Do you have a recognition and reward system?		
Do you have a system for measuring safety data?		
Is there a forum for measuring and reviewing this data?		
Is there an experienced and competent OH&S person available to provide advice and are they appropriately qualified?		
If you answer yes to all above you can continue as you have the pre-requisite commitment to be successful		

3.0 STEP 1 - Identify Hazards and Assess Risks

3.1 Practical Safety Approach to Hazard Identification and Risk Assessment

Effective and well understood hazard identification and risk assessment processes are vital as the foundation stone for building an effective safety system. There are different levels of risk assessment from the more holistic approach such as conceptual risk assessment to very specific risk assessment processes relating to individual plant, substances, tasks, equipment etc. The important factors to consider are:

1. A common organizational understanding of the difference between hazard and risk

2. A structured method for identifying hazards

3. A method defined for assessing risk

4. A method for assessing frequency of (likelihood) exposure and consequence

5. A simple method for calculating relative level of risk

6. A method of allocating priority for risk control actions based upon a relative level of risk calculation.

3.1.1 Hazard Identification

Firstly what is a hazard? The definition given in the Australian Standard AS4801 is:

> " A source or a situation with a potential for harm in terms of human injury or ill health, damage to property, damage to the environment, or a combination of these." [17]

This might seem a fairly obvious question with an obvious answer but is it really? Those who have spent many years looking at risk assessments will probably agree that this simple question is probably the least understood. In examining many risk assessments over the years I've been consistently amazed by how people confuse describing situations with hazards. When it boils down to it just how many hazards are there? The Victorian WorkSafe Authority in Australia[18] produced a hazard list several years ago that for me has provided an excellent basis for a common list of hazard types that provides for a disciplined approach to hazard identification. These hazard types included:

- Entanglement
- Crushing
- Cutting / Stabbing/ Puncturing
- Striking
- Slipping / Tripping
- Falling
- Shearing
- Friction
- High Pressure Fluid or gas
- Electrical
- Ergonomic
- Suffocation
- Fire and Explosion
- Chemicals
- Biological
- Temperature High or Low
- Noxious Fumes
- Environment
- Dust and other particulates
- Noise
- Vibration
- Weather
- Radiation (UV/EMR/Welding)
- Confined Space

The amazing revelation for me is that the list of hazard types is not endless. This has significant benefits in that these types can be taught and applied in many different situations. It also provides for more fundamental analysis of hazards in the workplace inf a common list of types is used. It also helps to separate hazards from causes. This is where the mistake is often made with many people describing the situation they see rather than the hazard that is present. Let's look at the example below in Fig 14.

Fig 14 Spot The Hazards[19]

> *E.g. Whilst there are a number of Hazards illustrated here, typically what I find is that an observer might conclude that the hose is the principal hazard. However the better interpretation is that there is a "tripping" hazard presented by the hose.*

This is a subtle message but a very important one to grasp. It requires a change in mindset of observers and auditors to achieve this level of maturity, but the benefits are immense. With a consistently applied list of standard hazard types one can analyse where the hazards occur and target the management of their risks appropriately. This also provides for consistency throughout the organization and builds competency around understanding in identifying common hazard types. Consistent reinforcement can then be engendered throughout the safety system in all processes. For example I print the hazard types list on job safety analysis and plant safety assessment process forms. It develops understanding and builds competency in the knowledge of hazards. It also provides a much easier route to consultation, provision of information, instruction and training.

3.1.2 Assessing Risks

There are many proprietary models in the market for assessing risk. The Australian Standard AS4360[20] is a good starting point in terms of a simple approach. It really does not matter which system is used or indeed if you develop your own, however the system employed needs to be robust and able to be used and understood by the entire workforce and must include the following fundamentals:

a. Some sort of risk weighting to allow comparison of risks associated with hazards across different situations

b. A measure of frequency and likelihood of exposure to the risk

c. A measure for assessing the consequences of exposure

d. A method of prioritizing risks for action

The real sticking point around risk assessment for me lies in the obsession by many to apply a residual risk ranking to hazards after risk controls are applied. The objective of the Practical Safety Process® is the attainment of zero harm. Risk must be eliminated or reduced as far as reasonably practicable such that, with appropriate risk controls work can be carried out safely. Elimination of risk is relatively clear in definition, but is often not easily accomplished. Reduction of risk in a reasonably practicable way occurs when all risk controls including ongoing management of change, monitoring, and review have been applied in a demonstrable process. In the Practical Safety Process®, practicability is well demonstrated particularly when the relative level of risk has been determined through consultation and the application of the hazard identification, risk assessment, prioritisation and implementation of risk control process. In such a process the relative level of risk is an essential factor in setting priorities for risk controls. Once the risk controls are in place the risk is eliminated or reduced as far as reasonably practicable.

Assessing risk is not about reducing risk scores! It's a subtle point, but an important one, especially in the eyes of operators in the work environment. They want to know how and when the risk associated with the hazard will be dealt with such that the work environment is safe. Debates over residual risk in this context add little positive value towards achieving the zero harm objective.

3.2 Hazard and Risk Management Assessment Processes

There are many different hazard and risk processes that may need to be addressed by an individual organization. See Table 6.

Table 6: Potential Hazard Identification and Risk Assessment Processes That May be Required

Plant Risk Assessment Process

Confined Space Risk Assessment Process

Dangerous Goods Risk Assessment Process

Hot Work Risk Assessment Process

Excavation Risk Assessment process

Hazardous Substances Risk Assessment Process

Electrical Risk Assessment Process

Falls Risk Assessment Process

Noise Risk Assessment Process

Asbestos Risk Assessment Process

Environmental Risk Assessment Process

Manual Handling Risk assessment process

Ergonomic Risk Assessment Process

Traffic Risk Assessment Process

Insurance Assessment Process

This is by no means an exhaustive list but due consideration needs to be given to the types of hazard potential in a workplace and what processes may need to be employed to identify them. Some of these processes will be situational and some processes like asbestos, confined spaces, workplace substances including dangerous goods and hazardous substances, manual handling, plant, environment have legislative requirements that must be addressed. See Step 3 Identify Compliance Requirements. It is important to have all the required information when establishing risk assessment processes.

In preparing for hazard identification, risk assessment and control of risk, the Practical Safety Process® approach is to start by developing various registers for such things as plant, workplace substances and other equipment and structures. These registers form the basis for disciplined management of change protocols and form the basis for control. This is particularly important for those that have regulatory requirements where it is important to ensure that:

1.   Assessment media is available – this should include checklists derived from legislation, national standards, company guidelines, and best practice.
2.   A system is in place for recording observations- forms, camera, etc.
3.   The appropriate people are involved – including shop floor level through a consultative process.
4.   A method for summarizing findings is in place
5.   A method for recording, prioritizing, and tracking actions is in place

All these components are important to the success of the process and hence effort needs to be made to ensure that they are all in place. See Fig.15

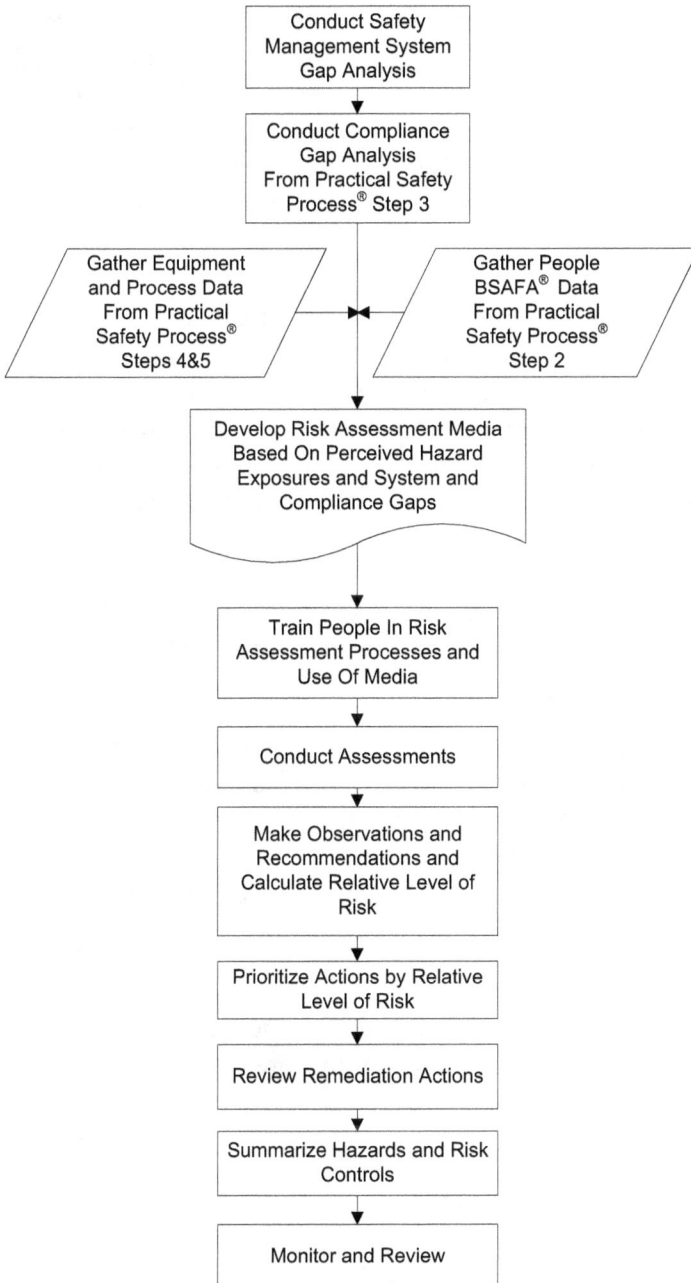

Fig 15 Practical Safety Hazard Identification and Risk Assessment Management Process

Getting started is a significant issue for many organizations. Risk assessment is time consuming and requires considerable effort. It also can be very subjective, especially if there is lack of preparation of background information. This should include having a knowledge of management systems gaps, compliance issues, the work environment and expected hazards requiring management.

Due to the fact that most of the participants in risk assessment processes are not safety professionals it is incumbent on the safety professional to provide such advice, training and instruction to the risk assessment team so that the risk assessment can be conducted successfully. It also means where the scope of the assessment is outside their own expertise, that appropriate professional or other advice should be obtained.

The development of hazard identification and risk assessment media can be quite beneficial in this regard. These might include such things as:

1. Regulatory requirements. e.g. regulations
2. National guidelines and codes of practice
3. Standards requirements
4. Industry best practice.
5. Company policy and procedure requirements
6. Various registers eg. plant, workplace substances, slings and chains, etc.

This media can be developed by the safety professional or someone who has expertise in the area of concern. e.g. Plant Hazard Checklist Fig 16.

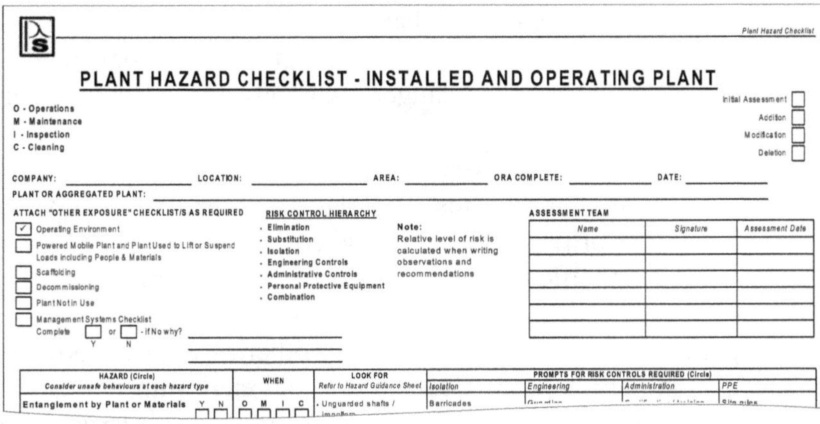

Fig 16 Plant Hazard Checklist

A plant hazard and risk assessment process is often a good starting point especially in a manufacturing environment as it can quite often highlight other areas for investigation especially if the standard hazards list is used.

One of the most difficult areas to address is that of workplace substances. It is highly regulated with many requirements and it can often be difficult to find expertise in this area. The requirements usually mean varying types and levels of assessment for substances that can, by regulatory definition be:

- Dangerous and hazardous
- Dangerous not hazardous
- Hazardous not dangerous
- None of the above but with health or other risks of a varying nature

At the basic recognition level, I refer to them as workplace substances. The workplace substances register is an important tool here and is used to record the name, location and particular nature of the substances. This ensures that:

- Management of change is controlled
- Material Safety Data Sheet currency is controlled
- Manifests for dangerous goods and other lists can be produced
- Workplace assessments for hazardous substances and dangerous goods can be appropriately prioritized, recorded and controlled.
- Specific health surveillance needs are managed

The approach here is no different to any other assessment process where it is important to conduct an external environment scan to find out what regulations, codes practice, standards and benchmark practices might apply. Once these are known the approach is to distill these requirements into the workplace substances register and checklists. This makes it easier for non experts to participate in the assessment process e.g. Fig 17

Fig 17 Workplace Substance Assessment Media

In this way the safety professional can also use the assessment process to impart valuable knowledge to participants.

However care should be taken that this does not reduce the risk assessment to a tick and flick exercise. The collection of objective evidence is crucial. With the advent of digital photography much of the data collection can be done through photographs. Care needs to be taken in media design to retain some flexibility for team members to raise unforeseen hazards and risks.

The most difficult issue in risk assessment is having the appropriate people participate. This is not always easy to achieve in a busy work environment, but the collective views of a team produces a much better result than an individual.

Consideration needs to be given to participation of:

a. Safety Professional
b. Safety Work Area Representative
c. Employees who work in the area concerned
d. The Supervisor of area
e. Expert in the field concerned
f. Consider maintenance people

Fig 18. Don't forget maintenance people in hazard identification and risk assessment [21]

The importance of involving the employees who work in the area should not be overlooked. Too often they are left out of risk assessment processes. This is a mistake, as these are the very people who are exposed to the most hazards on a daily basis. They are ultimately the ones that must sign off that the risk is acceptable given the controls that have been implemented. They are also the ones that can benefit most from taking time out to learn about the risks associated with the hazards in their area.

Another group is the maintenance crew. Whether employees or contractors these people need to manage risk to a different level and can provide valuable insights. Quite often in their work front line safeguards are removed and the work is more situationally based where normal operating risk controls may be removed.

Hence their depth of knowledge of the hazards, are and need to be, much greater. This knowledge can contribute greatly to the risk assessment outcomes.

Another consideration is whether the team selected has the required expertise. It's starts with their competency in the risk assessment process itself. Has there been training?   Equally important is whether there is sufficient competency in the group to deal with the issues at hand. Some risk controls may require expert advice from a trained professional. These experts should be brought in as required as part of the group. Resist the temptation to have them prepare a report independently of your own personnel. This reduces the learning opportunity of your people and does not provide for them to input into the expert assessment. Ultimately this leads to a substandard result through assumptions or omissions.

Hazard identification and risk assessment can be a complex multifaceted task but it is one that must be approached systematically and cautiously. Preparation and understanding of the nature of the potential hazard is critical as is some understanding of legislative and incorporated or referenced Standard requirements. For some of the more common risk assessments a set of example processes is shown in the Appendix.

3.3   Conclusion

The identification of hazards and the assessment of risks are fundamental to any safety process. The key in the Practical Safety Process® approach is to involve people from all levels in the organization. This is not a process that can be done at a desk, but must be carried out in the field and involve the very people expozed to the hazards to be successful.

3.4 Check Your Progress

Practical Safety Process® STEP 1 Gap Analysis	Y	N
IDENTIFY HAZARDS AND ASSESS RISKS		
Have you established a common understanding of what a hazard is?		
Do you have a system for assessing risks based on likelihood and consequence?		
Do you have a list of the hazards that need to be managed in your business?		
Have you established hazard identification and risk assessment processes? E.g.		
Plant		
Workplace substances		
Confined spaces		
Hot work		
Excavation		
Electrical		
Noise		
Asbestos		
Manual Handling		
Ergonomic		
Traffic		
Is the required assessment media available?		
Is training material available?		
Are competency assessment tools available?		
Is there a system in place for establishing and maintaining safety registers?		
Is there a system in place for recording assessment data?		
Are the appropriate people involved i.e. all levels?		
Is there a method for summarizing findings from assessments?		
Is there a method for prioritizing and tracking actions?		
Do you have a system for the creation, storage and retrieval of safety records?		

4.0 STEP 2 - Identify the Desired People Requirements BSAFA®

The importance of behavior in safety is being better understood with the work done by Scott Geller[22] and Thomas Krause [23, 24].

In chapter 1 we examined the importance of aligning people behaviors, skills, attitudes, feelings and attributes (BSAFA®) with organizational outcomes. This same exercise needs to be replicated at the plant, process or job level to determine what BSAFA® are required. This is just as important as identifying hazards, but very few organizations take the time to do this. Just as the quality fraternity learnt in the 80's that quality cannot be inspected in, so the safety fraternity needs to understand that safety cannot be inspected in. It's about assuring safety. Too often I see people conducting behavioral observations only to find that they have no idea what they are looking for. This results in more conditions being observed or even worse employees feeling like they have policeman waiting for them to do the wrong thing. The better approach is to Identify the Desired People Requirements BSAFA®s, communicate this to employees, train them, and then monitor. i.e. tell them what is expected up front. This is the fundamental difference in the Practical Safety Process® approach to safety. It is my belief that unless you have communicated to people what you expect, then you have no right to inspect. Identifying the Desired People Requirements BSAFA® is critical for success and should be given priority. People are important in the safety process and systems need to be in place that identify and encourage the desired BSAFA®s. This Practical Safety BSAFA® identification process is outlined in Fig. 19.

In order to identify the BSAFA® requirements a Job Person/People Analysis (JPA)® form is used. See Fig 20. It is much the same process as a job safety analysis except this time the focus is on identifying the desired BSAFA® requirements at each step rather than hazards. The process also examines the risk associated with employees not showing these desired BSAFA®s.

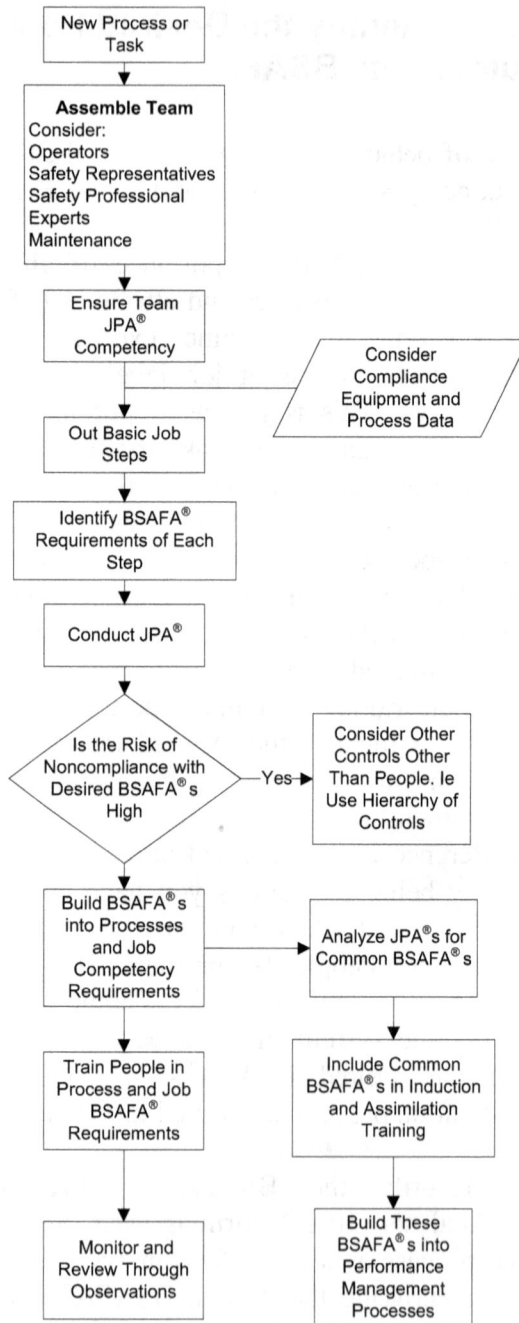

Fig 19 BSAFA® Identification Process

This knowledge of consequences can be used as a powerful motivator for employees and guide whether further controls are required beyond BSAFA® awareness or modification.

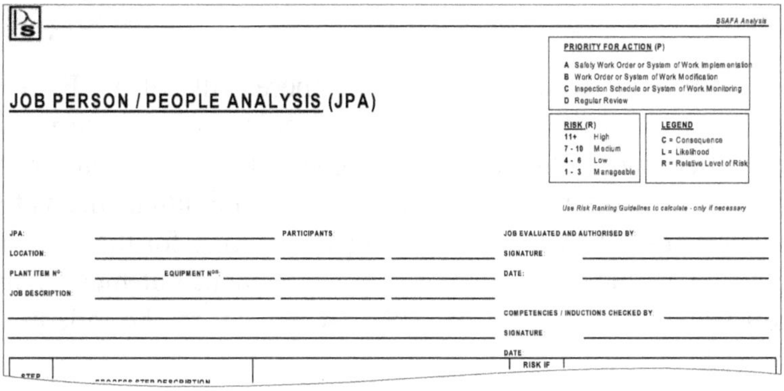
BSAFA Analysis

JOB PERSON / PEOPLE ANALYSIS (JPA)

PRIORITY FOR ACTION (P)
A Safety Work Order or System of Work Implementation
B Work Order or System of Work Modification
C Inspection Schedule or System of Work Monitoring
D Regular Review

RISK (R)
11+ High
7 - 10 Medium
4 - 6 Low
1 - 3 Manageable

LEGEND
C = Consequence
L = Likelihood
R = Relative Level of Risk

Use Risk Ranking Guidelines to calculate - only if necessary

JPA:
LOCATION:
PLANT ITEM Nº
EQUIPMENT NºS:
JOB DESCRIPTION:
PARTICIPANTS
JOB EVALUATED AND AUTHORISED BY
SIGNATURE
DATE:
COMPETENCIES / INDUCTIONS CHECKED BY
SIGNATURE
DATE
RISK IF

Fig 20 Extract of Job Person/People Analysis Form

Over a period of time you will find some common BSAFA®s are highlighted through different JPA®s or JSPA®s (Job Safety Person Analysis® or Job SPA®). The "Job SPA®" is useful once people have become familiar with using a JPA® first. It is essentially a combination of a traditional JSA and a JPA®.

These processes often yield BSAFA®s that are common to your type of industry and workplace. It is well worth the effort to distill these into a consolidated list over time. These common BSAFA®s should then be made part of general recruitment, induction and assimilation processes and should be considered for inclusion into performance review processes.

These BSAFA®s can also be used in recruitment to guide selection to ensure the best alignment to job requirements. I often use questioning, scenarios and work skill exercises in recruitment to explore a person's response to a BSAFA® requirement.

This means that in defining processes and job competency models the BSAFA® elements need to be considered. For processes this might mean building in BSAFA® prompts at key points in the process. For specific jobs BSAFA® competencies may also be required.

Apart from these common BSAFA®s there will still be BSAFA® requirements that are specific to a particular task. These need to be identified and included in competency models for that job. See Step 6 Assess Competency. Assessment of individuals needs to be completed against these models prior to working for the first time. This might include written and oral assessment but must include demonstrated assessment if BSAFA®s are to be adequately addressed.

As we concluded in chapter one all this assessment can be in vain if the required supporting systems are not employed. It also requires, at a conscious level, an understanding of the required BSAFA®s by management and supervision. These systemic reinforcers that influence and drive attitudes and behavior are so important to overall success. So much depends on the prevailing culture.

4.1   Conclusion

The Identification of the Desired People Requirements
BSAFA®s differentiates the Practical Safety Process® from other approaches to safety management. I do not believe that ultimately you can be successful in safety management without paying due attention to this important step. To define what is required of your people up front is fundamental to success not only in safety but in other aspects of the business as well.

4.2   Check Your Progress

Practical Safety Process® STEP 2 Gap Analysis	Y	N
IDENTIFY THE DESIRED PEOPLE REQUIREMENTS BSAFA®		
Is there a method for identifying the desired behaviors?		
Is there a method for identifying the desired skills?		
Is there a method for identifying the desired attitudes?		
Is there a method for identifying the desired feelings?		
Is there a method for identifying the desired attributes?		
Are systems in place to identify core BSAFA®		
Are there systems in place for identifying task specific BSAFA®		
Are there systems in place to build BSAFA® requirements into competency and performance model requirements?		
Is there a system in place to monitor BSAFA®?		
Do managers role model safety behaviors and show leadership and the correct attitude in development of safety improvement initiatives?		
Are managers aware of management system policies? Including OHS, rehab, harassment, quality & environment		
Where conflict exists between safety and other business priorities do management as far as practicable minimise risk to employees, the environment and the Company?		

5.0 STEP 3 – Identify Compliance Requirements

Compliance is about understanding what the level of community expectation is with respect to safety. It should be viewed as the minimum standard for risk controls that must be in place irrespective of internal Company policies. This might mean compliance with:

1. Acts

2. Regulations

3. Codes of Practice

4. Standards

5. Industry Guidance

6. Specific Authority Guidance

7. State or local Government

8. Council Bylaws etc.

Whatever business you are in, a base level understanding of potential compliance issues must be understood. This starts with understanding the Acts, Regulations and Codes of Practice of the jurisdiction. The safety professional must be in a position to support management in this area. They must ensure that access is available and that they have an understanding of which laws are applicable to their Company. This is often best done through a compliance register. It can be comprised of a simple spreadsheet that lists the appropriate legislation and it how it applies to the organization. See Fig 21. As legislation changes the register needs to be updated. Having identified what applies, the application of the requirements can be addressed. Likewise for standards it can be quite useful to distill these into similar checklists that provide a practical way for people to analyze a particular issue. See Fig 22.

Commonwealth				
Acts	**Regulations and Standards**	**Applies** Yes	No	**Status**
Australian Heritage Commission Act 1975				
Control of Workplace Hazardous Substances - National Model Regulation 1994				
Disability Discrimination Act 1992				
Endangered Species Protection Act 1992				
Environment Protection (Impact of Proposals) Act 1974				
	Environment Protection (Impact of Proposals) Regulations			
	Environment Protection (Impact of Proposals) Administrative Procedures			
Hazardous Waste (Regulation of Exports and Imports) Act 1989 (amended June 1996) (amended December 1996)				
	Hazardous Waste (Exports and Imports) (Fees) Regulations, 1990 (amended February 1999)			
Hazardous Waste (Regulation of Exports and Imports) Regulations (commenced December 1996)				
	Hazardous Waste (Regulation of Exports and Imports) (OECD Decision) Regulations (commenced December 1996) (amended May 1999)			
Industrial Chemicals (Notification and Assessment) Act 1989 (amended				
	October 1996) (amended June 1997 – commenced December 1997)			

Fig 21 Extract From Compliance Register

AS 1940 - 2004

VERIFICATION CHECKLIST - EXAMPLE

STORAGE AND HANDLING OF FLAMMABLE AND COMBUSTIBLE LIQUIDS (AS 1940 - 2004)

Note: Designed to supplement the use of this Standard. Only to be used by competent persons and only in conjunction with an updated version of the full text.

For non compliances complete Observations, Recommendations and Actions detailing actions to achieve equivalency

	STANDARD	UNDERSTOOD YES	NO	RELEVANT YES	NO	COMPLY YES	NO	ORA YES	NO
Section 1	Scope & General								
Section 2	Minor Storage								
2.1	Scope								
2.2.1	Minor storage quantities								
2.2.2	PG I								
2.2.3	Multiple storages								
2.2.4	Separation								
2.2.5	Open land								
2.2.6	Construction sites								
	Precautions (location)								

Fig 22 Extract From Storage and Handling of Flammable and Combustible Liquids.

This is often a good way for the professional safety person to transfer knowledge to others and build competency around standards interpretation. Compliance to standards is not always obligatory under law (unless they are incorporated in regulations) but nevertheless it is good practice to ascertain what guidance can be gained from them in developing safety controls.

Approved codes of practice that provide guidance on how to comply with regulations are often available. These are not mandatory to follow however failure to observe them may prove a contravention of the law as they may be seen as evidence of minimum compliance.

In addition quite often national safety bodies and industry groups will provide information through instruments like national standards and other guidelines. This information is freely available and provides significant information to be leveraged in the workplace.

Taking this practical approach means compliance can become the ally of the safety professional in setting the minimum standards for controls that need to be applied. The word minimum is not used lightly as compliance to the law, and standards, do not necessarily yield a safe work place. They should rather be seen as the foundation stones for achieving it.

5.1   Conclusion

The legal framework within which one operates defines the minimum requirements for controls that must be in place to manage risk. They reflect community expectations and must be understood. As these are minimum requirements they should not be relied upon to provide the ultimate guide to controls to achieve zero harm.

5.2 Check Your Progress

Practical Safety Process® STEP 3 Gap Analysis	Y	N
IDENTIFY COMPLIANCE REQUIREMENTS		
Is there a system in place to understand compliance obligations?		
Is there a system in place to assess standards requirements?		
Is there a system in place to track compliance changes?		
Is there a compliance strategy in place to either, cope, react or influence future legislation or standards?		
Are compliance assessments carried out?		
Is a compliance register maintained?		
Have specific notification/licensing requirements been identified?		
Cranes		
Pressure vessels		
Lifts		
Dangerous Goods		
Others not sure have you checked		
Are licensing obligations known?		
Are records available?		
Are recertification dates known and scheduled?		
Is there understanding of compliance with Plant Safety Regulations?		
Is there evidence of a Plant Register?		
Is prescribed Plant registered?		
Is there evidence of hazard identification, risk assessment and control? Plant, Systems of work		
Are risk controls in place?		
Are risk controls monitored and reviewed?		
Is there evidence of plant inspection and maintenance?		
Is there evidence of information, training and instruction for employees and contractors?		
Is there a management of change procedure?		
Do you design / manufacture / supply plant?		
Do you understand you obligations?		
Is there evidence of hazard and risk statements, requirements on requests for tender, contract and purchasing orders?		
Is there evidence of checking against specification in stores receiving?		
Is there understanding of compliance with Dangerous Goods/Hazardous Substances Regulations?		
Is there evidence that quantities and types have been minimized?		
Is there a need for Regulatory Notification or Fire Authority Written Advice?		
Is there a "gating" process to control procurement of substances (management of change)		
Is there evidence of a workplace substances register?		

Practical Safety Process® STEP 3 Gap Analysis continued	Y	N
Is there a need for a Dangerous Goods Manifest?		
Have you substances requiring health surveillance?		
Are there any Poisons Schedule implications?		
Are MSDS in date and relevant? Can they be found easily?		
Is there an MSDS review process?		
Is there evidence of hazard identification, risk assessment and control? How is this information provided to relevant personnel? Is there evidence of provision of information, training and instruction?		
For dangerous goods is there evidence of product identification and compliance to standards?		
Do you understand periodicity for regulated review?		
Has plant associated with dangerous goods been assessed?		
Are placards and signage appropriate?		
Are all substances labelled appropriately?		
Are all storage and handling facilities provided with placarding and appropriate safety signage?		
Is there a signage review process?		
Is there a knowledge of differences - hazardous substances / dangerous goods?		
Do you facilitate workplace assessment in a simple understandable way?		
Are risk controls in place?		
Are risk controls monitored and reviewed?		
Is there evidence of checking against specification in stores receiving?		
Are loaders, packers and consignors responsibilities relevant?		
Is there understanding of compliance with Manual Handling Regulations?		
Is there evidence of a task register?		
Is there evidence of hazardous manual handling tasks identified?		
Is there evidence of assessment?		
How is this information provided to relevant personnel to identify situational circumstances and need for other risk controls or permits?		
Is there evidence of provision of information, training and instruction?		
Is there evidence of control measure application?		
Are risk controls monitored and reviewed?		
Is there a management of change procedure?		
Is there understanding of compliance with Confined Space Regulations?		
Is there evidence of a confined space register?		
Is there evidence of confined space assessment?		
Are all spaces positively identified with signage?		
Is there evidence of JSA before use?		
How is this information provided to relevant personnel?		
Is there evidence of provision of information, training and instruction?		

Practical Safety Process® STEP 3 Gap Analysis continued	Y	N
Is the appropriate rescue and monitoring equipment available?		
Is air monitoring equipment appropriately calibrated?		
Is there evidence of confined space permit use?		
Is there evidence of permit retention in accordance with regulatory requirements?		
Are risk controls monitored and reviewed?		
Is there a management of change procedure?		
Is there understanding of compliance with prevention of falls regulations?		
Is there evidence of a register of relevant tasks?		
Is there evidence of assessment?		
How is this information provided to relevant personnel to identify situational circumstances and need for other risk controls or permits?		
Is there evidence of provision of information, training and instruction?		
Are risk controls monitored and reviewed?		
Is there a management of change procedure?		
Is there understanding of compliance with asbestos regulations?		
Is there a system that ensures compliance with asbestos regulations?		
Is there an asbestos register?		
Is there an asbestos management control plan?		
Have assessments been done?		
How is this information provided to relevant personnel, including contractors to identify situational work circumstances and the need for other risk controls or permits?		
Is there evidence of provision of information, training and instruction?		
Are risk controls monitored and reviewed?		
Has all labeling been erected and in clear view?		
Is there a management of change procedure?		
Is there understanding of Traffic Management Planning (Plant safety adjunct)?		
Do you separate people by time, distance or physical segregation?		
Is a Traffic Management drawing available?		
Have assessments been done for mobile plant or plant used to lift or suspend loads?		
Is all equipment inspected maintained and records kept?		
Are signage / marking appropriate?		
Is there evidence of provision of information, training and instruction?		
Are risk controls monitored and reviewed?		
Is there a management of change procedure?		
Is there understanding of compliance with environmental regulations?		
Is there a plan? Is there an environmental impact statement?		
What is done with environmental waste?		
Are emissions to air created?		

Practical Safety Process® STEP 3 Gap Analysis continued	Y	N
Are threats to stormwater / ground water created?		
Do you know where stormwater drains lead?		
Are provisions made to clean up?		
How would you protect the environment from fire water or clean up?		
Is there a site services drawing?		
Is there a management of change procedure?		
Where you have Emissions?		
Have all emissions been identified?		
Are emission compliance requirements known?		
Have emissions been verified against approved criteria?		
Is a licence to discharge in place and are its conditions known, monitored and reporting requirements met.?		
Where you have any trade waste discharges to sewer?		
Have all trade waste discharges been identified?		
Does the trade waste agreement with the authority cover all discharge types, quantities and discharge points?		
Are collection systems routinely maintained and samples taken to verify performance?		
. Are conditions of the licence being met?		
Are local authority requirements known?		
Are incident notification guidelines known for the local authorities and are contact details known along with the relevant forms available?		
Do the quantities of dangerous/hazardous substances stored require licensing/registration with the local authority?		
Where licensing is required are quantities stored within specified limits?		
Are the reporting requirements of the licence being met?		
Where hazardous/dangerous substances are disposed of, are local authority requirements known and complied with, including the use of an approved disposal contractor?		
Are authorities included in emergency planning procedures?		
Is your site likely to have any form of contamination?		
Has a comprehensive survey been conducted to identify all sources of contamination? PCB, lead, oils, solvents, paints etc.?		
Is there a control plan in place which ensures the safety of employees and the community and has an appropriate hierarchy of controls been employed. ie. Elimination, engineering, procedural, PPE etc?.		
Have all likely contamination areas been surveyed. e.g. Storm water, ground water, soil?		
Is there a system for managing pests and vermin?		
Are arrangements are in place for the control of vermin and other pests that may impact on the health and wellbeing?		
Are the type and nature of control measures known including appropriate hazardous substance assessments?		
Are application controls plans are in place and are appropriate (least req approach)		

Practical Safety Process® STEP 3 Gap Analysis continued	Y	N
Is there a system for managing the hygiene requirements on site?		
Are arrangements in place for the maintenance of hygiene?		
Are routine checks made?		
Are chemicals used are declared and assessments carried out?		
Are storage arrangements are appropriate?		
Are systems in place for the disposal of blood borne pathogens? Bloods needles?		
Is there understanding of compliance with noise regulations?		
Is it difficult to hear in the Plant?		
Are there noisy processes?		
Is there a noise map?		
Are risk controls monitored and reviewed?		
Is there a management of change procedure?		
Does your company have any evidence of offences?		
Are there any prosecutions or PIN Notices (are they resolved)?		

6.0   STEP 4 - Ensure a Safe Physical Work Environment

The Practical Safety Process is designed so that each step is completed in order. There is very good reason for this. Without the foregoing knowledge from Steps 1-3 there is no point attempting to examine the requirements of Step 4.

In this step we are looking at the physical work environment. The processes that often need to be addressed are:

- Emergency Management Process
- Essential Services Process
- First Aid and Hygiene Process
- Signage Process
- Security Process
- Equipment Guarding Process
- Equipment Maintenance Process
- Mobile Plant Process
- Lighting Management Process
- Electromagnetic Radiation Management Process
- Asbestos Management Process
- Lead Management Process
- Lifting Equipment Management Process
- Disability Access Process
- Working From Home Process
- Waste Management Process
- Traffic Management Process

- Work Layout design Process
- Housekeeping Process

The purpose here is not to go through every process but to highlight the importance of the physical work environment and its impact on safety.

In referring to a physical work environment I am referring to the technologies and facilities. Sometimes these technologies and facilities are old and outdated with many negative legacies. Even with new technologies and facilities there can be problems. Often they have been designed by people who have not always considered the impact that their decisions have on the safety of people. At the end of the day it's not an old or new argument. It's about creating a safe work environment.

In planning any change, whether it be to an existing place of work, a building, or a new technology, due consideration needs to be given to safety. It means involving people at all levels in decision making. It means applying Steps 1 to 3 and taking the information gathered into the design review process. Communication and input from all levels is paramount for success in this area.

Technology can often be a useful ally in eliminating hazards. However it comes at a cost and can often introduce its own new set of issues that must be addressed. So care needs to be exercised when relying purely on technology for safety improvement.

An area that is often overlooked, and one that deserves mention here, is aesthetics. I don't know about you, but there are places that when I walk into them that I immediately feel unsafe, and there are others that I am comfortable in. There is more at play here than physical structure and technology. It's about the way these are presented. The colors, the layout, the lighting, the posters etc all go towards creating an environment that looks and feels safer. More than that, the physical environment is conveying the message that safety is important here. Perhaps there is a place for a safety interior designer! See also the section on communication. Section 2.1.2.6

Designing a safe workplace is one thing but maintaining it is another. Housekeeping routines are important in this regard. For me housekeeping includes not only having a place for everything but also having standards for things such as measuring deterioration. e.g. When does a guard rail need repainting. Often visual factory concepts are used to convey such standards in a very simple way. The use of proprietary programs such as $5S+1^{32}$ can be very useful in this area.

6.1   Conclusion

Traditionally the provision of a safe place of work has received a significant proportion of the attention in most safety programs. This is well directed effort if it leads to safer workplace design but it needs to be implemented proportionately with the other Practical Safety Process® Steps. The processes employed must involve shop floor employees if they are to be successful and achieve the resultant buy in. Processes for setting and maintaining standards are significant for the ongoing success in this step. Management of change is equally important. See section 9.10

6.2 Check Your Progress

Practical Safety Process® STEP 4 Gap Analysis	Y	N
ENSURE A SAFE PHYSICAL WORK ENVIRONMENT		
Is there a site plan showing locations of workplace substance storages, primary service isolations, fire equipment, exits and major traffic routes.		
Have you implemented Emergency Management Arrangements? Do you understand the elements of: • Prevention • Preparedness • Response • Recovery		
Is there any formal regulatory requirement for Fire Authority intervention or written advice under Dangerous Goods, Major Hazards or any other Legislation?		
Do you have drawings for dangerous goods (linked to a manifest)?		
Do you have fixed fire protection drawings?		
Have all emergency planning assumptions been made and recorded		
Has Fire Protection been considered under the requirements of building codes?		
Is there a Business Recovery Plan?		
Do you have security sensitive assets or chemicals?		
Have security standard operating and response procedures been written?		
Is there an Emergency Control Organization?		
Is there an Emergency Planning Committee?		
Are there formal Emergency Response Procedures written against those exposures?		
Is there training for Wardens?		
Are visitors fully informed of the emergency management arrangements?		
Are the emergency management arrangements subject to Management of Change procedures?		
Are processes practiced routinely?		
Are essential service requirements being monitored?		
Are there provisions for first aid?		
Are first aiders trained?		
Is there a process for identifying signage requirements?		
Are there adequate security arrangements in place?		
Are equipment installations planned?		
Are plant hazard identification and risk assessments carried out in consultation with employees?		
Have the hierarchy of controls applied to machinery or is there opportunity for higher controls?		
Is there adequate machine guarding?		

Practical Safety Process® STEP 4 Gap Analysis continued	Y	N
Is there a system for monitoring and maintaining safeguards?		
Is there a system for maintaining plant and equipment?		
Is there a system for managing mobile plant safety?		
Is lighting adequate and appropriately maintained?		
Is electromagnetic radiation understood and managed?		
Have all lifting devices been identified and load limits defined?		
Are these devices being maintained?		
Are these devices labeled appropriately?		
Is there provision for disability access?		
Are home office environments controlled and monitored?		
Is there a traffic management plan in place?		
Are the redundancies of electronic control systems known?		
Are emergency stops really emergency stops or control stops?		
Can electronic safety circuits be bypassed ie. program versus hard wire?		
Are visual stimuli used to promote safety? E.g.		
Wall colors		
Painted walkways		
Posters		
Signage		
Electronic banners		
Process map displays		
Shadow boards		
Area safety boards etc		
Are there systems in place for waste disposal?		
Is recycling a component of this?		
Have housekeeping standards been set and monitored?		
Have noise levels been measured?		
Has noise suppression been considered?		
Has air quality been measured?		
Are there systems in place to improve air quality?		
Is temperature an issue?		
What measures have been put in place to manage temperature?		
For hot areas have cool vests been considered?		
Are there drinking water facilities available?		
Are they sufficient?		
Are the staff amenities adequate for number of people?		
Are they maintained to a high standard?		
Has the use of plants been considered?		
Are there isolation plans for all services?		
Are there any systems that have dual feeds?		
What safeguards have been put in place to address these?		

Practical Safety Process® STEP 4 Gap Analysis continued	Y	N
Are isolation plans documented clearly and included in emergency plans?		
Are plant isolation plans available for all equipment?		
Do they form part of employee training?		
Are all buildings structurally sound?		
Do they all meet current building standards?		
Is there a system for storing workplace substances?		
Have compliance requirements been considered?		
Has emergency requirements been considered? Eg. Eye wash, showers etc.		

7.0   STEP 5 - Develop Safe Systems of Work

In developing safe systems of work there is a need to understand the fundamental processes of the business. This needs to be done at the highest level and then broken down in the individual processes that are needed for operation.

7.1   Safety Processes

The safety processes that may need to be implemented will vary greatly from company to company. Some that may need to be considered regarding safe systems of work are:

- Recruitment Process

- Induction and Assimilation Process

- Training Process

- Work Instruction Process

- Situational or Adhoc Work Process

- Electrical Work Process

- Portable Hand Tools Process

- Materials Management Process

- Workplace Substances Process

- Housekeeping Process

- Office Safety Process

- Smoking, Drug and Alcohol Management Process

- Product Design Process

- Project Management Process

- Purchasing Process

- Transport Process

- Teleworking Process

- Travel Safety Process

- Contractor Process

- Acquisition and Divestment Process

- Waste Disposal Process etc.

This is not meant to be an exhaustive list but what it does illustrate is that within safety there are many processes that need to be formulated and managed appropriately. Combining this with the requirements of the other steps the list is even longer. Thus it is incumbent upon the safety professional to provide advice to management on the processes that require development and implementation to meet both the needs of the company and also its statutory obligations. It requires careful thought and planning as discussed in Chapter 1. One of the most important aspects is to try and integrate safety processes with other normal activities and to avoid where possible safety being seen as an add on. If this can be achieved safety will become an integral part of the business and its culture. i.e. it's the way we do things around here! There are example processes given in the Appendices for the more common safety processes required.

7.2 Writing Procedures

In developing procedures all the previous Practical Safety Steps are applied. See Fig 23. The starting point is to complete both a Job Safety Analysis (JSA) (note: sometimes called Safe Work Method Statements SWMS or Work Method Statements (WMS) and a Job Person/People Analysis (JPA)® or Job Safety Person Analysis (Job SPA®). Input is also required from Practical Safety Process Step 3 Assess Compliance, to ensure the base level requirements are known.

The Job Person/People Analysis (JPA)® and Job Safety Person Analysis (Job SPA®) have been previously discussed, however the Job Safety Analysis requires further discussion. See Fig 24.

This tool if used correctly is very powerful in helping to formulate safe systems of work. It involves noting the basic steps of the process and then the hazards associated with each step. These hazards are then assessed for risk and controls proposed. In proposing controls there is a hierarchy that must be considered which is commonly referred to as the hierarchy of controls. see Table 7. This hierarchy is important as it reflects the desirability of the various controls from most desirable on the left, to least desirable on the right. The reason for this is because the reliance on people increases as you move across the page.

As shown in Fig 23 compliance is an important input when identifying controls. Quite often there might be legislative issues, standards or industry practices that should be considered when evaluating controls. It is therefore imperative that the right people are involved as these control statements become the basis for developing Standard Operating Procedures (SOP).

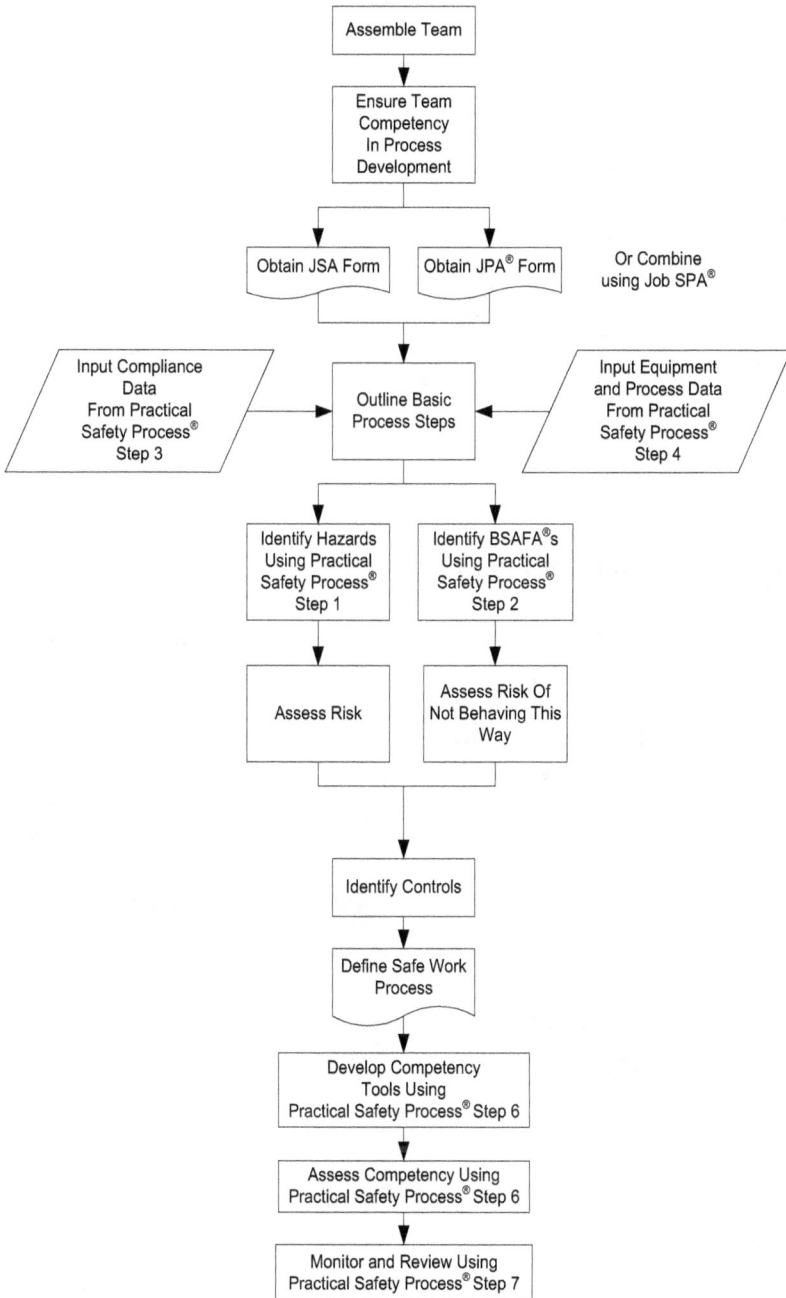

Fig 23 Developing Procedures Process.

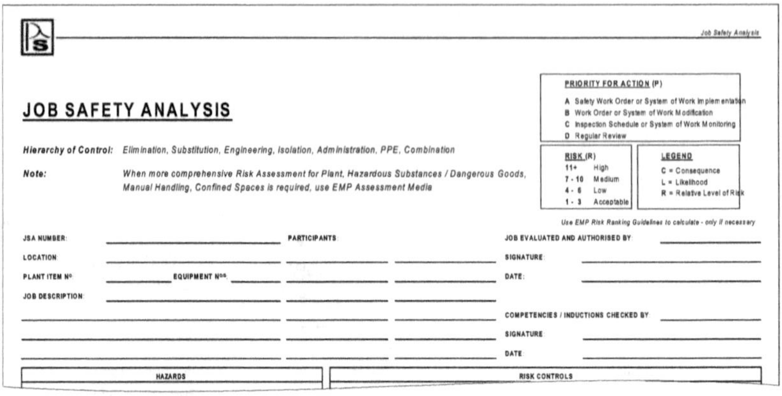

Job Safety Analysis

JOB SAFETY ANALYSIS

PRIORITY FOR ACTION (P)
A Safety Work Order or System of Work Implementation
B Work Order or System of Work Modification
C Inspection Schedule or System of Work Monitoring
D Regular Review

Hierarchy of Control: *Elimination, Substitution, Engineering, Isolation, Administration, PPE, Combination*

Note: *When more comprehensive Risk Assessment for Plant, Hazardous Substances / Dangerous Goods, Manual Handling, Confined Spaces is required, use EMP Assessment Media*

RISK (R)
11+ High
7 - 10 Medium
4 - 6 Low
1 - 3 Acceptable

LEGEND
C = Consequence
L = Likelihood
R = Relative Level of Risk

Use EMP Risk Ranking Guidelines to calculate - only if necessary

JSA NUMBER: ____ PARTICIPANTS: ____ JOB EVALUATED AND AUTHORISED BY: ____
LOCATION: ____ SIGNATURE: ____
PLANT ITEM Nº ____ EQUIPMENT Nºˢ ____ DATE: ____
JOB DESCRIPTION: ____
COMPETENCIES / INDUCTIONS CHECKED BY: ____
SIGNATURE: ____
DATE: ____

HAZARDS	RISK CONTROLS

Fig 24 Extract From a Job Safety Analysis Form

Table 7: Hierarchy of Controls

Eliminate	Substitute	Engineer	Isolate	Administration	PPE
Self Explanatory	Less Toxic Substance Alternative Process	Guards, Interlocks, Fortress Keys, Light Curtains, Limit switches, Stop /Go	Barricade, Bunting, Chains, Fence, Barrier, Crossings Cones, Chemical Cabinet, Fire Walls	JSA, Tagout Lockout, Site Rules, SOP's, MSDS, Toolbox, Observer, Dial/Dig, Housekeeping Training/ Licences, Dogging, Confined Space, Forklift, EWP, Harness, Crane, Heavy Vehicle, Induction	As Per MSDS, As Per Situation
Most Desirable					Least Desirable
Most Effective					Least Effective

There is an interesting dilemma faced here by anyone developing procedures. It relates to a potential trade of between the levels of detail required in the SOP versus the level of training. Too often I find procedures written that amount to several pages and many thousands of words. Whilst I'm sure the originator had the best intent, the practical value on the shop floor will be to gather dust. So what is the answer? In my view it's about keeping procedural documentation simple and holistic and then backing this up with detailed competency requirements.

To be effective procedures need to appeal to all types of thinking preferences. Whether employees are left or right brained in their thinking, this should not matter. This means though that procedural documentation needs to be visual, logical and detailed. e.g. Fig 25. In this example, which uses a proprietary template from Talsico International[25], there is a good balance achieved. There are safety and other prompts, a basic flowchart of the process, photographs and other checks that are included. There is significant information presented in a simple and concise way. It takes significant effort to create SOPs with this level of detail but the effort is worth it. Prompts are a particularly good feature that can be used to highlight hazards and their risk controls. At the other end of the scale information can be distilled into very basic but effective work instructions by extracting key issues for emphasis and just documenting these. See Fig 26.

7.3 Conclusion

It is imperative that a robust set of procedures are documented for all processes. This documentation needs to take into account all the information from the identification steps of the Practical Safety Process® (i.e. steps 1-3) and build in the risk control requirements. This then provides all the information required to safely carry out operations. The remaining action is to transfer this knowledge to employees through training and competency assessment.

Fig 25 Standard Operating Procedure Extract [25]

2. Reproduced with permission from Talsico International. Extracted from www.Talsico.com example Talsico ® Process Picture Maps ™

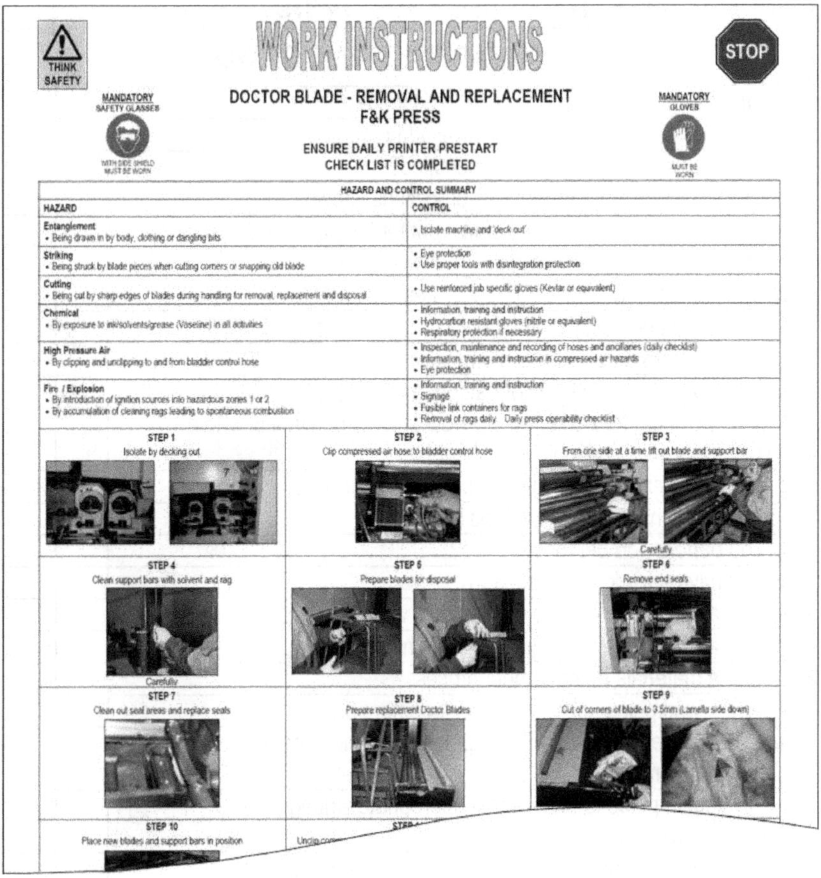

THINK SAFETY

WORK INSTRUCTIONS

STOP

MANDATORY SAFETY GLASSES

WITH SIDE SHIELD MUST BE WORN

DOCTOR BLADE - REMOVAL AND REPLACEMENT
F&K PRESS

ENSURE DAILY PRINTER PRESTART
CHECK LIST IS COMPLETED

MANDATORY GLOVES

MUST BE WORN

HAZARD AND CONTROL SUMMARY

HAZARD	CONTROL
Entanglement • Being drawn in by body, clothing or dangling bits	• Isolate machine and 'deck out'
Striking • Being struck by blade pieces when cutting corners or snapping old blade	• Eye protection • Use proper tools with disintegration protection
Cutting • Being cut by sharp edges of blades during handling for removal, replacement and disposal	• Use reinforced job specific gloves (Kevlar or equivalent)
Chemical • By exposure to ink/solvents/grease (Vaseline) in all activities	• Information, training and instruction • Hydrocarbon resistant gloves (nitrile or equivalent) • Respiratory protection if necessary
High Pressure Air • By clipping and unclipping to and from bladder control hose	• Inspection, maintenance and recording of hoses and ancillaries (daily checklist) • Information, training and instruction in compressed air hazards • Eye protection
Fire / Explosion • By introduction of ignition sources into hazardous zones 1 or 2 • By accumulation of cleaning rags leading to spontaneous combustion	• Information, training and instruction • Signage • Fusible link containers for rags • Removal of rags daily. Daily press operability checklist

STEP 1
Isolate by decking out

STEP 2
Clip compressed air hose to bladder control hose

STEP 3
From one side at a time lift out blade and support bar
Carefully

STEP 4
Clean support bars with solvent and rag
Carefully

STEP 5
Prepare blades for disposal

STEP 6
Remove end seals

STEP 7
Clean out seal areas and replace seals

STEP 8
Prepare replacement Doctor Blades

STEP 9
Cut of corners of blade to 3.5mm (Lamella side down)

STEP 10
Place new blades and support bars in position

Fig 26 Work Instruction example using a hazard checklist and risk control summary demonstrating the Practical Safety approach[30].

Reproduced with permission from APEX Plastics Extrusions Pty Ltd, Melbourne 2008.

7.4 Check Your Progress

Practical Safety Process STEP 5 Gap Analysis	Y	N
DEVELOP SAFE SYSTEMS OF WORK		
Has the basic business process been defined?		
Is there an understanding of the value add processes?		
Are non value adding processes identified?		
Are the BSAFA® requirements for processes known?		
Are people trained before they start work for the first time?		
Are competency requirements defined for all jobs?		
Are recruitment processes aligned to these requirements		
Are induction and assimilation training systems in place?		
Do they address corporate, site and specific area of work?		
Do such systems extend to contractors and visitors?		
Is there a system for documenting work instructions that is whole brained eg. visual and logical?		
Is there a system for managing adhoc work situations?		
Do you perform job safety analysis?		
Do you perform job person analysis?		
Do you have a work permit system?		
Is there a system for managing electrical work?		
Is there a system for managing portable hand tools?		
Is there a materials management process?		
Is there a workplace substances management process?		
Have personnel who use the workplace substances been appropriately trained?		
Is a system in place to ensure that appropriate signage and labeling is provided?		
Does this include facility, storage and product labelling (including decanted materials containers)		
Where hazardous and dangerous goods are to be transported are appropriate controls in place in accordance with legislative requirements?		
Are emergency arrangements in place and practiced, including; spill control processes, eye wash stations, etc.?		
Is there an office safety process?		
Is there a smoking, drug and alcohol management process?		
Is there a product design process?		
Are Company products/services assessed for potential hazards?		
Is there a need to provide the recipients of these products/services with the appropriate information regarding the hazards and appropriate risk control measures?		
Is there a project management process?		

Practical Safety Process STEP 5 Gap Analysis continued	Y	N
Does this process address all stages from design, tendering, manufacture, supply, install, erect and handover to operations?		
Does this include information transfer from design to fabrication to installation to commissioning to operation with regard to: hazard analysis, technical standards, notification and verification, fabrication installation and operation, equipment guarantees, training, decommissioning?		
Is there a procurement process?		
Does the selection of vendors and contractors include an assessment of their safety management system and does this include an assessment of past performance?		
Do contracts include specific safety and compliance obligations, the degree to which shall depend on the hazards and risks identified?		
Are the safety requirements of equipment and materials, which have the potential to affect the health and safety of people, specified prior to purchase, hire or lease and is compliance with these specifications verified?		
Are there systems established to maintain and control the quality of maintenance consumables and replacement parts to ensure that there is no adverse effect on safety?		
Does the purchasing process address the special requirements of workplace substances? Ie. quantities, storage and information and instruction?		
Is there a system for maintaining MSDS sheets?		
Do purchasing protocols include the provision of an MSDS prior to purchase for the first time and a system for ensuring MSDS has currency for ongoing orders?		
Is there a transport process?		
Is there a teleworking process?		
Is there a travel safety process?		
Does it address immunization, travel alerts and health insurance?		
Is there a process for managing acquisitions and divestments?		
Are the responsibilities and authorities of all personnel with respect to safety identified, defined, documented and understood in a responsibility chart?		
All personnel understand they have the authority to intervene/stop any behavior/condition which they believe to be unsafe?		
Effective initiatives are in place to promote and encourage a healthy lifestyle and to improve the general health of employees?		
Are appropriate company policies in place, authorised and relevant?		
Do these policies express responsibilities and commitment for all personnel?		
Are policies communicated appropriately?		

Practical Safety Process STEP 5 Gap Analysis continued	Y	N
Do employees know about them?		
Do they have regulatory compliance statements?		
Do your policies state the overall risk management context of the business?		
Do they have a consultation with employees statement? (particularly OH&S)		
Does a policy consider harassment?		
Is there a Rehabilitation and Return to Work policy?		
Does a policy consider equal opportunity?		
Is any safety or environmental system accredited?		
Does it need to be?		
Are safety management groups structured appropriately, proactive and trained?		
Is there a written constitution to formalize a safety committee?		
Are there formal agendas and minutes?		
Is there evidence of LTI injury frequency statistics?		
Is there evidence of recording all injuries?		
Is there evidence of how agenda items get to the meeting?		
Is there evidence of how issues are resolved?		
Is there evidence of pro-action by the Committee, for example compliance projects?		
Is there evidence of how and to whom meeting determinations and minutes are circulated?		
Is there evidence of members being elected?		
Is there balance in Employer / Employee representation?		
Is consultation with employees and H&S representatives carried out with all people affected?		
Is there a management of change procedure containing requirements for consultation for additions, modifications and deletions to plant and substances and systems of work?		
Are toolbox meetings and workplace communication meetings held?		
Is there evidence of Toolbox discussions and frequency? Look for recording		
Are safety issues managed appropriately?		
Is there a Safety Issue Resolution procedure?		
Does it include a risk assessment process so that specifics are identified and generalities excluded?		
Is there formal evidence of Observations, Recommendations and Management Actions? (if necessary)		
Is the issuing of PIN's understood?		
Do you have complete control over our contractors large and small?		
Are contractors selected, inducted and trained appropriately?		
Is there written evidence of formal selection, review of qualification and induction for contractors?		

Practical Safety Process STEP 5 Gap Analysis continued	Y	N
Is there evidence of provision of information, training and instruction, particularly for hazard identification, risk assessment and control of risk:- Plant safety Hazardous substances Confined spaces Manual handling Falls Noise		
Do you demand proof of a Safety Management System from your contractors?		
Do you ask for their insurance and liability information?		
Is management of maintenance/engineering and capital work effective?		
Can the system identify plant recognized under plant safety regulation.		
Does a management of change procedure correlate with any "maintainable" asset register?		
Is there evidence of an appropriate work request and authorization system?		
Do you plan work to optimize resource requirements? Trades / Hours / Parts / Tools / Costs		
Do you conduct maintenance routines on time on production parameters?		
Do you coordinate maintenance with production?		
Can you recognize discrete scheduled maintenance requirements in a process stream?		
Is capital work controlled by the work management system?		
Is there regular backlog reporting to production and maintenance? (Things not done)		
Is it sorted by exception e.g. missed due date/priority?		
Can the work management system reschedule?		
Does a management of change procedure correlate with the work management system?		
Is there evidence of condition checklists for equipment, eg: forklifts, mobile plant, pumps?		
Is there a formal work order system?		
Is there a formal work priority system (eg safety/work orders)?		
Is maintenance history recorded?		
Is there a structured JSA process for job step planning?		
Do all contractors use JSA?		

Practical Safety Process STEP 5 Gap Analysis continued	Y	N
Does the JSA process trigger permits against hazards recognized at the job step? For example; electrical, confined space, digging, heights, power lines (up and down) (otherwise how are they generated?)		
Is there a procedure for cancellation of permits?		
Is there a procedure to file permits in accordance with regulatory requirements, e.g. confined spaces?		
Are there documented work procedures and instructions?		

8.0   STEP 6 - Assess Competency

Whilst the idea of competency assessment has been around for some time in our educational systems it would be fair to say that industry is only just beginning to grasp its application in more recent years. If you haven't heard already the "buddy" training days are gone. It's no longer sufficient to put a new employee with an experienced one to learn the ropes. There needs to be a process of assessing competency prior to the person working for the first time. In fact the competency assessment process begins at the selection phase.

The role of gatekeeper is extremely important in determining who can enter the organization. Selection processes have now developed to a much more sophisticated level where personality profiling along with ability testing are now becoming the normal practice. Having experienced some of these, I'm not convinced that all organizations know why they do tests, or indeed what the testing results mean. However I am an advocate when they are used in the right way.

The Practical Safety Process® approach begins with the desired BSAFA®s. These are defined at the corporate level for overall cultural alignment, and at the job level for job alignment. A key finding for me over the years is that you can select people that have a higher propensity for safety than others. The complexity of the selection processes employed will depend on the nature of the work. This could entail many aspects such as those shown in Table 8.

Table 8: Selection Process Components

1. Ability testing	Numerical Reasoning, Mechanical Reasoning, Abstract Reasoning, Verbal Reasoning, Spatial Reasoning. Measures potential upside as well as current ability
2. Personality Profiling	To determine cultural fit
3. Work Skill Testing	Ability to do job
4. Role Playing	Simulating work environment challenges
5. Interviewing	Personal interview
6. Reference Checking	Previous performance

However before any of the selection process is initiated time needs to be spent understanding the job requirements. The Practical Safety Process® approach is illustrated in Fig. 27.

The process begins with establishing a Performance Model for a particular position. The best way I have found to do this is to start with the best performer in a particular job or position and define what they do. The supervisor of an area knows who these people are, but they will not necessarily know what makes them better than everyone else. The process of gathering this information is through interview and observation techniques. The things to look for are process knowledge, special skill requirements, and any particular behaviors or attitudes that they demonstrate that are critical to the job. Some of the most interesting information is gathered when there is process variability. i.e. When the process is not performing to standard. Quite often I find that this is what makes a standout performer. There are various tools that can be used for examining this, but one tool that I have found quite useful is a common variance chart[26]. See Fig 28.

Define Task

Identify an Exemplary Performer

Determine Their Activities

Identify External Best Practice and Competency Standards

Identify Where Possible What Makes Them The Best.
(Contrast BSAFA® s)

Gather Appropriate Work Procedures See Practical Safety Process® Step 5

Gather BSAFA® Information See Practical Safety Process® Step 2

Gather Compliance Information See Practical Safety Process® Step 3

Evaluate Industry Competencies Where They Exist

Define Success Criteria In a Performance Model

Review Each individual Against the Performance Model.
Theory and Practice

Identify Gaps and Assess Development Requirements

Define Individual Training Plan

Monitor and Review Performance See Practical Safety Process®
Step 7

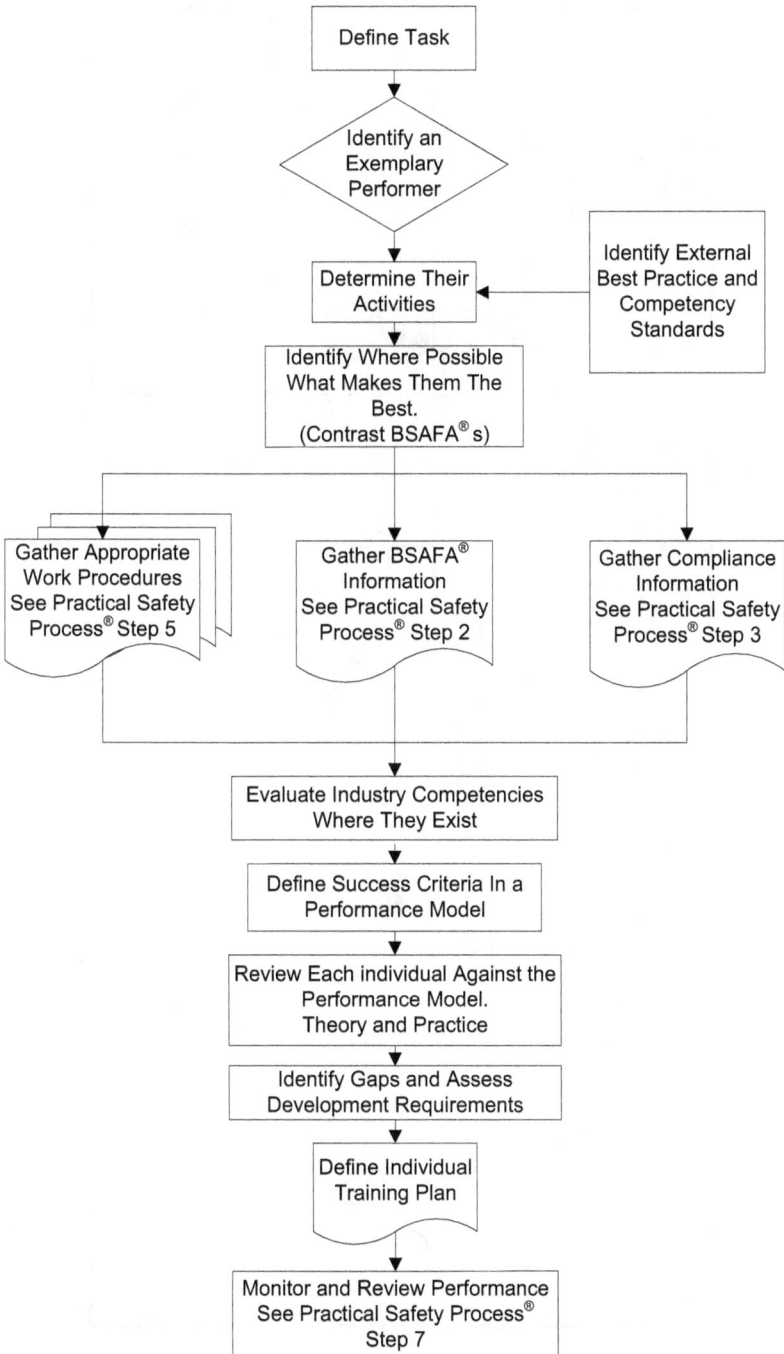

Fig 27 Developing a Performance Model and Assessing Competency

PROCESS STEPS	Frequency	Consequence	VARIANCES
Cut The plate	Daily	Lost Time Injury	
	Monthly	Failed Part/LTI	
	Monthly	Failed Part/LTI	
	Rarely	Failed Part	
	Daily	Waste/Costs	
	Rarely	Failed Part	
	Daily	Lost Part	
Weld Plate	Monthly	Failed Part	
	Rarely	Failed Part	
	Rarely	Failed Part	
	Rarely	Lost Time Injury	
Inspect Part	Rarely	Failed Part	
	Weekly	Failed Part	
	Daily	Failed Part	
Label with Conformance Tag	Daily	Failed Part	

Variances:
1 Ensure Guard In Place
2 Edges burred
3 Jagged cut
4 Not straight
5 Scrap Plate
6 Edge not parrallel
7 Label with Tag
8 Weld splatter
9 Poor weld penetration
10 Part warped when welded
11 Weld Flash To Eyes
12 Part out of shape
13 Part out of specification
14 Quality Mix up

Safety Variance Summary	1	2	3	4	5	6	7	8	9	10	11	
Environmental Variance Summary	2	3	4	5	6	7	8	9	10	11	12	13	14
Process Variance Summary	2	3	4	5	6	7	8	9	10	12	13	14

Insert Row
Delete Row

Fig 28 Variance Chart

These charts are quite useful in examining a process and distilling out issues that may arise. Quite often a brainstorming type session may be useful in determining the bulk of the issues but always go back to the exemplary performer to find out more.

I didn't realize the significance of this until one day I was interviewing an operator when he just stopped me, grabbed a grease gun and greased a bearing. When he returned I asked what he just did. He said to me, "Didn't you hear that bearing squealing? If I hadn't greased it, we would be down for 2 hours, as it is now, we can change it at the next changeover." This is the type of action that makes an exemplary performer, and it is this knowledge that needs to be captured and taught to others.

In the example shown in Fig 28. the safety, environmental and process variances have been captured. In most cases these would be done separately, especially for someone with little experience. The process is similar to a Job Safety Analysis or Job Person/People Analysis JPA® in that the first step is to outline the job steps. The next step is to establish the common things that can go wrong, their frequency and the potential consequences. At this stage it is sufficient just to capture the data, as what is desired is a free flow of information from the operator to the interviewer. The interrelationships of these variances on each other can be determined later to establish downstream effects.

In the example shown "Variance 2- Edge Burred" can contribute to "Variance 13- Part out Of Specification". This is indicated by the number 3 being entered on the variance 13 line. Establishing these interrelationships helps prioritize effort by taking into consideration the downstream effects, frequencies and consequences of each variance.

Finally the impact of the various variances on safety, environmental and process performance is summarized at the bottom of the chart.

Having established the Variance Chart, the controls for each variance should be established and prioritized in Pareto order. i.e.

Most likely to least likely. In this way it is possible to capture critical knowledge capital around a process. See Table 9.

Table 9: Variance Control Table

Process Step	Variance	Controls
Cut The Plate	Edges Burred	1. Guillotine gap too wide – check and adjust as per SOP 1234.
		2. Blade Blunt – Check blade sharpness as per SOP 5678
		Etc.

As shown the most likely controls are listed in Pareto order according to the information gathered from most likely control to least likely control. These variance control tables, along with operating procedures, desired behaviors and compliance elements can then be used to feed process information into the Performance Model. The components of a performance model for a particular job might include:

1. Position Description

2. Prerequisite requirements
    a. Skill requirements
    b. Common Core Behavioral/Value requirements
    c. In-house training
    d. Position requirements
    e. Physical Attributes

3. Process Performance Requirements
    a. Process Steps
    b. Key activities and reference SOPs
    c. Competencies
    d. Attitude and Behaviors
    e. Performance Indicators
    f. Obstacles/Variance Control (Must Know hot spots)

4. Written Assessment

5. Demonstrated Performance Assessment

6. Verbal Assessment.

This list is not exhaustive by any means but there is a need to be thorough here. The performance model is where all the information gathered to date is collated and summarized so that it can be taught to others. An example is shown in Fig 29. This example shows an extract from a Cutter Welder Performance Model. The first sheet shows the components along with the prerequisites of this position. The other 2 pages show examples of competency clusters for Safety and Process control. Each of these clusters has a set of activities and competencies that need to be addressed. Linkage is made to standard operating procedures and the behavioral elements. Other common competency clusters might include environment, quality, finance/costs and maintenance etc. These models provide for a common assessment against requirements and provide for tailored interventions for individuals based on gaps found. This speeds up competency development and knowledge transfer.

The assessment activity involves either written, oral, demonstrated or a combination assessment against each of the criteria mentioned. With respect to safety, demonstrated performance should be the key assessment methodology. The competency of the assessor is not to be overlooked either. There is a real need for assessors to be trained to ensure success.

B.2 PERFORMANCE CLUSTER   Process

Key Performance Result   Guillotine Blade changed over in a timely and accurate manner.

B. PERFORMANCE MODEL   Cutter Welder

B1. PERFORMANCE CLUSTER   Safety

POSITION DESCRIPTION

Cutter Welder

Performance Model

Each Performance Model is captured in the following documents:

Position Description
Process Performance Requirements
Written & Verbal Assessment
Performance Demonstration
Performance Observation

A. Prerequisites

1. Welding trade certificate or equivalent
2. Guillotine Operation Assessment
3. Company Induction
4. Area Induction
5. Aptitude Testing
6. Medical Testing

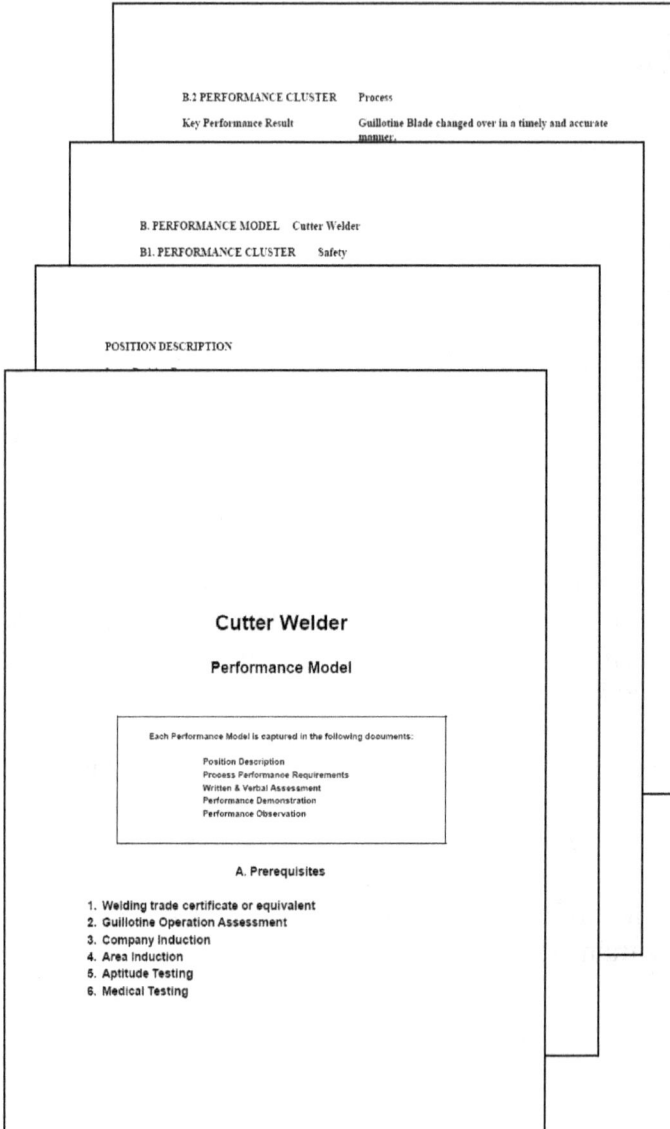

Fig 29 Extract From a Performance Model

In Australia there is a Certificate IV training program for assessors that could be considered the minimum requirement. With all this time and effort there is a need to secure management commitment. Considerable effort is required to achieve the desired results in both time and resources. This needs to be understood, and cooperation at all levels must be achieved. It requires significant contributions from Safety, Quality, Environmental, Human Resource and Supervisory staff. However the benefits in terms of safety and increased productivity outcomes can be significant. These same models can be used in the initial selection process to better understand potential candidate matching.

A key tool for any supervisor in this area is the skills/competency matrix. This is a key tool for understanding staff abilities whilst providing for allocation of tasks.

In recent times I have expanded on this traditional use to better map capabilities using the BSAFA® approach. I include the BSAFA®s in the traditional matrix along with job competencies as defined in the performance models. See Table 10. In the example the BSAFA®s become the non negotiables in terms of whether the person is to be selected or not. The core competencies (CC) are developed within the organization and provide for a development path for each individual. I've found it useful to divide these competencies into 2 parts, core competencies (CC) and application of core competencies (AP). In the example there are 2 welders that are tradesmen. The core competencies required are listed as CC1-CC4 which each one must pass. These core competencies are pre-requisites for various parts of the production environment. As shown CC1 is a prerequisite for AP1. In this example the welders must demonstrate their ability to apply CC1 competency to Product 1 in accordance with the requirements of SOP 1234. It is this second stage that allows the welders to be released to the production environment. The application competency AP1 allows the operator to make product or be certified to a particular process competency.

Table 10: Example Skill/Competency Matrix

Requirements	Measures	Person 1	Person 2
Ability Scores	Verbal >60 Numerical > 50	V 65 N 60	V 70 N 80
B	Attention to detail	Pass	Pass
S	Welding	Trade certificate	Trade Certificate
A	Enthusiastic	Yes	Yes
F	Proud of Work	Yes	Yes
A	20/20 vision	Pass	Pass
Core Competencies (CC)			
CC1	Mig Weld Mild steel	Pass	Pass
CC2	Mig Weld Aluminium	Pass	NYC
CC3	Mig Weld Mild Steel vertical	Pass	NYC
CC4	Flux Core Weld Mild Steel	NYC	NYC
Application of Core Competencies (AP)			
AP1	Apply CC1 to Product 1 6 fillet welds as per SOP 1234	NYC	Pass

Each must demonstrate competency in accordance with defined requirements prior to working for the first time. This is a standard requirement in all safety legislation. For me it also makes good business sense to have people understand the job requirements!

8.1 Conclusion

Competency assessment is the key to ensuring understanding. It is the result of significant effort with respect to assembling the requisite information, preparing training and development pathways and materials, and then finally training and assessing individuals. The rewards are significant not only in terms of safety but productivity as well.

8.2　Check Your Progress

Practical Safety Process STEP 6 Gap Analysis	Y	N
ASSESS COMPETENCY		
Are performance models defined for all jobs and do they contain?		
Position description?		
Prerequisite BSAFA® requirements?		
Process performance requirements including BSAFA®, process steps, reference SOP's, competencies, performance indicators and Variance controls?		
Do the performance models build in the information from Steps 1 to 5		
Assessment criteria verbal, written or demonstrated?		
Does the criterion include core competencies as well as application competencies related to products/processes for example?		
Does training include training required by legislation?		
Is safety a component of these?		
Are supervisors adequately trained to assess competency?		
Is a competency matrix available?		
Do selection processes align to performance models?		
Are records maintained and secured?		

9.0   STEP 7 - Monitor and Review Performance

The final step is to monitor and review performance. Unfortunately this is where most Company's start their Safety journey. As was shown in the previous chapters significant effort is required to assure success through the appropriate provision of infrastructure, information, instruction and training.

Monitoring is about measuring the performance and effectiveness of the safety system implementation against the desired outcomes. The common processes that need to be considered are:

1. Measuring and Reporting

2. Auditing

3. Housekeeping and Workplace Inspection

4. Safety Observations

5. Health Assessment

6. Rehabilitation

7. Incident Investigation

8. Corrective Action

9. Change Management

10. Safety Recognition

11. Records Management

9.1   Measuring and Reporting

Great care needs to be taken in establishing the measuring and reporting processes to be implemented. Essentially these processes can be divided into 2 areas.

1. Latent Measures
2. Proactive Measures

In the early seventies Bird[27] developed the safety triangle that has been a cornerstone in guiding management thinking in terms of what measures are important. It is also sometimes referred to as the "Iceberg Principle[28]" in safety. See Fig 30.

The iceberg metaphor asserts that by addressing minor issues below the waterline that you can prevent injuries from occurring as illustrated above the waterline. It also asserts that there are progressively more issues to manage as you move from the tip to the bottom of the iceberg.

For example for every fatality you could expect to find more lost time injuries, even more medical treatment injuries etc. This can be a very powerful tool when examining statistical data. Quite often reporting issues can be highlighted when the principle is applied.

A few years ago when I started work for a major corporation I found that despite having a lost time frequency rate of 5 LTI/million person hours worked, the first aid frequency rate was 1FAI/million person hours worked. This did not make sense if you apply the iceberg principle. Indeed it was found that a reporting issue did exist with respect to first aid injuries. Subsequently, after some intervention, the next batch of data showed a dramatic increase in first aid injuries. This increase continued in the months that followed for a period of 4 years before a reduction started to occur once again. This change in first aid incidents reported amounted to a 10 fold increase in the 4 years. In this same period there was a 75% reduction in lost time injuries. It's not an overnight success story, as changing a reporting culture takes time. What it does show though is that gathering data is one thing, but using and interpreting the data to guide intervention is another.

Fig 30 Adaption of Birds Safety Triangle[31]

Many of the latent measures are dictated by legislation, and guided by Standards. Indeed many jurisdictions require notification to local authorities for specific types of injuries. The safety professional must understand and advise on such requirements. Thus latent measures are important in safety.
These indicators may include:

- Fatalities

- Lost Time Injury Frequency Rate (LTIFR)
  (Categorized according to type of injury, severity, part of the body, agency of injury, mechanism of injury, circumstances, area, time, type of work, etc)

- Number of days lost due to lost time injury's

- Days away on restricted duties – DART rates

- Medical Treatment Injury Frequency Rate (categorised as above)
- First aid injury Frequency Rate (categorized as above)
- All injury Frequency rate
- Occupational illnesses
- Number of days lost due to occupational illnesses

To enable a better comparison of performance particularly across multiple sites and Company boundaries, measures are often converted to frequency rates. e.g. LTIFR – lost time injury frequency rate expressed as a ratio of injuries per million person hours worked. Likewise medical treatment, first aid and all injury frequency rates are often used. It is important to realize that quite often different Countries/Companies will use different numbers of hours worked in calculating their ratios, so care needs to be taken when reviewing data from multiple sources. It is important to make best use of this data by tracking trends and determining intervention strategies. It's not sufficient to produce a report showing data without using it to make informed intervention strategies.

The proactive measures represent data that can be gathered on performance prior to an injury occurring. Changes in this data can often be used as lead indicators in injury prevention. These indicators can include:

- Unsafe Acts/hour
- Safe Acts/hour
- Unsafe Conditions/Inspection hour
- Training hours/month versus plan
- Toolboxes/month versus plan
- Safety Observations versus plan

- Audits conducted versus plan

- Risk assessments completed versus planned

- Actions completed versus planned

- Employee competency assessments planned versus completed

- Employee hazard notifications/month

- Procedures written versus planned

- System implementation status

- Maintenance activities planned versus completed etc.

As shown most of these indicators are expressed ratios as this allows comparison across multiple sites and organizations. Others relate to specific internal goals that are specific to system improvement and development, and hence will be more aligned to individual entities. The important thing to note is that over time the effort being spent must lead to a reduction in injuries. Careful analysis of these ratios over time can yield some interesting correlations when compared with the latent indicators.

Reporting of incidents is sometimes required by authorities as per the applicable statutory requirements. For example the following incidents normally require reporting.

- Fatalities
- Injuries requiring hospitalisation
- Any person requiring immediate medical treatment as a result of exposure to chemicals

The extent and nature of reporting will depend on the different authorities. In addition some authorities also require reporting of near miss type incidents such as:

- The collapse, overturning, failure, malfunction or damage to plant.

- The collapse or failure of an excavation or of any shoring supporting an excavation

- The collapse or partial collapse of all or part of a building or structure

- The fall or release from a height of any plant, substance or object

- An interruption to ventilation in mines

- A leak or spill of workplace substances etc.

These are examples only and therefore it is incumbent upon the Safety Professional to be aware of such requirements and be in a position to advise on such matters.

9.2   Auditing

Safety auditing is concerned with the status of implementation of the safety systems. It requires that the desired system is known, its elements and success criteria are defined and that an audit tool is available. This tool should be simple to use and provide the criteria. See Fig 31.

COMPLIANCE	Weighting	Total
Element 1 Legislative Compliance (AS4801 4.3.2, 4.4.7)		
C1 Site Issues applicable: (circle relevant): Emissions…… Trade Waste………… Authorities Insurance……. Asbestos………. Contamination………… Plant……………… Confined Spaces……… Hazardous….EPA…… Substances (see supplementary checklists for requirements)		
1. All relevant legislative and regulatory requirements applicable to the operation have been identified and this is demonstrated through a compliance register.	40	
2. Plans are formulated, documented and implemented to achieve full compliance.	30	
3. Arrangements are in place to ensure that any changes to legislative requirements are identified and acted upon.	10	
4. Systems are developed to ensure that all compliance reporting and recording requirements are met. Including compliance inspections	10	
5. Due diligence requirements extend to customers, contractors visitors and the community.	10	
	TOTAL	
PEOPLE		
Element 2 Leadership and Commitment (AS4801 4.2,4.3.4,4.4.1.1)		
1. People component of Business Plan and dialogues addresses corporate safety objectives	20	
2. HSE action plan in place and the plan is supported and reviewed	20	
3. Involvement of employees to improve HSE performance through consultative process	5	
4. Management and employees are involved in Management System review processes, ie. Audits, observations.	10	
5. Sufficient human, material and financial resources are provided for the effective ……		

Fig 31 Audit Tool

In this example the various elements have performance criteria listed which are given a relative weighting so performance can be judged. The level of detail required in such a tool is really dependent on the expertise of the auditors concerned.

Where people have limited safety system knowledge or where multiple sites or many different auditors are involved the level of detail will need to be increased to ensure consistency. Reporting should also be considered in this planning stage. The audience is an important consideration here but experience has lead me to believe that to be effective there needs to be:

1.   Summary of findings
10 Detail of observations and recommendations
11 Photos of findings
12 A cross link to legislation as appropriate

Care needs to be exercised in the summary as this is the only part many managers will read. The key points need to be presented to ensure that they understand what is required of them in terms of support and follow-up. I have found that a simple graphical summary of the performance against the audit elements along with a summary of the key points can normally be completed on a single page. See Fig 32.

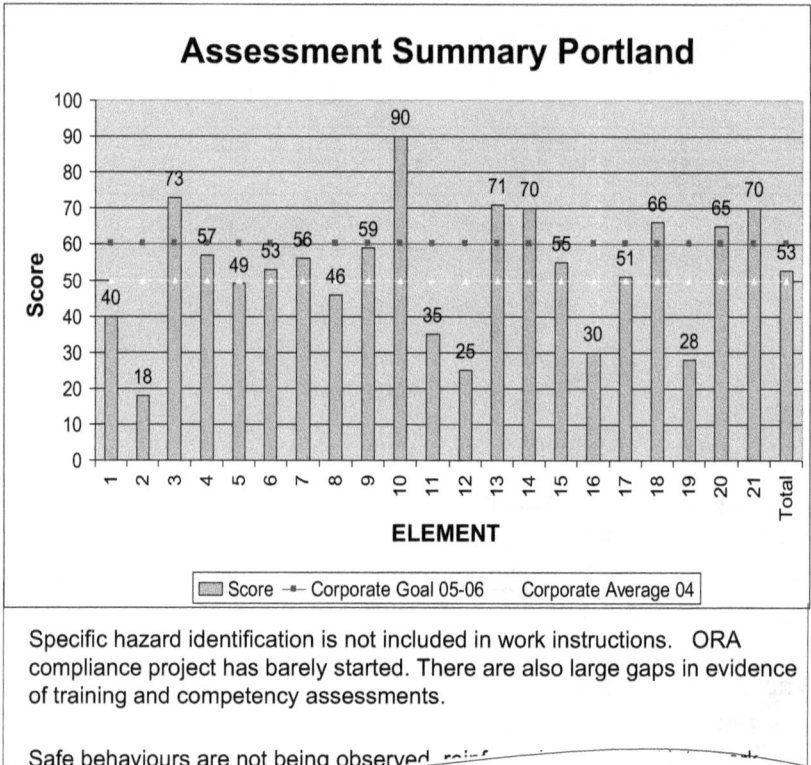

Assessment Summary Portland

Specific hazard identification is not included in work instructions. ORA compliance project has barely started. There are also large gaps in evidence of training and competency assessments.

Safe behaviours are not being observed

Fig 32 Audit Report Extract

The photographic evidence is also particularly important in that it can convey an irrefutable message to all levels of the organization. It removes the subjective arguments about what was present at the time and allows issues to be addressed.

A summary of the Internal Audit process is shown in Flowchart 9.2.

9.2 Audit Process

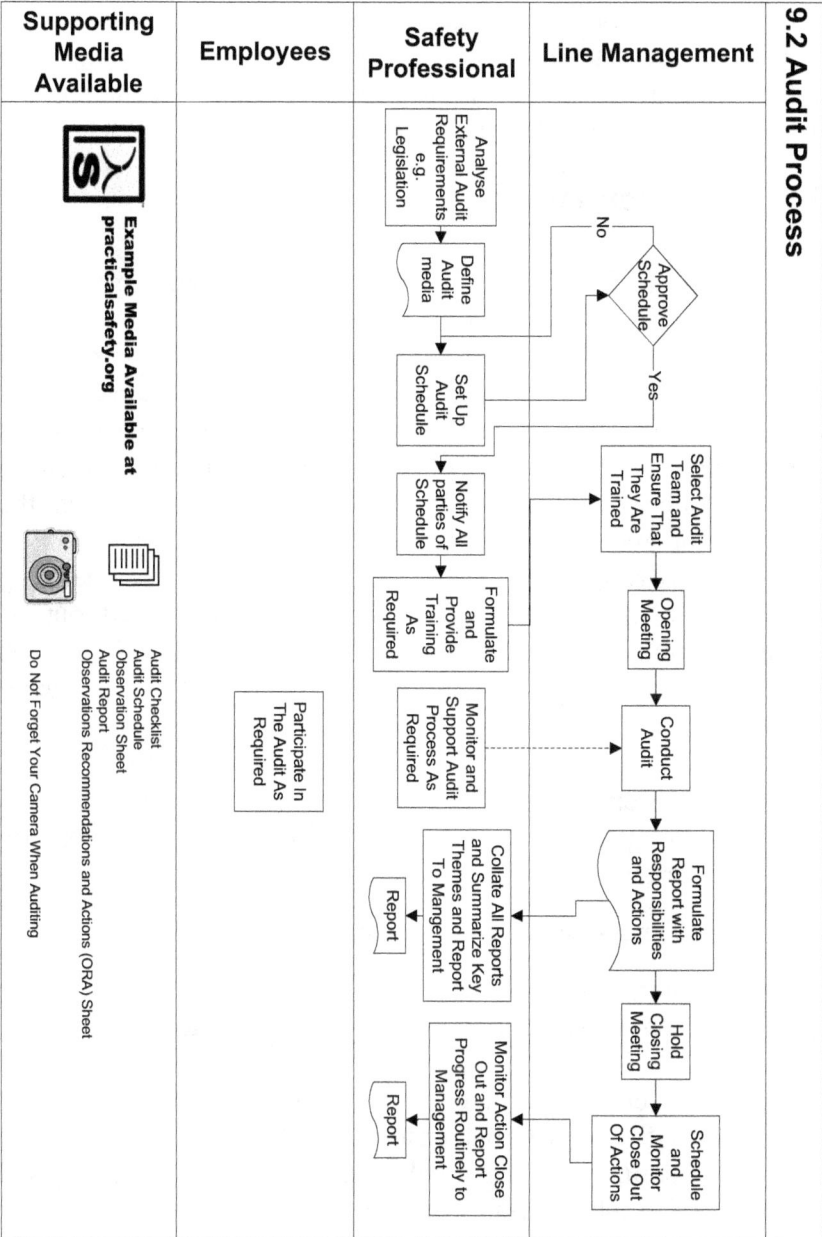

Supporting Media Available	Employees	Safety Professional	Line Management

Safety Professional flow:
- Analyse External Audit Requirements e.g. Legislation
- Define Audit media
- Set Up Audit Schedule
- Notify All parties of Schedule
- Formulate and Provide Training As Required
- Monitor and Support Audit Process As Required
- Collate All Reports and Summarize Key Themes and Report To Management → Report
- Monitor Action Close Out and Report Progress Routinely to Management → Report

Line Management flow:
- Approve Schedule? — No / Yes
- Select Audit Team and Ensure That They Are Trained
- Opening Meeting
- Conduct Audit
- Formulate Report with Responsibilities and Actions
- Hold Closing Meeting
- Schedule and Monitor Close Out Of Actions

Employees:
- Participate In The Audit As Required

Supporting Media Available:

Example Media Available at practicalsafety.org

- Audit Checklist
- Audit Schedule
- Observation Sheet
- Audit Report
- Observations Recommendations and Actions (ORA) Sheet

Do Not Forget Your Camera When Auditing

Not all audits can be planned rigidly and there needs to be scope for adhoc audits to be conducted. These could be generated out of internal events or can sometimes be promulgated by external authorities. It should also be noted that some audits and assessments in specific areas may be required by legislation and these should be identified and addressed.

9.3   Observations

As discussed in Step 2, the importance of understanding what the desired BSAFA®s are cannot be underestimated. Employees need to have been given the opportunity of knowing what is required before observations take place. This should be done as part of the work instructions and competency assessment steps. This removes the policeman attitude and self righteousness that can often be linked to safety observation. Having said that, carried out with the right attitude and preparation, observations are very significant to safety improvement. I make a distinction here between observations and inspections. Observations are carried out on people behavior, where as inspections are carried out on workplace conditions. Observations can be carried out in several ways:

- Observations of demonstrated performance as part of competency assessment processes against set job criteria.

- General observations against desired core BSAFA®s

- Non Specified behavior observations (need caution here to avoid "policemen" culture developing)

The biggest challenge here is not so much conducting the observations themselves but ensuring that the observer has the courage to confront At Risk behaviors, and to also praise good behaviors. The intervention needs to be timely and appropriate. I have found that not many people are comfortable intervening. Different people will react in different ways to being observed, and it is often the fear of this reaction, that stops the intervention.

There needs to be a culture developed where intervention is acceptable, and expected, by everyone. The success here comes not so much from what is observed but what is done about what is observed. It's not about taking a list of observations back to the office and writing a report. It's more about how many interventions did you make as a result of the observations made, that makes the difference. The old saying of "You get the level of safety you are prepared to walk past" is a good one to remember here.

As a result of the intervention requirements not everyone will be suited to making observations. Thus care needs to be taken in the selection of observers, and training needs to be given. This training must include:

- People personality types/groups

- Understanding of their own personality

- Intervention strategies for different people

- Role playing intervention

Observers should also be supported by documentation that can prompt and support the activity. See Fig 33. Such documentation should have the desired behaviors listed to aid the observer in what is expected. As with audits, observations need to be scheduled routinely to be effective. As was discussed in Chapter 2.1.2 safety commitment is best demonstrated by management actively participating in the workplace. A significant proportion (up to 5%) of management time needs to be spent in observations for a system to be effective. Management by walking around has significant value. The types and nature of the interventions provides valuable data that should be analyzed and used to direct safety effort. In Chapter 2.1.1 Fig 11 page 45 we saw the advantage of such analysis in a project setting.

Safety Observation Form

Area			Date	
Tasks Observed	Pendant Crane Operation			
Observation Team				
Time Started				
Time Finished		Total Observation Time		

BSAFA™ Performed

	BSAFA™ Observation Checklist	Yes	No
B1	When using pendant crane does operator always walk forwards		
B2	Is the load always placed in front of operator		
B3	Did the operator scan the area before initiating crane movement		
B4	Was load ever suspended over other people		

			Follow up ORA No.
		Other Observations	
		OBSERVATION SUMMARY	
		At Risk Acts/Hr Observation	
		Safe Acts/Hr Observation	

Fig 33 Observation Form

Observations reinforce the desired behaviors and test the effectiveness of the work instructions and competency assessment processes. As such they are critical to any safety effort.

9.4 Workplace Inspections

Workplace inspections arise out of the need to maintain consistency in workplace standards. As with behaviors, expectations must be defined for workplace standards. The principle here is "everything in its place and a place for everything."

Probably one of the most effective methods in this area is the application of the "visual factory" concept. In applying this to the workplace consider:

- Photographs showing good/bad
- Color-coded pipes and wires
- Painted floor areas for good stock, scrap, trash, etc.
- Shadow boards for parts and tools
- Visual displays on performance[29]
- Indicator lights
- Workgroup display boards with charts
- Procedures with photographs and graphics
- Production status boards
- Work Console design

All these things have one motive, and that is to drive the desired BSAFA®s. It's about making it easier for people to do, and want to do, the right thing rather than the wrong thing. These systems also make inspections very straightforward and help supervision maintain standards on a routine basis.

As with the other forms of monitoring, workplace inspections need to be planned and scheduled. Results again need to be analysed and interventions planned appropriately. It sometimes helps to have checklists to prompt inspectors. These can be general in nature or specific to a particular area or topic of interest. See Fig 34. Some of the more mature systems have photographs on their checklists to guide inspections further on what is acceptable.

Other types of inspections may include those required by an External Authority, OHS Representatives, or Union Representatives.

SAFETY INSPECTION CHECK LIST				
Designated area for Inspection:			Inspection Date:	
Details	Y/N	Comments	ORA No.
A	**Floors**			
	1. Even surface, free from defects			
	2. Dropped objects			
	3. Oil and/or grease spots			
	4. Off-cuts/rubbish/excessive dirt			
	5. Stock material cluster			
	6. Floor openings safely covered			
	7. Clear of electrical leads			
B	**Aisles/ designated walk ways**			
	1. Wide enough for traffic			
	2. Even surface, free from defects			
	3. Boundary marked with yellow lines			
	4. Clear of cases/materials and rubbish			
	5. Clear of trolleys, hand trucks etc.			
	6. Clear of electrical leads			
	7. Unobstructed vision at intersections			
	8. Exits clearly marked			
C	**Machines etc**			

Fig 34 Safety Inspection Checklist

9.5   Health Assessment

Health assessments are an integral part of any safety system. The health of an employee has a direct relationship to productivity, and potentially directly affects the safety of the individual employee and that of their colleagues. In addition some health assessments are required by law especially where there is exposure to a particular hazard. e.g. Noise, Lead

Some of the types of assessments that need to be considered are:

1.   Pre- employment – where the potential employee is checked to ensure their physical health attributes match the criteria for the job.

2.   Job Change – Reassessment against new job requirements

3. Specific Duty Assessments – some duties require assessments e.g. Forklift Drivers, Crane Operators, Miners, railway workers etc.

4. Assessments as part of injury treatment and rehabilitation

5. Assessments as part of health monitoring. e.g. hearing, eyesight, spirometry etc.

6. Assessments as part of workplace surveillance e.g. Drug and alcohol testing.

The essence of all this testing is to ensure the health and wellbeing of the individual and his/her work colleagues. It is important to maintain confidentiality with respect to health information but equally it is important to share information with employees about their health. Such records need to be maintained in a secured place and maintained indefinitely.

When considering health assessment requirements it is important to know the scope and nature of the work, the physical attribute requirements, the hazard exposures, legal requirements and standards that apply.

Health assessments conducted as part of a health surveillance regime normally require employee consultation prior to implementation. This is to ensure all personnel understand under what circumstances testing will be carried out and the potential consequences.

9.6   Rehabilitation

Rehabilitation is to be provided to any employee who has suffered an injury or illness as a result of their work. The legal framework around this must be understood for the various jurisdictions that are operated in.

Policies and procedures need to be communicated to all employees. This should also include an understanding of the escalation process in terms of notification of injury. e.g. Fig 35.

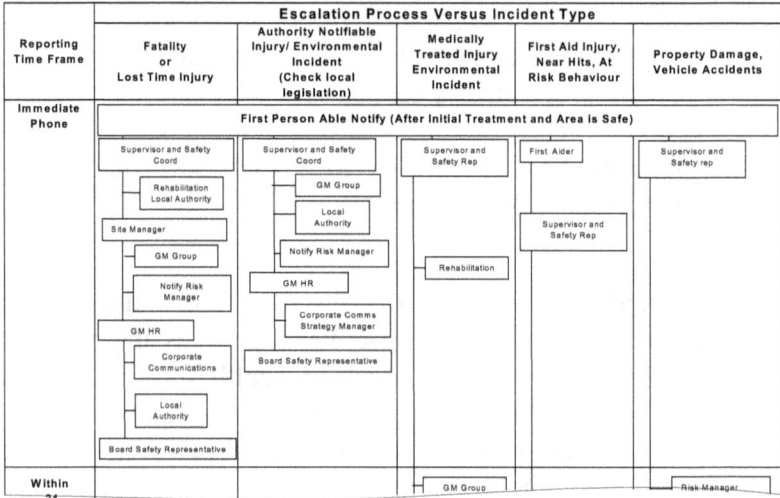

Reporting Time Frame	Escalation Process Versus Incident Type					
	Fatality or Lost Time Injury	Authority Notifiable Injury/ Environmental Incident (Check local legislation)	Medically Treated Injury Environmental Incident	First Aid Injury, Near Hits, At Risk Behaviour	Property Damage, Vehicle Accidents	
Immediate Phone	First Person Able Notify (After Initial Treatment and Area is Safe)					
	Supervisor and Safety Coord	Supervisor and Safety Coord	Supervisor and Safety Rep	First Aider	Supervisor and Safety rep	
	Rehabilitation Local Authority	GM Group				
	Site Manager	Local Authority		Supervisor and Safety Rep		
	GM Group	Notify Risk Manager	Rehabilitation			
	Notify Risk Manager	GM HR				
	GM HR	Corporate Comms Strategy Manager				
	Corporate Communications	Board Safety Representative				
	Local Authority					
	Board Safety Representative					
Within			GM Group		Risk Manager	

Fig 35 Example Extract From Escalation Process

Nothing causes more frustration than a poor understanding and application of this process. Thus all employees must understand how the rehabilitation and escalation processes apply to them.

One aspect that must be considered in any rehabilitation program is the need for the employee to maintain contact with workmates and colleagues. This is significant for their psychological healing. By contrast psychological detachment from the workplace can occur if the employee is left to their own devices at home.

As shown in the example in Flowcharts 9.6.1-2. the rehabilitation process can be quite complex and involve considerable effort. It is much better to spend the effort avoiding injury in the first place rather than managing the consequences.

Manipulation of the rehabilitation system can occur by over zealous management trying to avoid lost time injuries and also by employees who want to manipulate the system. This means that it is an area that must attract careful management scrutiny and monitoring to avoid potential problems.

However, used correctly, rehabilitation is a valuable process in ensuring an employee is cared for and returned to the workforce in a timely manner. For this to occur a carefully thought out return to work program needs to be implemented which includes the potential for alternative duties or job retraining. Such a program is normally developed and agreed in consultation with the employee, treating doctor and a company representative. It is desirable to have a list of possible alternative duties that can be sent to a treating doctor at the time the injury occurs. This enables the doctor to make an informed decision about what duties can be performed given the employees reduced capacity. In the case where the employee is unfit for any duties a schedule of retesting should be put into place. In some unfortunate cases it may not be possible to rehabilitate the employee for any duty. In these cases support mechanisms need to be in place to support the ongoing issues that often accompany serious injuries. Such support should extend to the families involved. e.g. Employee Assistance Programs.

9.6.1 Rehabilitation

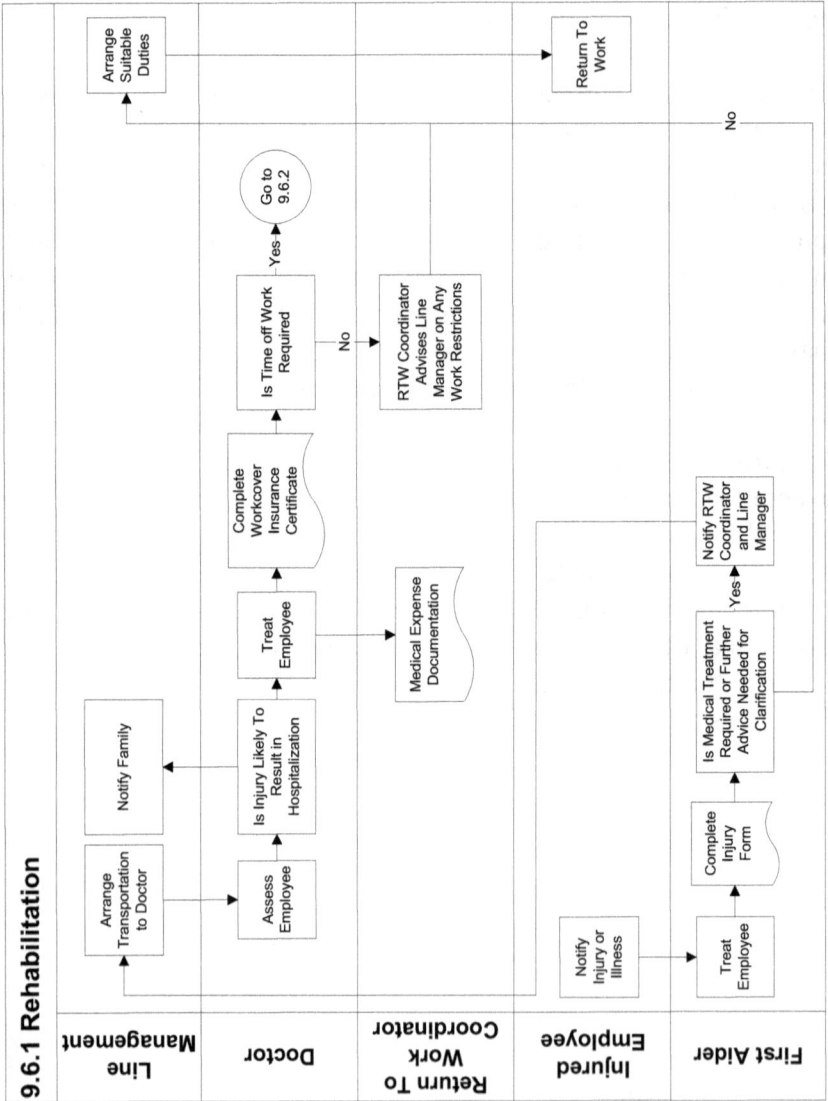

Line Management · **Doctor** · **Return To Work Coordinator** · **Injured Employee** · **First Aider**

Flowchart elements:

- Line Management: Arrange Transportation to Doctor → Notify Family; Arrange Suitable Duties
- Doctor: Assess Employee → Is Injury Likely To Result in Hospitalization → Treat Employee → Complete Workcover Insurance Certificate → Is Time off Work Required (Yes → Go to 9.6.2; No)
- Return To Work Coordinator: Medical Expense Documentation; RTW Coordinator Advises Line Manager on Any Work Restrictions → Return To Work
- Injured Employee: Notify Injury or Illness
- First Aider: Treat Employee → Complete Injury Form → Is Medical Treatment Required or Further Advice Needed for Clarification (Yes → Notify RTW Coordinator and Line Manager; No)

9.6.2 Rehabilitation

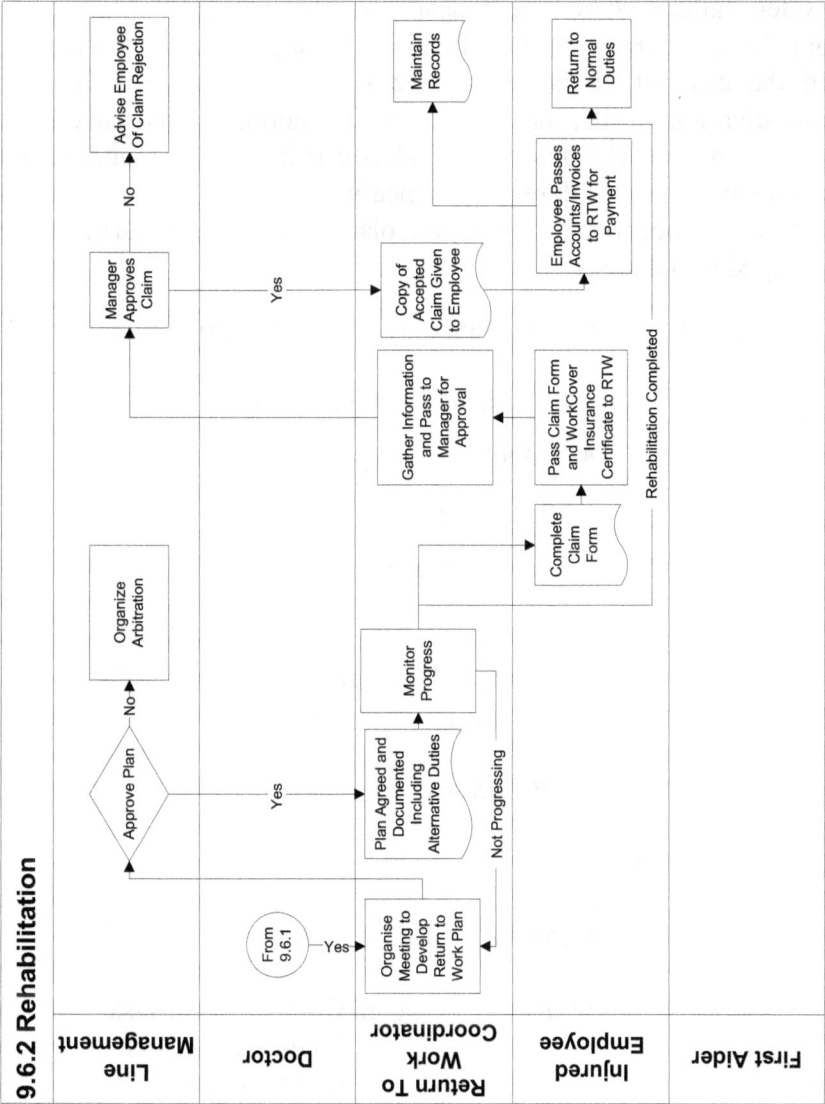

Line Management	Doctor	Return To Work Coordinator	Injured Employee	First Aider

Flowchart elements:

- Approve Plan (decision) — No → Organize Arbitration → Manager Approves Claim
- Approve Plan — Yes → Plan Agreed and Documented Including Alternative Duties
- Manager Approves Claim — No → Advise Employee Of Claim Rejection
- Manager Approves Claim — Yes → Copy of Accepted Claim Given to Employee
- From 9.6.1 — Yes → Organise Meeting to Develop Return to Work Plan
- Plan Agreed and Documented Including Alternative Duties → Monitor Progress
- Monitor Progress — Not Progressing
- Monitor Progress → Complete Claim Form
- Complete Claim Form → Pass Claim Form and WorkCover Insurance Certificate to RTW
- Gather Information and Pass to Manager for Approval
- Copy of Accepted Claim Given to Employee → Maintain Records
- Employee Passes Accounts/Invoices to RTW for Payment
- Rehabilitation Completed → Return to Normal Duties

9.7   Incident Investigation

Learning from system failures is another crucial component of any safety system. In the unfortunate situation where there has been a system failure where injury, near miss, unsafe condition or unsafe acts have occurred it is beneficial to investigate such occurrences. In the case of an injury I have never been involved in any investigation yet that has concluded that nothing could have been done to prevent the occurrence. Thus it is important to understand causes of system failures and hence what can be done to prevent them from occurring in the first place. Causes can normally be grouped into 2 areas.

1.   Environmental causes.(Hazards and Conditions)

- Physical work environment
- Mechanical design
- Housekeeping
- Maintenance
- Prevailing weather
- Surrounding area
- Schedules
- Processes etc

2.   BSAFA®s

i. Behaviors - e.g.		Cutting Corners, Pre-occupied, etc.
ii. Skills	- e.g.	Competent for task, Licences/Certificates up to date, training, etc.
iii. Attitudes	- e.g.	It won't happen to me, etc.
iv. Feelings	- e.g	Tired, etc.
vi. Attributes	- e.g.	Physically capable, etc.

Investigations are not blame exercises, but are rather driven out of a genuine desire to improve the workplace. To this end the investigation team needs to be competent for the task and involve those people necessary to act on findings. This might include a technical expert. In addition, responsible line managers should have the authority to suspend work in the area where the incident has occurred, or to suspend similar work, until the investigation has been completed.

The method of conducting investigations will usually involve a number of facets that might include:

- Interviews of person in area
- Interviews of colleagues
- Examining work area
- Examining maintenance records
- Procedures
- Determining any recent changes, people, surrounds, processes, equipment etc.
- Reviews of training
- Equipment being used and condition
- Notable deficiencies
- Performance statistics
- OHS statistical history of area
- Work Schedules
- Time sheets
- Employee History
- Production increases/decreases
- Any out of ordinary occurrences etc

This list is not exhaustive but serves to illustrate that in order to conduct proper investigations there is considerable information that needs to be gathered. It is not a simple exercise that can be done in a few sentences on an investigation form. The lack of time available to conduct proper investigations has lead to some Companies truncating this process to a point where it adds little value. Frequently I see one page investigation reports that fail to determine root causes. This is despite the learnings from such investigations having the potential to prevent further injuries. These truncated investigations also have the potential to lead to prosecution due to lack of adequacy.

In some cases such as significant injuries, incidents in major hazard facilities, or in the case of notifiable incidents, incident investigations may be required from a statutory requirement perspective. Some of these investigations may require legal advice to determine whether they need to be conducted under privilege.

The investigative process needs to be seen more in the light of a proactive process in injury prevention for it to attract the time and effort it deserves.

9.8   Corrective Action

In safety there is a lot of time spent on identifying things that have the potential to or actually impact on safety. Sometimes difficulty arises with the sheer volume of issues that need to be addressed. To some extent the risk process can help prioritise issues. However a robust corrective action process is absolutely crucial to any safety system. It actually helps if there is just one company wide system for corrective action so that the extent of effort can be gauged in the light of other priorities. The process is quite simple and involves normally just a few steps:

1.   Identify the issue
2.   Identify short term work around where required
3.   Determine root causes
4.   Determine long term solution and costs
5.   Prioritize implementation
6.   Allocate responsibility for implementation
7.   Allocate time line
8.   Monitor Implementation
9.   Evaluate success of implementation

Some companies have automated these processes using various electronic tools as part of their Quality Management Systems or even work management and maintenance systems whereby work backlog and progress to plan is readily available. Others use simple forms as the basis for ongoing monitoring. e.g. Fig 36.

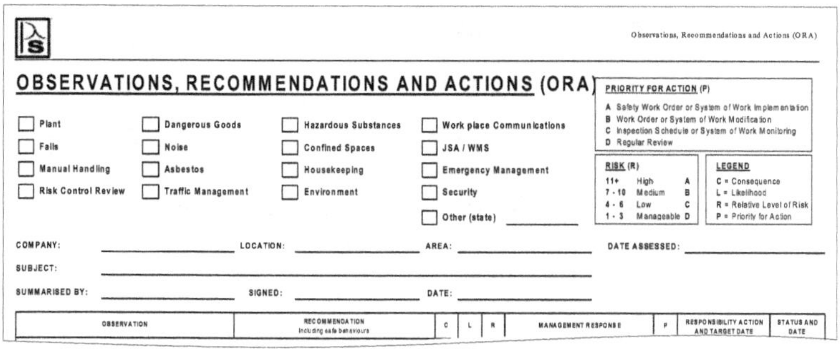
Observations, Recommendations and Actions (ORA)

OBSERVATIONS, RECOMMENDATIONS AND ACTIONS (ORA)

☐ Plant ☐ Dangerous Goods ☐ Hazardous Substances ☐ Work place Communications
☐ Falls ☐ Noise ☐ Confined Spaces ☐ JSA / WMS
☐ Manual Handling ☐ Asbestos ☐ Housekeeping ☐ Emergency Management
☐ Risk Control Review ☐ Traffic Management ☐ Environment ☐ Security
☐ Other (state) ________

PRIORITY FOR ACTION (P)
A Safety Work Order or System of Work Implementation
B Work Order or System of Work Modification
C Inspection Schedule or System of Work Monitoring
D Regular Review

RISK (R)
11+ High A
7 - 10 Medium B
4 - 6 Low C
1 - 3 Manageable D

LEGEND
C = Consequence
L = Likelihood
R = Relative Level of Risk
P = Priority for Action

COMPANY: ________ LOCATION: ________ AREA: ________ DATE ASSESSED: ________
SUBJECT: ________
SUMMARISED BY: ________ SIGNED: ________ DATE: ________

OBSERVATION	RECOMMENDATION Including safe behaviours	C	L	R	MANAGEMENT RESPONSE	P	RESPONSIBILITY ACTION AND TARGET DATE	STATUS AND DATE

Fig 36 Simple Corrective Action Form Extract

Whatever method is used, the key is to ensure the timely close out of actions and that the issue is satisfactorily resolved and that accurate records are kept to substantiate closure.

Corrective actions arise out of system failures that can be highlighted through many different avenues such as:

- Injuries
- Mechanical failure
- Identified hazards
- Discrete Risks Assessments on
    - Plant
    - Dangerous Goods
    - Hazardous Substances
    - Falls
    - Noise
    - Manual Handling etc

- Process Evaluation
- Statutory Infringement
- Audit non-compliance
- Workplace inspection non-compliance
- A management review
- An incident
- Statistical analysis
- Employee or Public complaint
- A legal claim
- Customer complaints
- Issue Resolution
- Toolbox discussions

Thus it is critical that the system does not end up with a different corrective action process for each otherwise it will become too unwieldy to manage.

Management attention needs to be placed on the effective close out of corrective actions to ensure that they are resourced appropriately and that importance of closure is understood and maintained. This should include managing the accountability for such actions.

9.9   Recognition

Monitoring is not only about conducting audits, observations and inspections it is also about reviewing system performance and recognizing good performance. This reinforces the desired BSAFA®s and boosts morale in the workplace. This recognition should be refined to the proactive measures, values and behaviors. There is danger in recognizing latent indicators as it can drive management behavior towards hiding injuries. This of course is not desirable and should be avoided.

9.10   Change Management

Change management is not merely a corrective action process. It is a process whereby the change is evaluated based on multiple impacts that might include:

- Regulatory
- Financial
- Employees
- Buildings and structures
- Systems
- Processes
- Customers
- Environment including neighbors etc.

Notwithstanding the above, the change management system requires a disciplined process to strictly control the introduction, modification or deletion of plant, substances and systems of work within the organization. The process must ensure commitment by all to consultation, training and instruction to those that will be affected by any change. It's not a simple process and should not be taken lightly. Input (consultation) by others to change is integral to compliance with performance based health and safety legislation. Input by operational, maintenance and other personnel will have a positive effect on the outcomes of change. The process must facilitate identification of potential health, physiochemical, environmental and security risks associated with changes to:-

- Plant and equipment
- Substances
- Dangerous goods
- Hazardous substances
- Other substances with health, physiochemical or environmental risks

- Systems of work
- Competencies and training
- Maintenance and repair arrangements
- Emergency procedures
- Training
- Supervision
- Processes
- Critical controls
- The organization and/or culture

Initiation of change media should be in the form of a written proposal with supporting documentation, e.g.

- Marked up P & ID's (Process and Instrumentation Drawings)
- Calculations and sketches
- MSDS for any substances involved
- Revised organizational structure and position descriptions if appropriate
- Hazard Identification and Risk Management Assessments

Quite often this type of discipline is shown in capital expenditure type proposals but is somewhat lacking in day to day change management activities. The change proposal should identify:-

- Potential health, safety and environmental issues including emergency management and security issues
- Other systems affected
- Regulatory requirements
- Risk assessment requirements
- People requirements (BSAFA®s)
- Competency and Training requirements

It should be noted that in some jurisdictions Regulatory approvals must be obtained and formal Notification provided in areas such as:-

- Dangerous goods
- Design notification and registration
- Environment
- Fire Authority for emergency planning
- Fire Authority for fire protection
- Building Code (Local Government)

Risk assessment must also be considered and arrangements made for formal risk control documentation to be available relating to:-

- Design
- Manufacture
- Install/Erect
- Environment
- Plant
- Dangerous goods
- Hazardous substances
- Manual handling
- Confined spaces
- Radiation
- Noise
- Other as identified

Consultation and communication is essential in any change process. Communication plans may be required for more complex changes. In other instances the consultative requirements can often be met by circulation of the change proposal for review and notation by :-

- Affected health and safety representatives, operators and involved personnel
- Affected operations and engineering personnel
- Others affected by systems and / or procedural changes

The review by the affected personnel should consider:-

- Impact on other systems
- Relevant safety issues
- Appropriateness of hazard identification, risk assessment and control of risk
- Statutory approvals
- Changes to Emergency Management Arrangements

Flowchart 9.10.1-2 shows an example change management process.

Changes need to be fully documented and reviewed for the desired affect taking into account the broad implications of the change. In a safety sense this often entails the need for some form of hazard identification and risk assessment, behavioral review, compliance review, process review and competency review. This means evaluating the change against all aspects of the Practical Safety Process®.

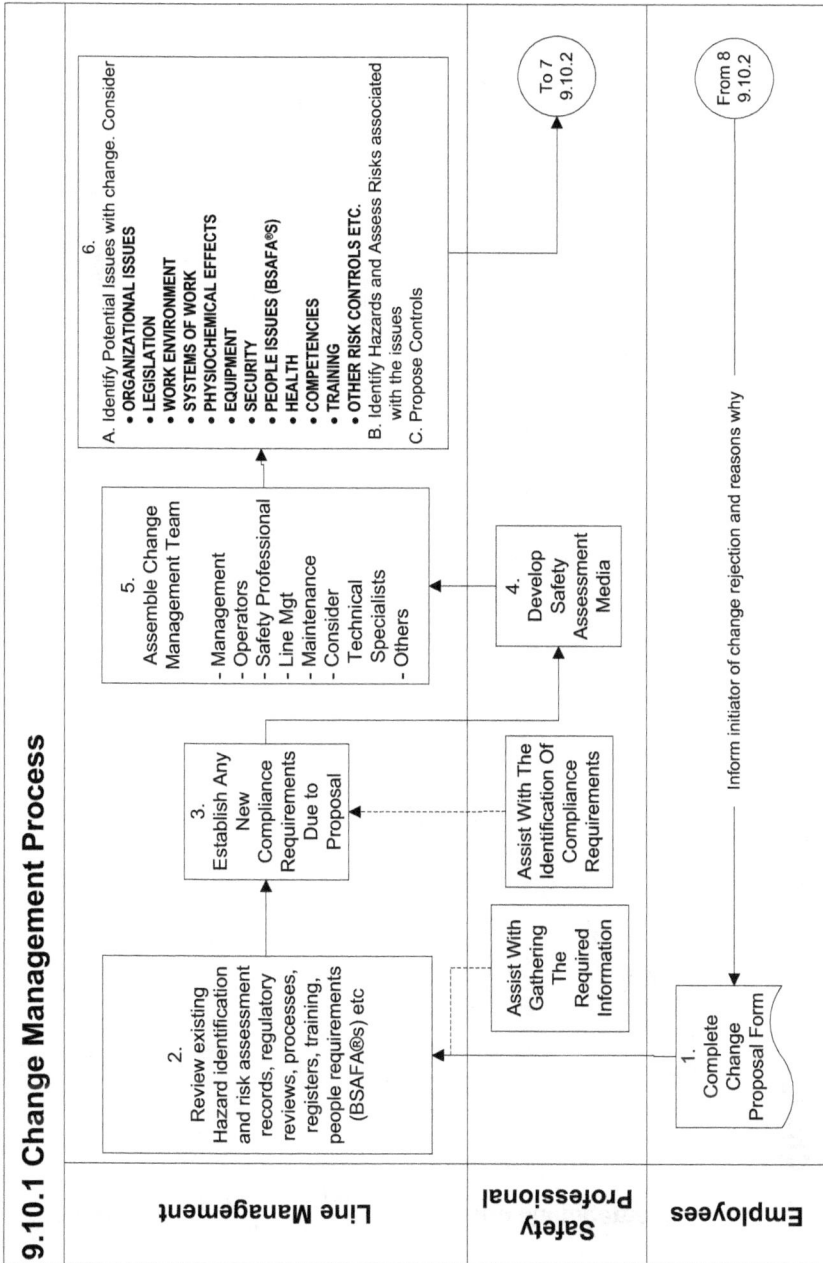

9.10.1 Change Management Process

Line Management

2.
Review existing Hazard identification and risk assessment records, regulatory reviews, processes, registers, training, people requirements (BSAFA®s) etc

3.
Establish Any New Compliance Requirements Due to Proposal

5.
Assemble Change Management Team
- Management
- Operators
- Safety Professional
- Line Mgt
- Maintenance
- Consider Technical Specialists
- Others

6.
A. Identify Potential Issues with change. Consider
• **ORGANIZATIONAL ISSUES**
• **LEGISLATION**
• **WORK ENVIRONMENT**
• **SYSTEMS OF WORK**
• **PHYSIOCHEMICAL EFFECTS**
• **EQUIPMENT**
• **SECURITY**
• **PEOPLE ISSUES (BSAFA®S)**
• **HEALTH**
• **COMPETENCIES**
• **TRAINING**
• **OTHER RISK CONTROLS ETC.**
B. Identify Hazards and Assess Risks associated with the issues
C. Propose Controls

Safety Professional

Assist With Gathering The Required Information

Assist With The Identification Of Compliance Requirements

4.
Develop Safety Assessment Media

To 7
9.10.2

Employees

1.
Complete Change Proposal Form

Inform initiator of change rejection and reasons why

From 8
9.10.2

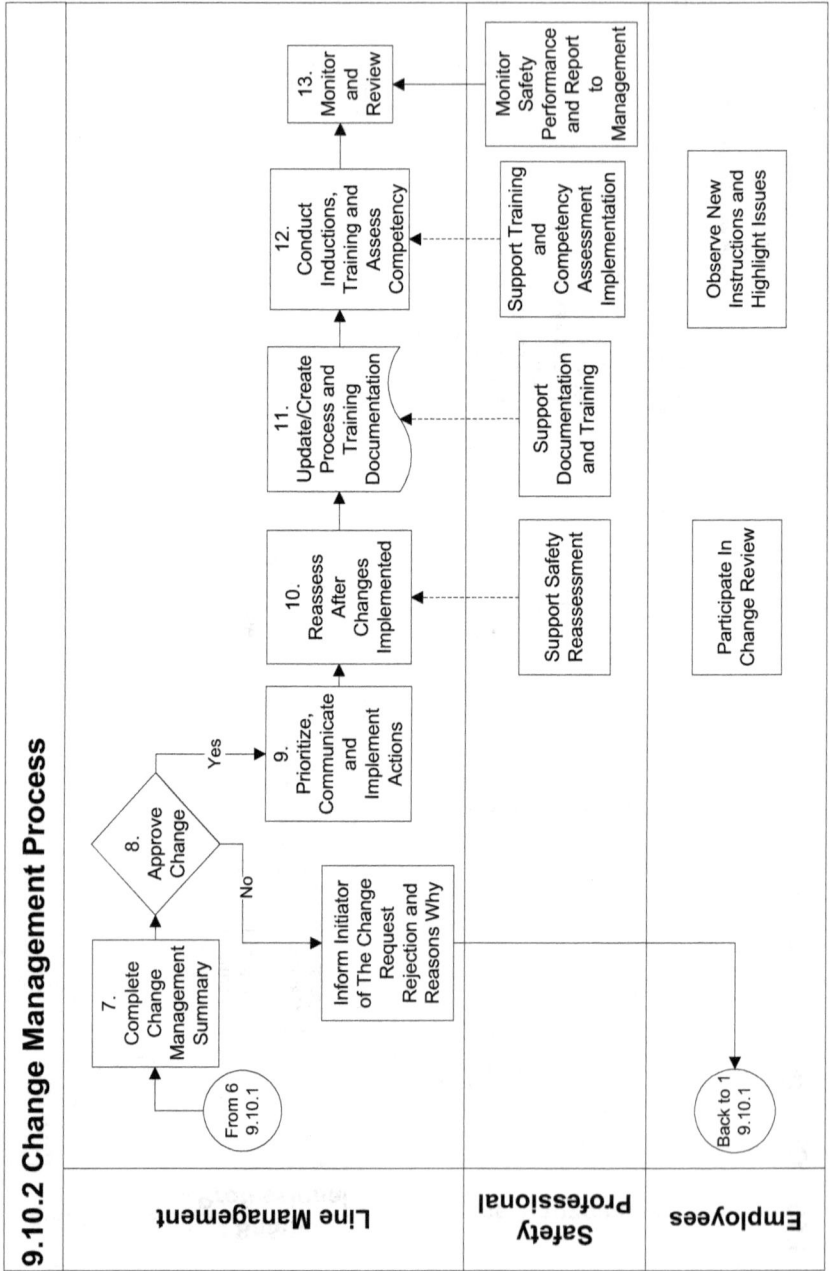

9.10.2 Change Management Process

Line Management

From 6
9.10.1

7. Complete Change Management Summary

8. Approve Change

Yes

No

Inform Initiator of The Change Request Rejection and Reasons Why

9. Prioritize, Communicate and Implement Actions

10. Reassess After Changes Implemented

11. Update/Create Process and Training Documentation

12. Conduct Inductions, Training and Assess Competency

13. Monitor and Review

Safety Professional

Support Safety Reassessment

Support Documentation and Training

Support Training and Competency Assessment Implementation

Monitor Safety Performance and Report to Management

Employees

Participate In Change Review

Observe New Instructions and Highlight Issues

Back to 1
9.10.1

9.11   Records Management

Safety management involves a considerable amount of effort in maintaining accurate and accessible records. Some of these records are required to be maintained by law especially when they relate to individuals. Procedures need to be written to take into account these statutory needs and those of the business with respect to records management. The responsibility for maintaining such records, and the period of time they are to be kept needs to be defined. Record registers should be considered to define these requirements. e.g. Fig 37.

Essential Service	Date of Maintenance Schedule	Maintenance Responsibility		Level Of Performance Required	Test or Inspection Frequency	Position Responsible	Record Location
		In House or Contractor Name	Contractor Contact Address PhoneNo				
Air Conditioning Systems				AS 1668, BCA Part F4	Monthly to AS 1851.1 & 3666		
Emergency Lighting				AS 2293.1, BCA E4	6 monthly AS 2293.2		
Emergency Power Supply				BCA G3.8	6 Monthly		
Emergency Warning & Intercommunication Systems				AS 2220, BCA E4.9 Spec. E1.5 & Spec. E1.7	Monthly to AS 1851.10		
Exit Doors				BCA D	3 monthly to ensure doors are intact, operational and fitted with conforming hardware.		
Exit Signs				AS 2293.1, BCA E4	6 monthly to AS 2293.2		
Fire Brigade Connection				Vic. H103	Weekly to AS 1851.1		
Fire Control Centre				BCA Spec. E1.8	Annual Inspection		
Fire Control Panels				AS 1603.4, BCA Vic. H101	Weekly to AS 1851.8		
Fire Curtains				BCA H1.3	Annual Inspection		
Fire Dampers				AS 1682.2	Annual inspection to AS 1851.6		
Fire Detector & Alarm				AS 1670			

Fig 37 Extract From Essential Services Records Register

In the example shown the record is defined, along with its performance standard, its frequency of creation, its location, its type and who is responsible for maintenance of the record.

Such registers help clarify what can otherwise be a relative unknown in many organizations. They can also be used as a precursor to electronic record management systems to ensure requirements are known and clarified. Traceability of records also becomes an easier task.

Records storage is by no means an easy task with many records associated with employees having to be stored indefinitely. Thus particular attention needs to be given to not only what has to be stored, but in what form will it be stored and where. e.g. paper hard-copies, microfilms, or as electronic records

Care needs to be taken when considering electronic media with respect to the formats and types of systems that data is stored in. A consideration needs to be the redundancy in the software needed to access such files as time goes on. Consideration often has to be given to document conversion.

9.12   Conclusion

Whilst Monitor and Review Performance is an important step it is the last step in the Practical Safety Process®. There is good reason for this. The process steps are designed to build on the information of each previous step so that by the time this last step is reached we already have a fully implemented safety management process. The monitoring then becomes a reinforcement tool. For so many organizations this last step is still their first step, and they fail to escape the endless cycle of fire fighting brought about by inadequate implementation of the first 6 steps.

I also would like to reinforce the importance of the change management process discussed in this chapter. It is critical that there is a robust change management process if success is to be sustained into the future. So much of what we see in investigations is that someone changed something that resulted in someone being hurt. As soon as you hear the word "change" mentioned, alarm bells should ring for you to ensure that appropriate plans are be put into place to ensure that the change is managed effectively.

9.13   Check Your Progress

Practical Safety Process® STEP 7 Gap Analysis	Y	N
MONITOR AND REVIEW PERFORMANCE		
Is there a safety measuring and reporting system in place?		
Does this contain both proactive and reactive measures?		
Is the information analysed and reported to all levels of management and employees?		
Is there a safety audit process?		
Do you conduct planned and scheduled inspections?		
Are planned and scheduled workplace inspections carried out? (in addition to scheduled maintenance)		
Is there evidence of Site Condition inspection (monthly)?		
Is there evidence of essential services check-listing and frequency? (Fire Equipment and Ancillaries)		
Is there evidence of housekeeping inspection?		
Is there evidence of first aid provision inspection?		
Is there evidence of a monitoring and risk control review program particularly Risk Control Review?		
Is there formal evidence of Observations, Recommendations and Actions being raised when exposures are identified?		
Do you use "new eyes" methods?		
Do people understand how to do inspections?		
Are visual systems in evidence for setting standards?		
Are visual performance feedback systems used?		
Are safety observations performed?		
Is health monitoring a requirement?		
Is there a rehabilitation process?		
Is there a trained RTW coordinator?		
Do you have an Incident and Near Miss Investigation and reporting procedure (internal and external)?		
Are all incidents / near misses and hazards in the workplace identified?		
Is there a hazard reporting system?		
Do people know how to use it?		
Is there documentation system that enables incidents to be reported promptly with reply back to the originator?		
Is there an investigation procedure and a process (who and how) of communication of findings back to involved personnel?		
Is there a knowledge of regulatory reporting requirements (do we know what a regulated near miss or incident is?)		
Is there documentation enabling incidents and near misses to be reported properly and in accordance with standards?		

Practical Safety Process® STEP 7 Gap Analysis continued	Y	N
Have there been any incidents to notify?		
Do you know how to preserve and control an incident at Site?		
Do you record all lost time, medical treatment and first aid injuries for review?		
Do you record unsafe and safe acts?		
Do you record audits\observations planned versus carried out?		
Have you set management targets for percentage time in the workplace?		
Is there a corrective action system in place?		
Is there a change management system?		
Are mechanisms in place to communicate the effects of changes and the potential/actual impact on safety?		
Is there a safety recognition system in place that rewards proactive measures?		
Is there a records management system?		
Is there a performance management system in place?		
Are management and employees are involved in Management System review processes, i.e. Audits, observations?		
Is there a system in place to share safety statistics with all employees, and can they interpret the results?		
Are mechanisms in place which provide an opportunity for employees to report safety concerns		
Are suitable forums for the ongoing involvement and consultation of all personnel in the development, implementation and review of safety initiatives and programs established e.g. safety committee?		
Is a system is in place to ensure compliance to statutory and corporate performance requirements?		
Are systems in place to ensure the maintenance of plant and equipment which may have the potential to impact on safety? This might include inspection, testing and calibration of equipment.		
Is the frequency of such testing is appropriate for the level of risk associated with the equipment and the appropriate legal requirements?		
Is a system in place for the review of work practices on a routine basis to ensure relevance, appropriateness and currency?		
Is the safety performance of contractors and vendors monitored?		
Do you understand the cost of safety i.e. consequential cost versus proactive costs?		

10. ESSENTIAL QUALITIES OF A SAFETY PROFESSIONAL

The most interesting aside for a safety professional is that they don't actually manage safety. They support the management of safety through others. Therefore to be successful as a Safety Professional I believe there are certain qualities that a person must possess. These include:

1.   Passionate about safety

2.   Tenacity

3.   Endurance

4.   Patience and self control

5.   Ability to manage up and through

6.   Powers of observation

7.   Technical aptitude

8.   Attention to detail

9.   Record keeping skills

10.   Self confidence

11.   Courage

12.   Business Acumen

To some extent these are not all learnt skills but rather personality traits essential for success. These traits require both left and right brained thinking. The most successful safety managers I find are those that are driven out of a passion for safety. This drive may have been driven out of personal experience with injury to themselves or a colleague. This passion will give the safety professional the tenacity and endurance required to push safety management to the forefront of management minds. However to balance this passion there needs to be attention to detail to manage records, evaluate legal documents, and to establish the facts.

Failure to do this will lead to emotive debate that will not add value, but destroy self confidence and undermine the safety effort. I see many safety professionals sitting in the back room office feeling satisfied with themselves that they "told them so". This is not good enough and demonstrates a lack of effectiveness. It's not about "them and us" it's about being willing to be part of the solution and doing whatever it takes to get the safety messages translated into action. This sometimes requires significant courage. Courage of your convictions to do or say what is necessary to ensure safety is maintained or enhanced.

It's also about applying advanced powers of observation to identifying hazards, and to observing the people you work with, and then being able to use this information to effect positive change. In order to enhance these powers of observation there also needs to be a degree of competency in mechanical aptitude. The safety professional must deal with often complex work environments and machinery. As such unless they can interpret drawings and evaluate complex and often automated machinery they will not be effective.

In order to communicate your message effectively you will often need to put yourself in the other person's shoes and speak in their language and on their terms. Safety terminology can often be so foreign to some of the biggest influencers in a business. For example if you are presenting to a finance manager who understands costs and spreadsheets very well, you will need to have an understanding of the cost benefit analysis of any proposal and have the data and facts at your disposal.

As was seen from chapter one the safety professional must also be organizationally aware to the extent necessary to be able to enter into important organizational debates that lay the foundations for the safety effort. Failure to do this will lead to a very frustrating and ultimately debilitating life for the safety professional.

I think being a Safety Professional has tremendous rewards in terms of self satisfaction that you have played a part in making the workplace safer. However you will often need to be satisfied with working through others to achieve this, and be secure enough in yourself to understand that the credit will not always come your way.

11. APPENDICES

APPENDICES INDEX

Example Process Flowcharts

1	Plant Risk Management Process	161
2.1-3	Confined Space Risk Management Process	162
3.1-4	Dangerous Goods and Hazardous Substances Risk Management Process	165
4	Hot Work Risk Management Process	169
5	Excavation Break In Risk Management Process	170
6	Electrical Risk Management Process	171
7.1	Isolation Lock Out Tag Out Risk Management Process	172
7.2	Practical Isolation Process	173
8	Falls Risk Management Process	174
9	Noise Risk Management Process	175
10.1	Asbestos Risk Management Process	176
10.2	Working With Asbestos Risk Management Process	177
11	Manual Handling Risk Management Process	178
12	Ergonomics Risk Management Process	179
13	Traffic Risk Management Process	180
14	Lead Risk Management Process	181
15	Electromagnetic Radiation EMR Risk Management Process	182
16.1-2	Emergency Management Process	183
17	Essential Services Management Process	185
18	First Aid Provision Management Process	186
19	Managing Adhoc Work Through Work Permits	187
20	Lifting Equipment Management Process	188
21	Smoking, Drugs Alcohol Management Process	189
22	Teleworking Management Process	190
23	Engineering Design Safety Management Process	191
24	Contractor and Project Management Information Flowchart	192

Appendix 1 Plant Risk Management Process

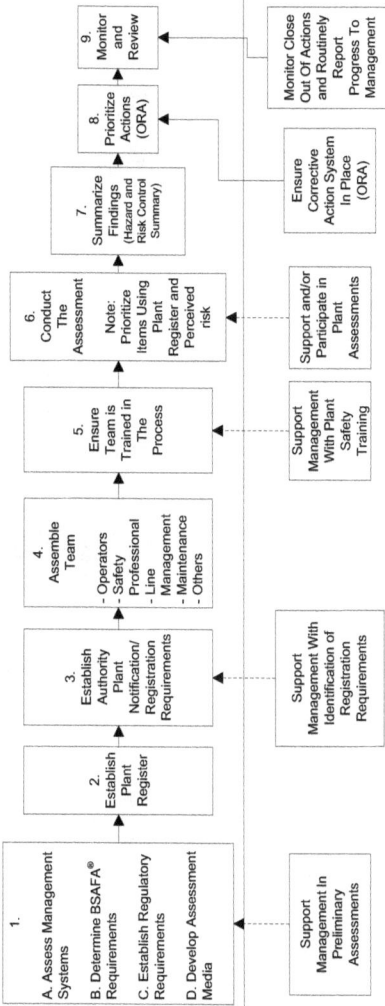

Line Management

1.
A. Assess Management Systems
B. Determine BSAFA® Requirements
C. Establish Regulatory Requirements
D. Develop Assessment Media

2. Establish Plant Register

3. Establish Authority Plant Notification/ Registration Requirements

4. Assemble Team
- Operators
- Safety Professional
- Line Management
- Maintenance
- Others

5. Ensure Team is Trained in The Process

6. Conduct The Assessment
Note: Prioritize Items Using Plant Register and Perceived risk

7. Summarize Findings (Hazard and Risk Control Summary)

8. Prioritize Actions (ORA)

9. Monitor and Review

Safety Professional

Support Management In Preliminary Assessments

Support Management With Identification of Registration Requirements

Support Management With Plant Safety Training

Support and/or Participate in Plant Assessments

Ensure Corrective Action System In Place (ORA)

Monitor Close Out Of Actions and Routinely Report Progress To Management

Employees

Participate in Plant Assessments

Supporting Media Available

Plant Register Template
Plant Hazard Checklist
Risk Assessment Sheet
Plant Notification and Registration Register
Hazard and Risk Control Summary
Observations Recommendations and Actions (ORA) Sheet
Job Person Analysis JPA® Form

Plant Safety Project Managers Manual
Plant Safety Manual

Example Media Available at practicalsafety.org

Appendix 2.1 Confined Space Risk Management Process

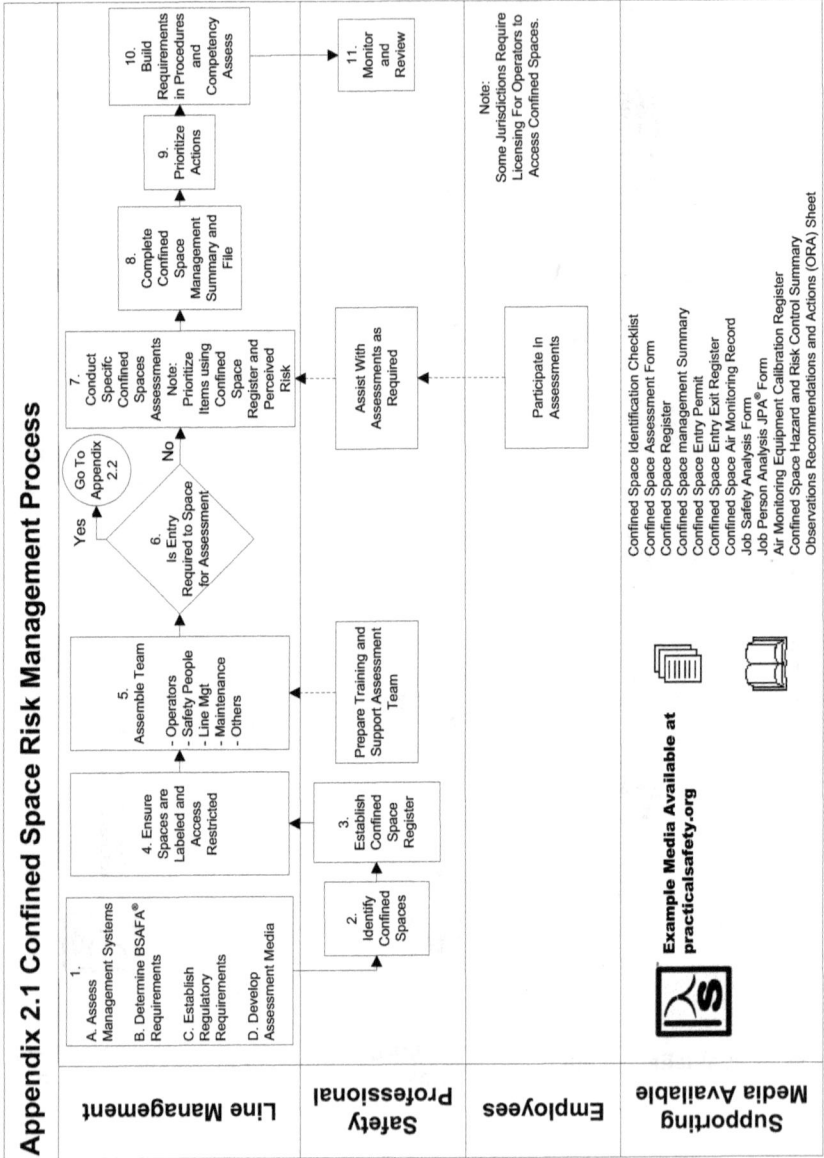

Line Management

1.
A. Assess Management Systems
B. Determine BSAFA® Requirements
C. Establish Regulatory Requirements
D. Develop Assessment Media

2. Identify Confined Spaces

3. Establish Confined Space Register

4. Ensure Spaces are Labeled and Access Restricted

5. Assemble Team
- Operators
- Safety People
- Line Mgt
- Maintenance
- Others

6. Is Entry Required to Space for Assessment
— Yes → Go To Appendix 2.2
— No →

7. Conduct Specific Confined Spaces Assessments
Note: Prioritize Items using Confined Space Register and Perceived Risk

8. Complete Confined Space Management Summary and File

9. Prioritize Actions

10. Build Requirements in Procedures and Competency Assess

11. Monitor and Review

Safety Professional

Prepare Training and Support Assessment Team

Employees

Assist With Assessments as Required

Participate In Assessments

Note:
Some Jurisdictions Require Licensing For Operators to Access Confined Spaces.

Supporting Media Available

Example Media Available at practicalsafety.org

Confined Space Identification Checklist
Confined Space Assessment Form
Confined Space Register
Confined Space management Summary
Confined Space Entry Permit
Confined Space Entry Exit Register
Confined Space Air Monitoring Record
Job Safety Analysis Form
Job Person Analysis JPA® Form
Air Monitoring Equipment Calibration Register
Confined Space Hazard and Risk Control Summary
Observations Recommendations and Actions (ORA) Sheet

Appendix 2.2 Confined Space Risk Management Process

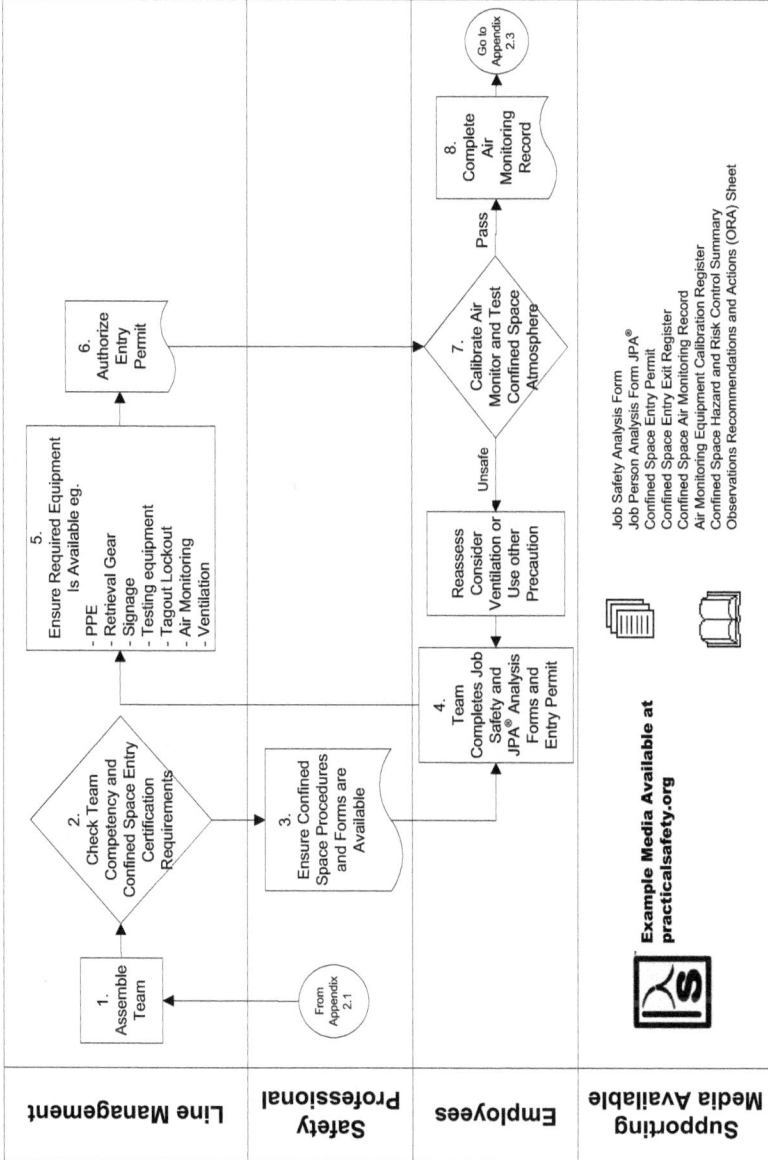

Line Management

From Appendix 2.1

1. Assemble Team

2. Check Team Competency and Confined Space Entry Certification Requirements

5. Ensure Required Equipment Is Available eg.
- PPE
- Retrieval Gear
- Signage
- Testing equipment
- Tagout Lockout
- Air Monitoring
- Ventilation

6. Authorize Entry Permit

Safety Professional

3. Ensure Confined Space Procedures and Forms are Available

Employees

4. Team Completes Job Safety and JPA® Analysis Forms and Entry Permit

Reassess Consider Ventilation or Use other Precaution

7. Calibrate Air Monitor and Test Confined Space Atmosphere

Unsafe

Pass

8. Complete Air Monitoring Record

Go to Appendix 2.3

Supporting Media Available

Example Media Available at practicalsafety.org

Job Safety Analysis Form
Job Person Analysis Form JPA®
Confined Space Entry Permit
Confined Space Entry Exit Register
Confined Space Air Monitoring Record
Air Monitoring Equipment Calibration Register
Confined Space Hazard and Risk Control Summary
Observations Recommendations and Actions (ORA) Sheet

Appendix 2.3 Confined Space Risk Management Process

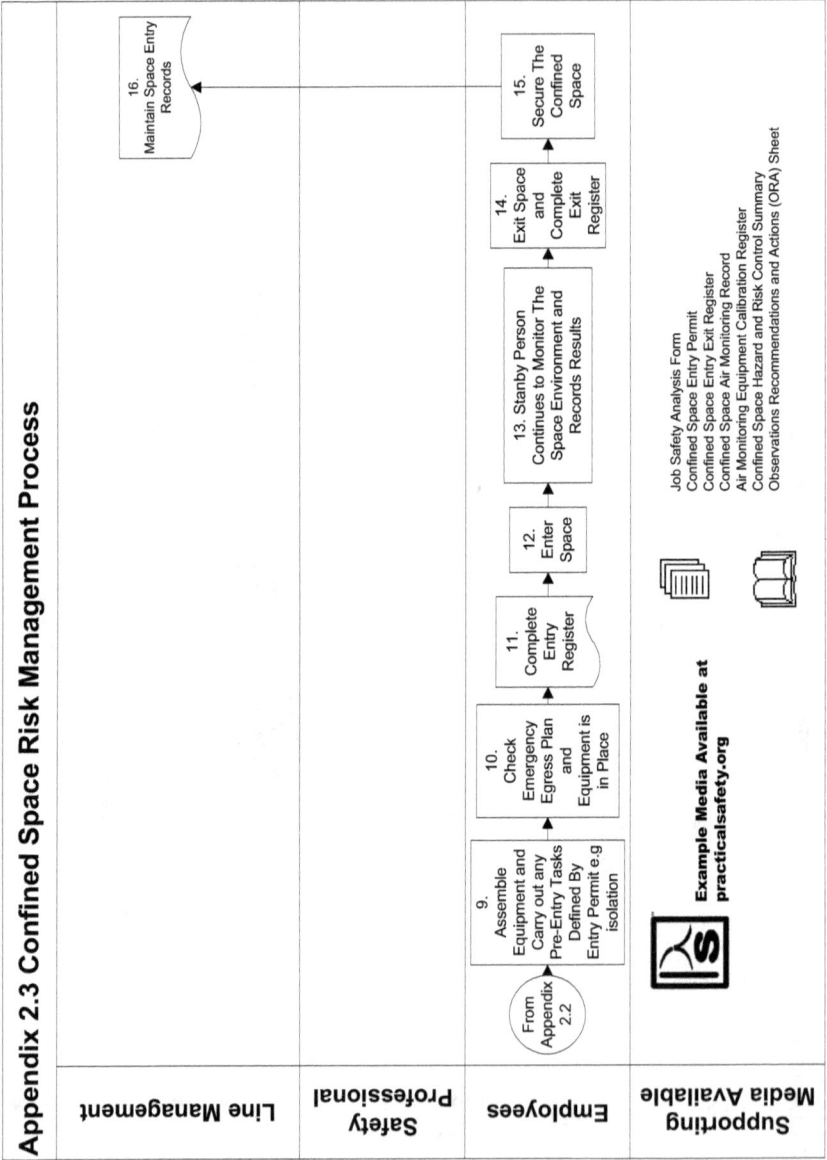

Line Management

16. Maintain Space Entry Records

Safety Professional

Employees

From Appendix 2.2

9. Assemble Equipment and Carry out any Pre-Entry Tasks Defined By Entry Permit e.g isolation

10. Check Emergency Egress Plan and Equipment is in Place

11. Complete Entry Register

12. Enter Space

13. Stanby Person Continues to Monitor The Space Environment and Records Results

14. Exit Space and Complete Exit Register

15. Secure The Confined Space

Supporting Media Available

Example Media Available at practicalsafety.org

Job Safety Analysis Form
Confined Space Entry Permit
Confined Space Entry Exit Register
Confined Space Air Monitoring Record
Air Monitoring Equipment Calibration Register
Confined Space Hazard and Risk Control Summary
Observations Recommendations and Actions (ORA) Sheet

Appendix 3.1 Dangerous and Hazardous Substances Risk Management Process

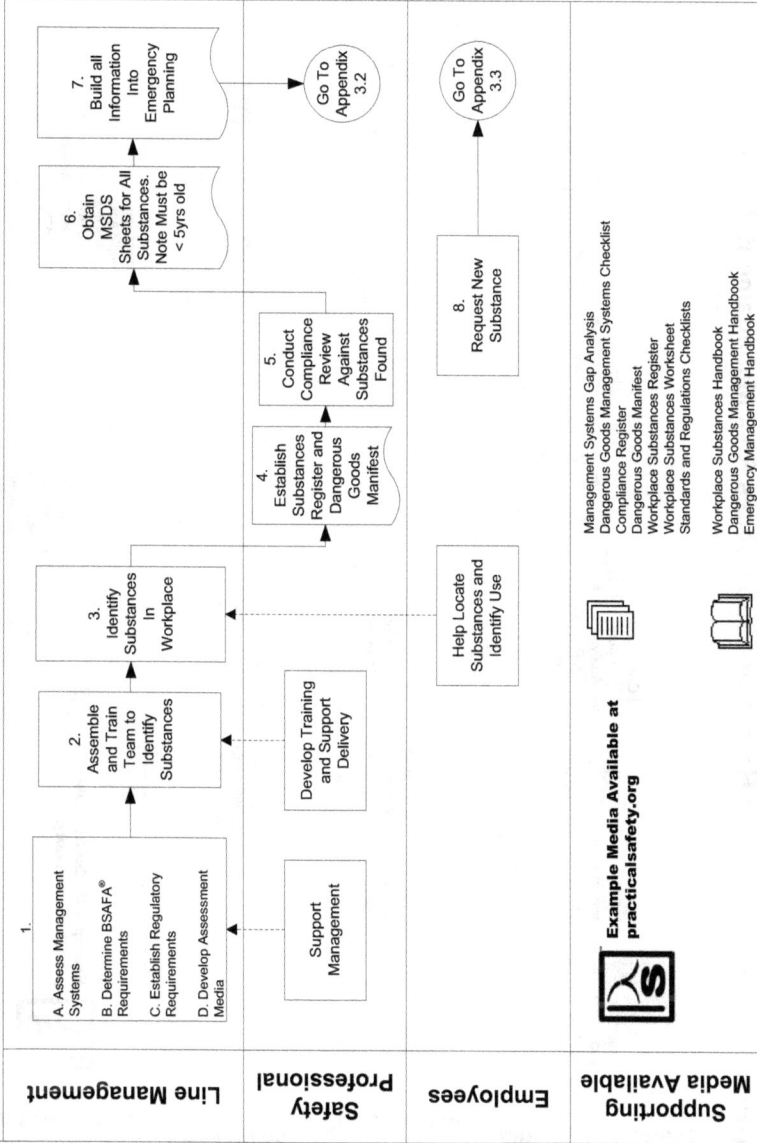

Line Management

1.
A. Assess Management Systems
B. Determine BSAFA® Requirements
C. Establish Regulatory Requirements
D. Develop Assessment Media

2.
Assemble and Train Team to Identify Substances

3.
Identify Substances In Workplace

6.
Obtain MSDS Sheets for All Substances. Note Must be < 5yrs old

7.
Build all Information Into Emergency Planning

Go To Appendix 3.2

Safety Professional

Support Management

Develop Training and Support Delivery

4.
Establish Substances Register and Dangerous Goods Manifest

5.
Conduct Compliance Review Against Substances Found

Employees

Help Locate Substances and Identify Use

8.
Request New Substance

Go To Appendix 3.3

Supporting Media Available

Example Media Available at practicalsafety.org

Management Systems Gap Analysis
Dangerous Goods Management Systems Checklist
Compliance Register
Dangerous Goods Manifest
Workplace Substances Register
Workplace Substances Worksheet
Standards and Regulations Checklists

Workplace Substances Handbook
Dangerous Goods Management Handbook
Emergency Management Handbook

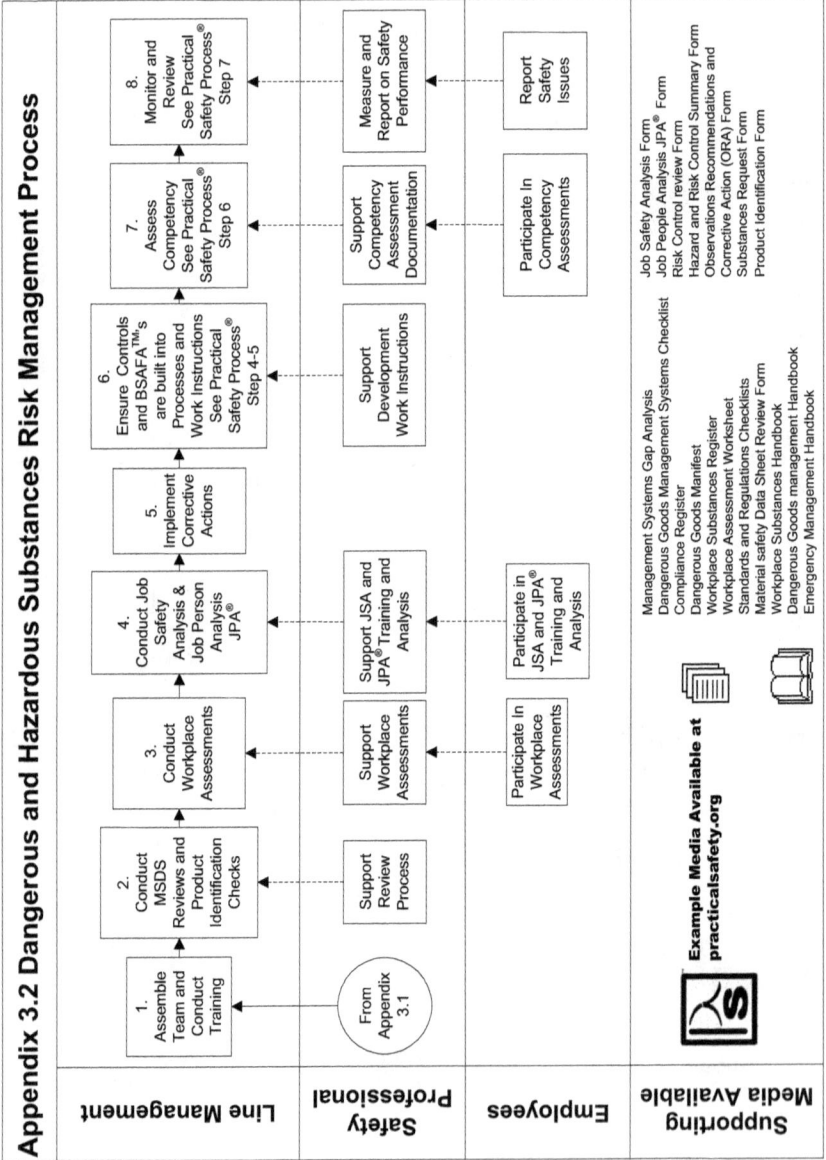

Appendix 3.2 Dangerous and Hazardous Substances Risk Management Process

Line Management

1. Assemble Team and Conduct Training

2. Conduct MSDS Reviews and Product Identification Checks

3. Conduct Workplace Assessments

4. Conduct Job Safety Analysis & Job Person Analysis JPA®

5. Implement Corrective Actions

6. Ensure Controls and BSAFA™'s are built into Processes and Work Instructions See Practical Safety Process® Step 4-5

7. Assess Competency See Practical Safety Process® Step 6

8. Monitor and Review See Practical Safety Process® Step 7

Safety Professional

From Appendix 3.1

Support Review Process

Support Workplace Assessments

Support JSA and JPA® Training and Analysis

Support Development Work Instructions

Support Competency Assessment Documentation

Measure and Report on Safety Performance

Employees

Participate In Workplace Assessments

Participate in JSA and JPA® Training and Analysis

Participate In Competency Assessments

Report Safety Issues

Supporting Media Available

Example Media Available at practicalsafety.org

Management Systems Gap Analysis
Dangerous Goods Management Systems Checklist
Compliance Register
Dangerous Goods Manifest
Workplace Substances Register
Workplace Assessment Worksheet
Standards and Regulations Checklists
Material safety Data Sheet Review Form
Workplace Substances Handbook
Dangerous Goods management Handbook
Emergency Management Handbook

Job Safety Analysis Form
Job People Analysis JPA® Form
Risk Control review Form
Hazard and Risk Control Summary Form
Observations Recommendations and
Corrective Action (ORA) Form
Substances Request Form
Product Identification Form

Appendix 3.3 Dangerous and Hazardous Substances Risk Management Process

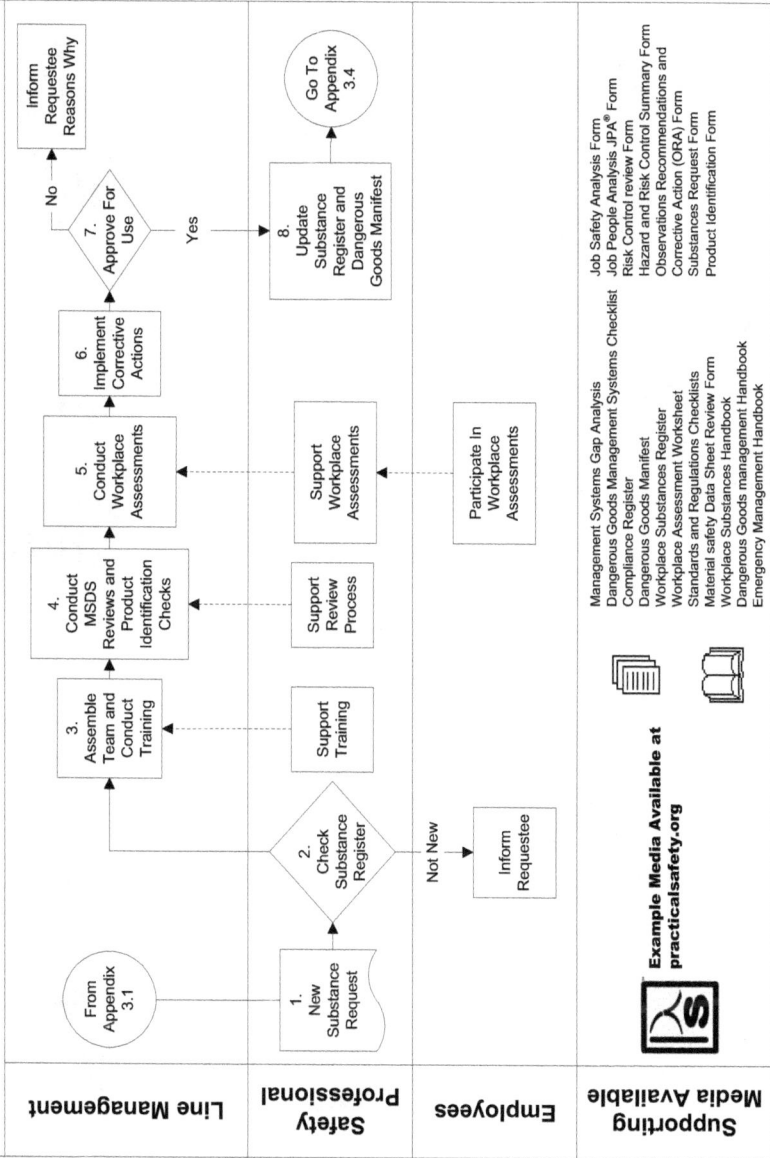

Line Management	From Appendix 3.1 → 1. New Substance Request → 2. Check Substance Register → 3. Assemble Team and Conduct Training → 4. Conduct MSDS Reviews and Product Identification Checks → 5. Conduct Workplace Assessments → 6. Implement Corrective Actions → 7. Approve For Use — No → Inform Requestee Reasons Why; Yes → 8. Update Substance Register and Dangerous Goods Manifest → Go To Appendix 3.4
Safety Professional	Support Training, Support Review Process, Support Workplace Assessments
Employees	Participate In Workplace Assessments
Supporting Media Available	

From flow: 2. Check Substance Register — Not New → Inform Requestee

Example Media Available at practicalsafety.org

Management Systems Gap Analysis
Dangerous Goods Management Systems Checklist
Compliance Register
Dangerous Goods Manifest
Workplace Substances Register
Workplace Assessment Worksheet
Standards and Regulations Checklists
Material safety Data Sheet Review Form
Workplace Substances Handbook
Dangerous Goods management Handbook
Emergency Management Handbook

Job Safety Analysis Form
Job People Analysis JPA® Form
Risk Control review Form
Hazard and Risk Control Summary Form
Observations Recommendations and
Corrective Action (ORA) Form
Substances Request Form
Product Identification Form

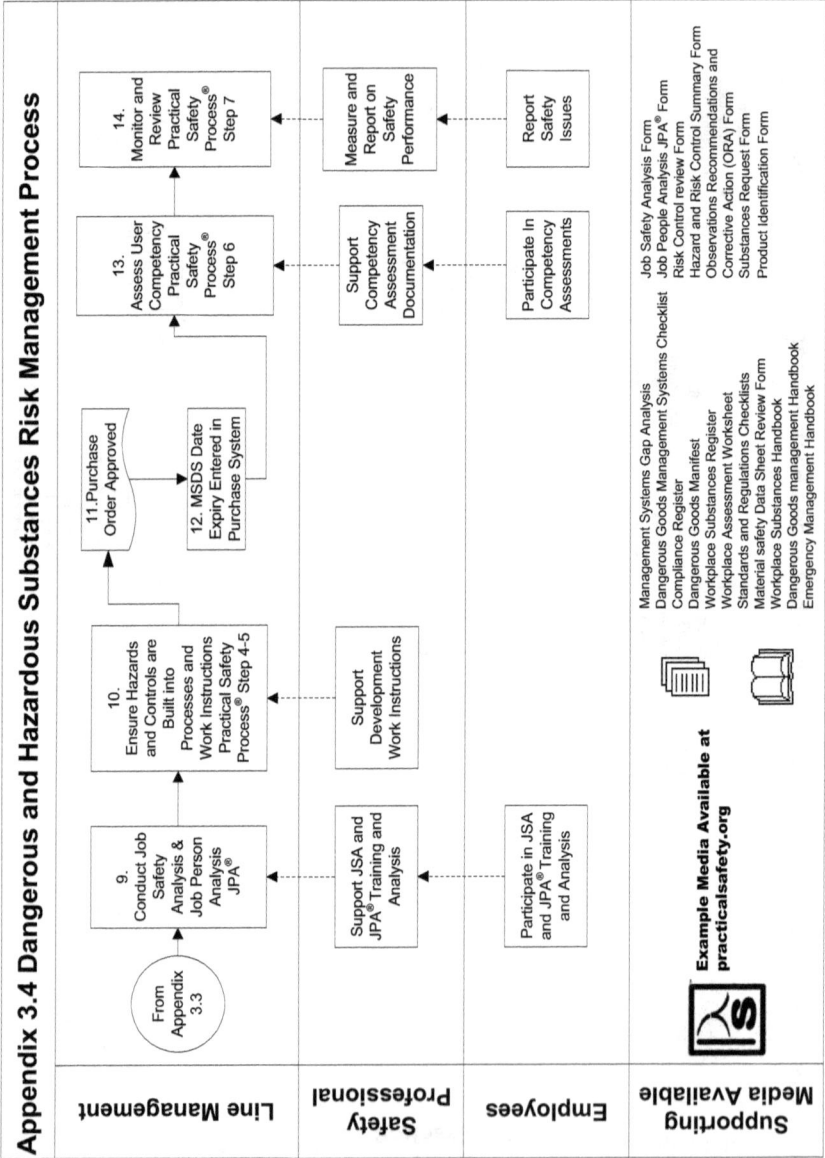

Appendix 3.4 Dangerous and Hazardous Substances Risk Management Process

Line Management	Safety Professional	Employees	Supporting Media Available

Line Management

From Appendix 3.3

9. Conduct Job Safety Analysis & Job Person Analysis JPA®

10. Ensure Hazards and Controls are Built into Processes and Work Instructions Practical Safety Process® Step 4-5

11. Purchase Order Approved

12. MSDS Date Expiry Entered in Purchase System

13. Assess User Competency Practical Safety Process® Step 6

14. Monitor and Review Practical Safety Process® Step 7

Safety Professional

Support JSA and JPA® Training and Analysis

Support Development Work Instructions

Support Competency Assessment Documentation

Measure and Report on Safety Performance

Employees

Participate in JSA and JPA® Training and Analysis

Participate In Competency Assessments

Report Safety Issues

Supporting Media Available

Example Media Available at practicalsafety.org

Management Systems Gap Analysis
Dangerous Goods Management Systems Checklist
Compliance Register
Dangerous Goods Manifest
Workplace Substances Register
Workplace Assessment Worksheet
Standards and Regulations Checklists
Material safety Data Sheet Review Form
Workplace Substances Handbook
Dangerous Goods management Handbook
Emergency Management Handbook

Job Safety Analysis Form
Job People Analysis JPA® Form
Risk Control review Form
Hazard and Risk Control Summary Form
Observations Recommendations and Corrective Action (ORA) Form
Substances Request Form
Product Identification Form

Appendix 4 Hot Work Risk Management Process

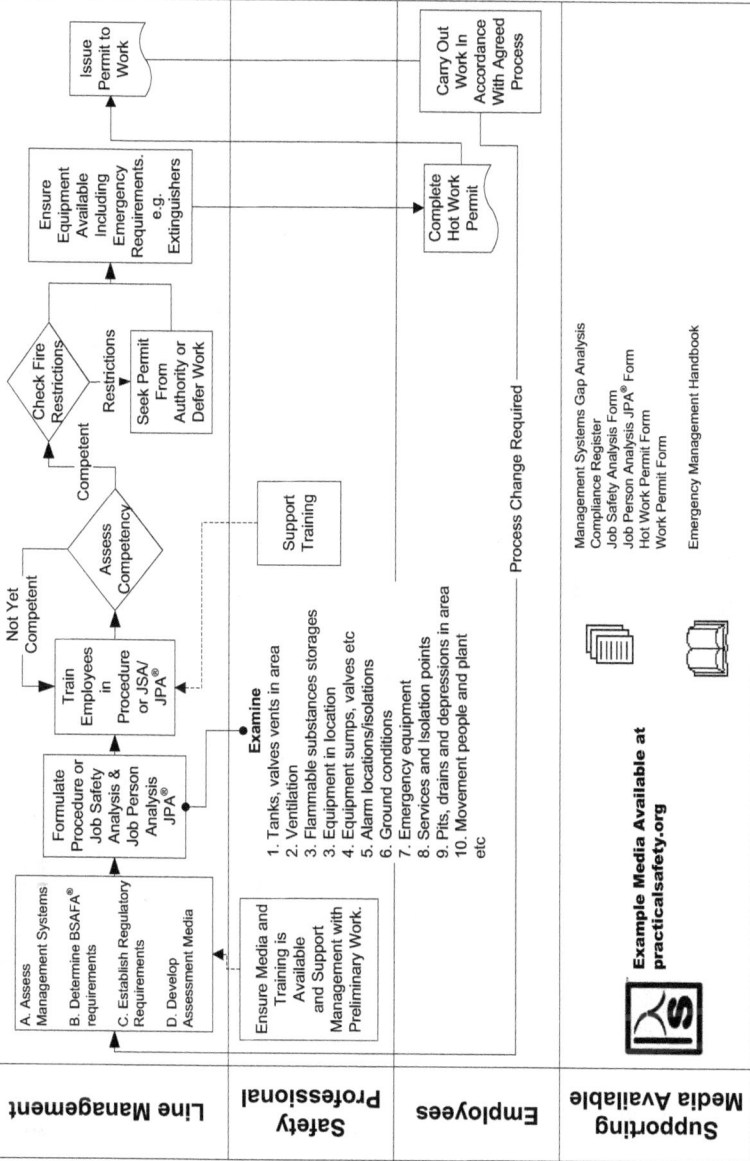

Line Management

A. Assess Management Systems

B. Determine BSAFA® requirements

C. Establish Regulatory Requirements

D. Develop Assessment Media

Formulate Procedure or Job Safety Analysis & Job Person Analysis JPA®

Train Employees in Procedure or JSA/ JPA®

Not Yet Competent

Assess Competency

Competent

Check Fire Restrictions

Restrictions

Seek Permit From Authority or Defer Work

Ensure Equipment Available Including Emergency Requirements. e.g. Extinguishers

Issue Permit to Work

Safety Professional

Ensure Media and Training is Available and Support Management with Preliminary Work.

Support Training

Process Change Required

Employees

Examine
1. Tanks, valves vents in area
2. Ventilation
3. Flammable substances storages
4. Equipment in location
5. Equipment sumps, valves etc
6. Ground conditions
7. Emergency equipment
8. Services and Isolation points
9. Pits, drains and depressions in area
10. Movement people and plant etc

Complete Hot Work Permit

Carry Out Work In Accordance With Agreed Process

Supporting Media Available

Example Media Available at practicalsafety.org

Management Systems Gap Analysis
Compliance Register
Job Safety Analysis Form
Job Person Analysis JPA® Form
Hot Work Permit Form
Work Permit Form

Emergency Management Handbook

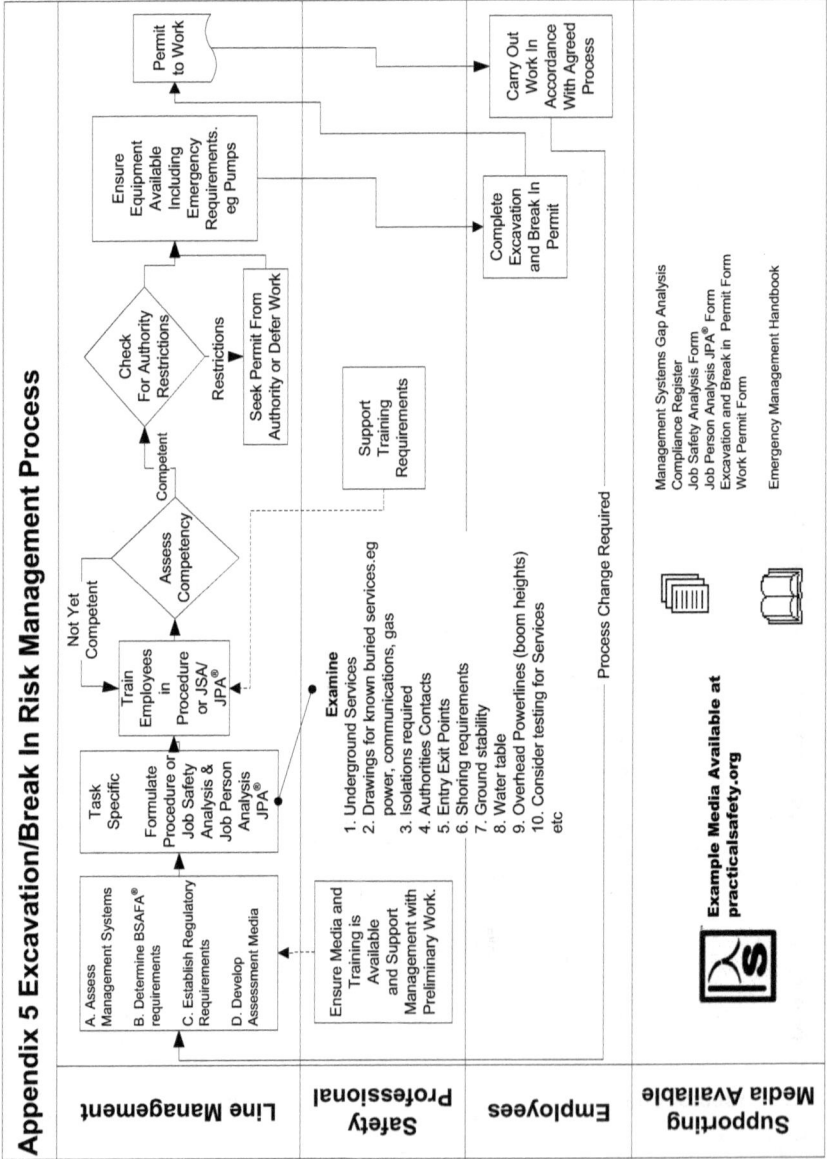

Appendix 5 Excavation/Break In Risk Management Process

Line Management

A. Assess Management Systems

B. Determine BSAFA® requirements

C. Establish Regulatory Requirements

D. Develop Assessment Media

Task Specific

Formulate Procedure or Job Safety Analysis & Job Person Analysis JPA®

Train Employees in Procedure or JSA/ JPA®

Not Yet Competent

Assess Competency

Competent

Check For Authority Restrictions

Restrictions

Seek Permit From Authority or Defer Work

Ensure Equipment Available Including Emergency Requirements. eg Pumps

Permit to Work

Carry Out Work In Accordance With Agreed Process

Complete Excavation and Break In Permit

Safety Professional

Ensure Media and Training is Available and Support Management with Preliminary Work.

Support Training Requirements

Process Change Required

Employees

Examine

1. Underground Services
2. Drawings for known buried services.eg power, communications, gas
3. Isolations required
4. Authorities Contacts
5. Entry Exit Points
6. Shoring requirements
7. Ground stability
8. Water table
9. Overhead Powerlines (boom heights)
10. Consider testing for Services etc

Supporting Media Available

Example Media Available at practicalsafety.org

Management Systems Gap Analysis
Compliance Register
Job Safety Analysis Form
Job Person Analysis JPA® Form
Excavation and Break In Permit Form
Work Permit Form

Emergency Management Handbook

Appendix 6 Electrical Risk Management Process

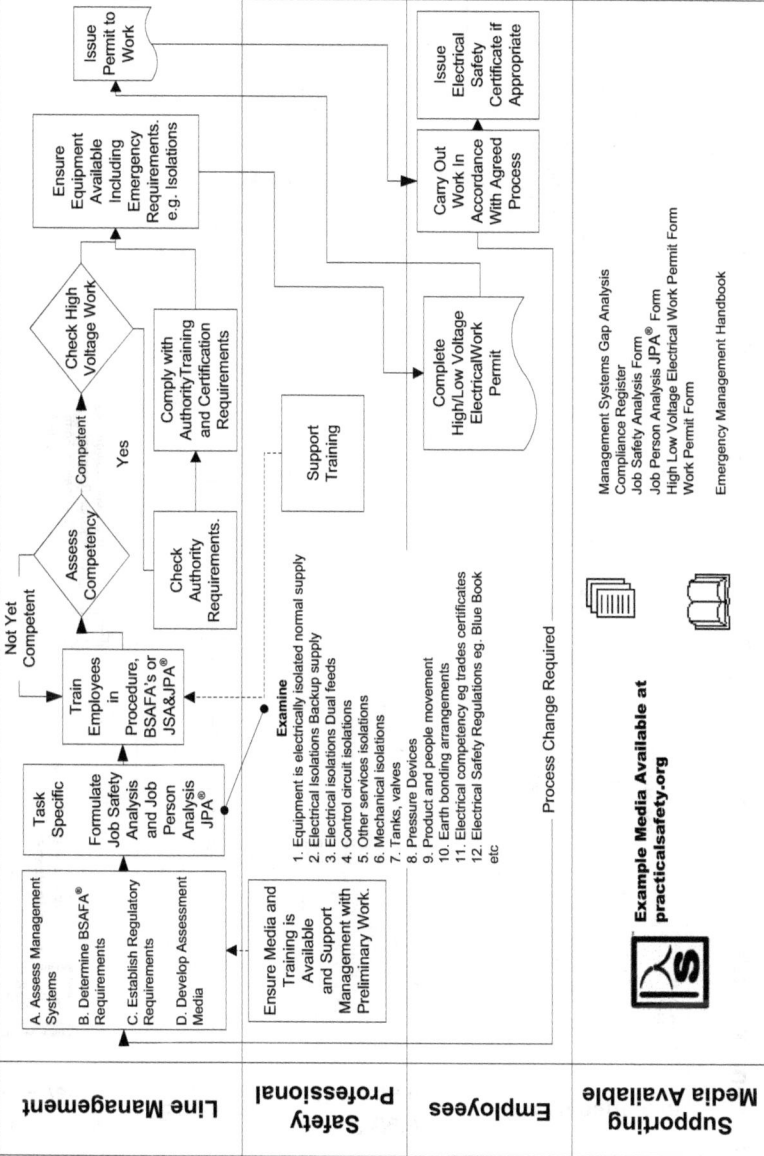

Line Management

- A. Assess Management Systems
- B. Determine BSAFA® Requirements
- C. Establish Regulatory Requirements
- D. Develop Assessment Media

Task Specific

Formulate Job Safety Analysis and Job Person Analysis JPA®

Train Employees in Procedure, BSAFA's or JSA&JPA®

Not Yet Competent

Assess Competency → Competent

Yes

Check High Voltage Work

Ensure Equipment Available Including Emergency Requirements. e.g. Isolations

Issue Permit to Work

Comply with Authority Training and Certification Requirements

Issue Electrical Safety Certificate if Appropriate

Carry Out Work In Accordance With Agreed Process

Complete High/Low Voltage Electrical Work Permit

Safety Professional

Ensure Media and Training is Available and Support Management with Preliminary Work.

Check Authority Requirements.

Support Training

Employees

Examine
1. Equipment is electrically isolated normal supply
2. Electrical Isolations Backup supply
3. Electrical Isolations Dual feeds
4. Control circuit isolations
5. Other services isolations
6. Mechanical Isolations
7. Tanks, valves
8. Pressure Devices
9. Product and people movement
10. Earth bonding arrangements
11. Electrical competency eg trades certificates
12. Electrical Safety Regulations eg. Blue Book
etc

Process Change Required

Supporting Media Available

Management Systems Gap Analysis
Compliance Register
Job Safety Analysis Form
Job Person Analysis JPA® Form
High Low Voltage Electrical Work Permit Form
Work Permit Form

Emergency Management Handbook

Example Media Available at practicalsafety.org

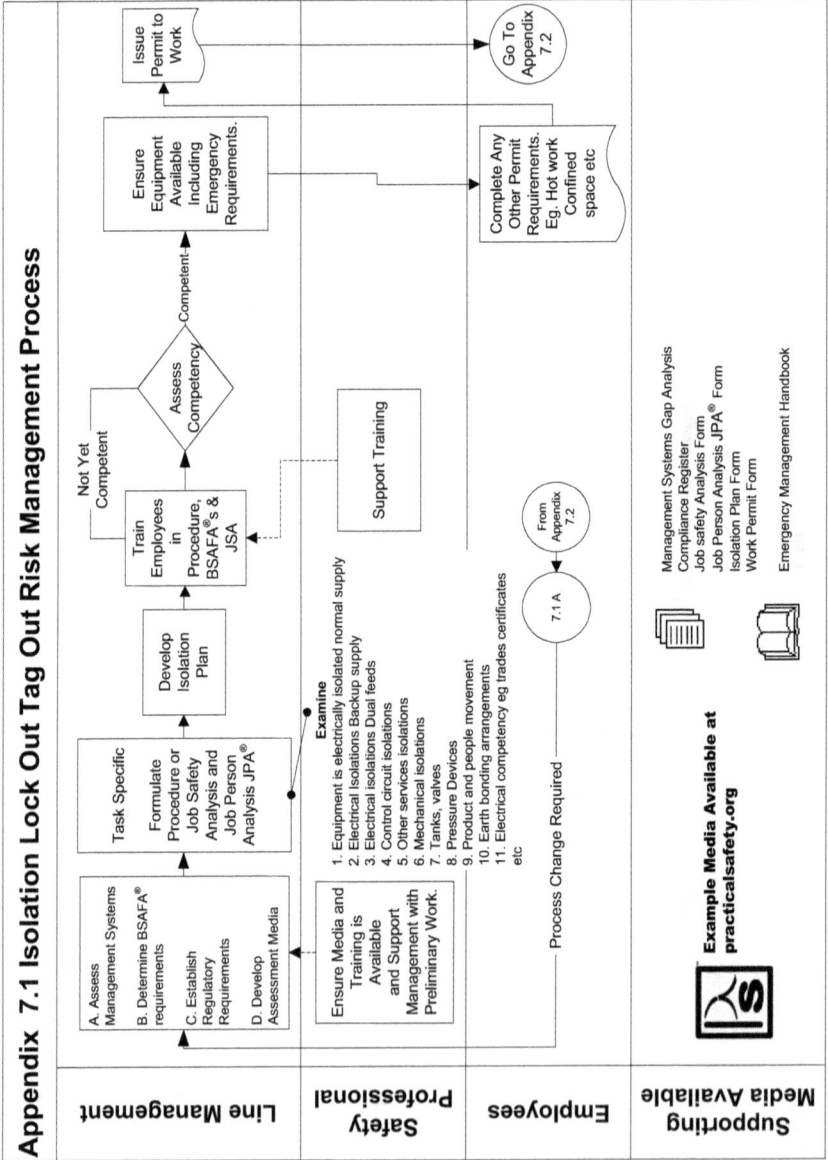

Appendix 7.1 Isolation Lock Out Tag Out Risk Management Process

Line Management	A. Assess Management Systems B. Determine BSAFA® requirements C. Establish Regulatory Requirements D. Develop Assessment Media → Task Specific → Formulate Procedure or Job Safety Analysis and Job Person Analysis JPA® → Develop Isolation Plan → Train Employees in Procedure, BSAFA®'s & JSA → Assess Competency
	Not Yet Competent (loop back to Train Employees) Competent → Ensure Equipment Available Including Emergency Requirements. → Issue Permit to Work
Safety Professional	Ensure Media and Training is Available and Support Management with Preliminary Work. Support Training
Employees	**Examine** 1. Equipment is electrically isolated normal supply 2. Electrical Isolations Backup supply 3. Electrical isolations Dual feeds 4. Control circuit isolations 5. Other services isolations 6. Mechanical isolations 7. Tanks, valves 8. Pressure Devices 9. Product and people movement 10. Earth bonding arrangements 11. Electrical competency eg trades certificates etc Process Change Required 7.1 A From Appendix 7.2 Complete Any Other Permit Requirements. Eg. Hot work Confined space etc → Go To Appendix 7.2
Supporting Media Available	Management Systems Gap Analysis Compliance Register Job safety Analysis Form Job Person Analysis JPA® Form Isolation Plan Form Work Permit Form Emergency Management Handbook **Example Media Available at practicalsafety.org**

Appendix 7.2 Practical Isolation Process

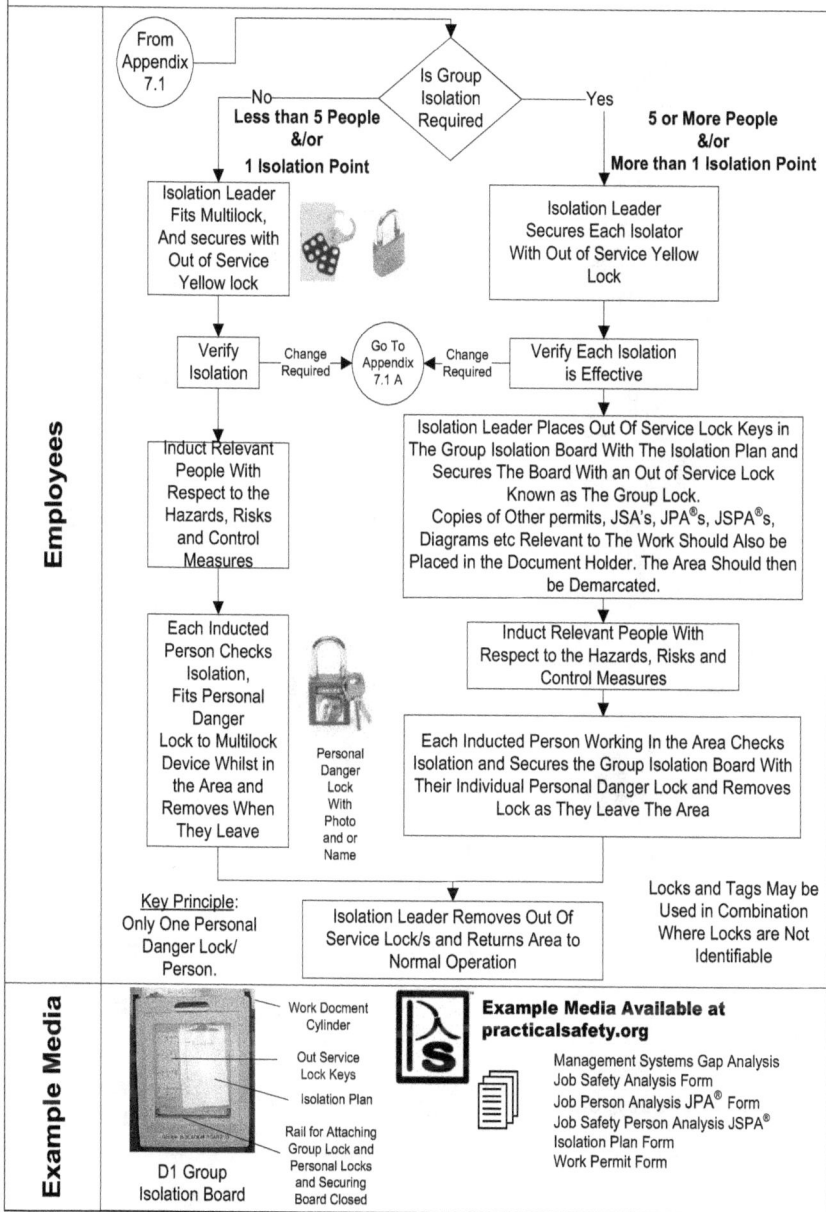

Employees

From Appendix 7.1

Is Group Isolation Required

No — **Less than 5 People &/or 1 Isolation Point**

Yes — **5 or More People &/or More than 1 Isolation Point**

Isolation Leader Fits Multilock, And secures with Out of Service Yellow lock

Isolation Leader Secures Each Isolator With Out of Service Yellow Lock

Verify Isolation — Change Required → Go To Appendix 7.1 A ← Change Required — Verify Each Isolation is Effective

Induct Relevant People With Respect to the Hazards, Risks and Control Measures

Isolation Leader Places Out Of Service Lock Keys in The Group Isolation Board With The Isolation Plan and Secures The Board With an Out of Service Lock Known as The Group Lock.
Copies of Other permits, JSA's, JPA®'s, JSPA®'s, Diagrams etc Relevant to The Work Should Also be Placed in the Document Holder. The Area Should then be Demarcated.

Each Inducted Person Checks Isolation, Fits Personal Danger Lock to Multilock Device Whilst in the Area and Removes When They Leave

Personal Danger Lock With Photo and or Name

Induct Relevant People With Respect to the Hazards, Risks and Control Measures

Each Inducted Person Working In the Area Checks Isolation and Secures the Group Isolation Board With Their Individual Personal Danger Lock and Removes Lock as They Leave The Area

Key Principle:
Only One Personal Danger Lock/ Person.

Isolation Leader Removes Out Of Service Lock/s and Returns Area to Normal Operation

Locks and Tags May be Used in Combination Where Locks are Not Identifiable

Example Media

Work Docment Cylinder
Out Service Lock Keys
Isolation Plan
Rail for Attaching Group Lock and Personal Locks and Securing Board Closed

D1 Group Isolation Board

Example Media Available at practicalsafety.org

Management Systems Gap Analysis
Job Safety Analysis Form
Job Person Analysis JPA® Form
Job Safety Person Analysis JSPA®
Isolation Plan Form
Work Permit Form

Appendix 8 Falls Risk Management Process

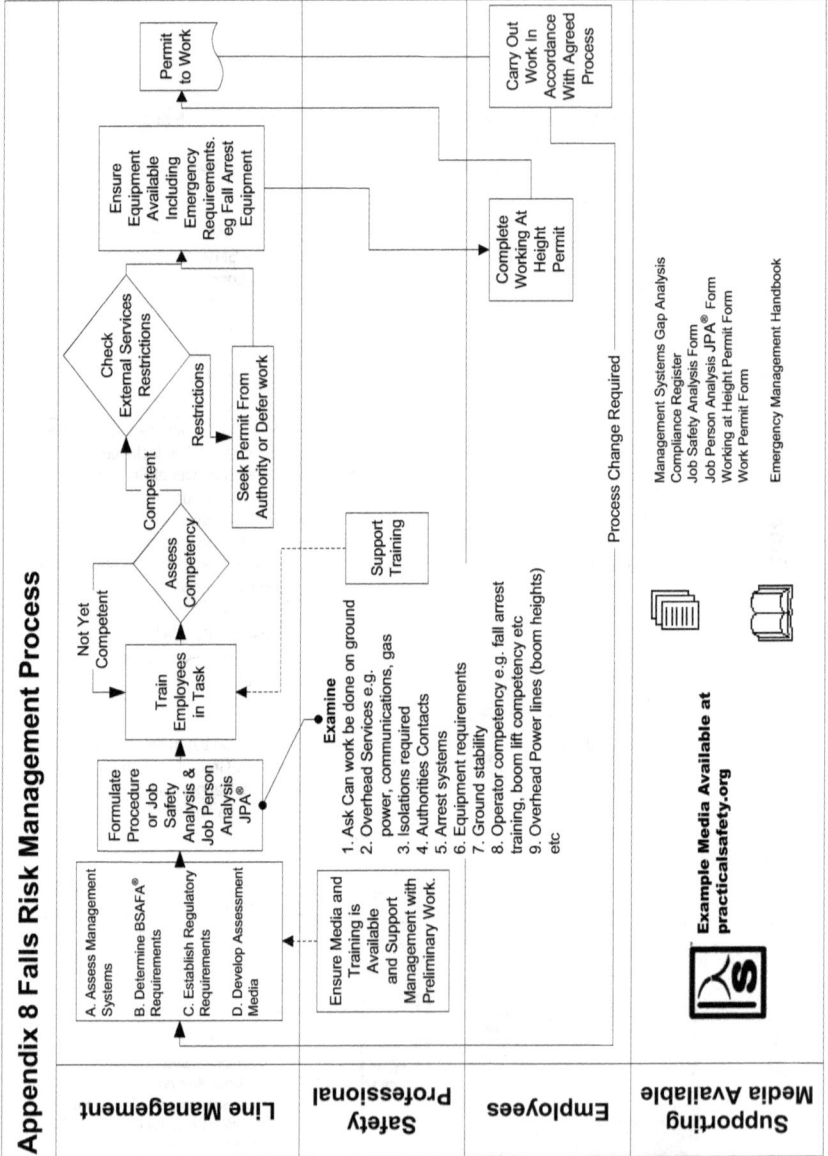

Line Management

A. Assess Management Systems

B. Determine BSAFA® Requirements

C. Establish Regulatory Requirements

D. Develop Assessment Media

Formulate Procedure or Job Safety Analysis & Job Person Analysis JPA®

Not Yet Competent

Train Employees in Task

Assess Competency

Competent

Check External Services Restrictions

Restrictions

Seek Permit From Authority or Defer work

Ensure Equipment Available Including Emergency Requirements. eg Fall Arrest Equipment

Permit to Work

Safety Professional

Ensure Media and Training is Available and Support Management with Preliminary Work.

Support Training

Employees

Examine

1. Ask Can work be done on ground
2. Overhead Services e.g. power, communications, gas
3. Isolations required
4. Authorities Contacts
5. Arrest systems
6. Equipment requirements
7. Ground stability
8. Operator competency e.g. fall arrest training, boom lift competency etc
9. Overhead Power lines (boom heights) etc

Complete Working At Height Permit

Carry Out Work In Accordance With Agreed Process

Process Change Required

Supporting Media Available

Management Systems Gap Analysis
Compliance Register
Job Safety Analysis Form
Job Person Analysis JPA® Form
Working at Height Permit Form
Work Permit Form

Emergency Management Handbook

Example Media Available at practicalsafety.org

Appendix 9 Noise Risk Management Process

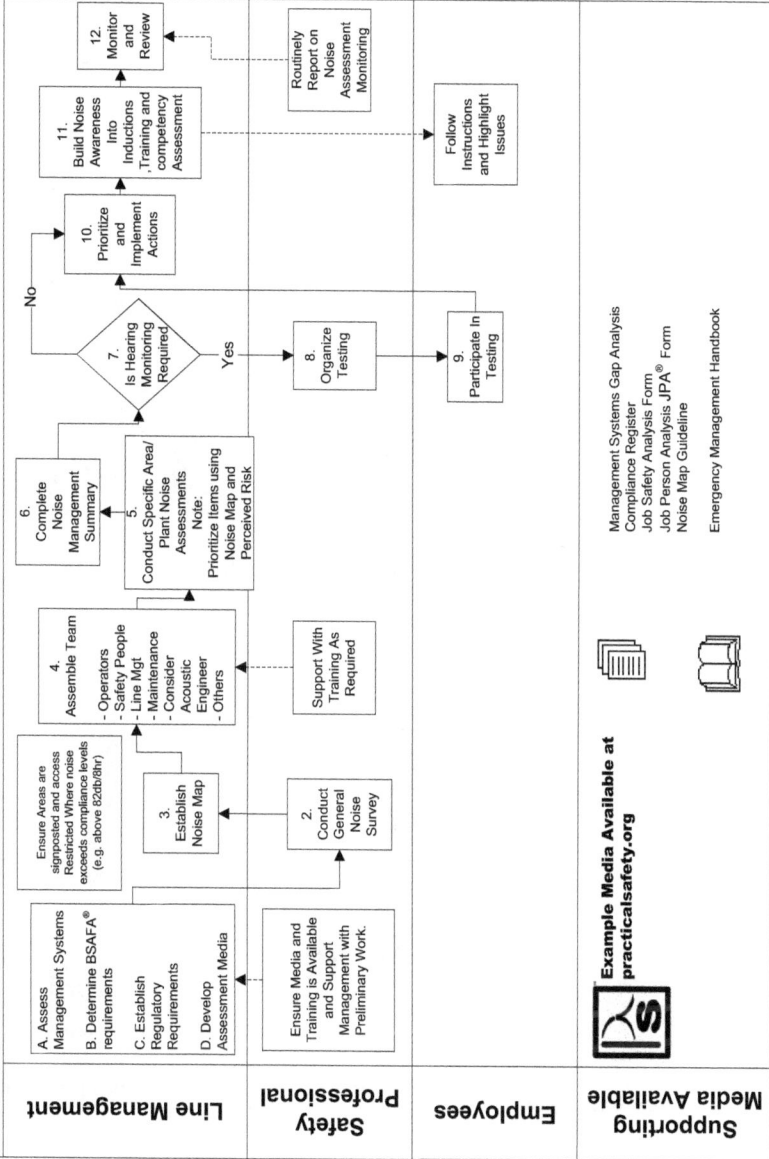

Line Management	A. Assess Management Systems
	B. Determine BSAFA® requirements
	C. Establish Regulatory Requirements
	D. Develop Assessment Media

Ensure Areas are signposted and access Restricted Where noise exceeds compliance levels (e.g. above 82db/8hr)

4. Assemble Team
- Operators
- Safety People
- Line Mgt
- Maintenance
- Consider Acoustic Engineer
- Others

3. Establish Noise Map

6. Complete Noise Management Summary

5. Conduct Specific Area/ Plant Noise Assessments
Note: Prioritize Items using Noise Map and Perceived Risk

11. Build Noise Awareness Into Inductions, Training and competency Assessment

12. Monitor and Review

10. Prioritize and Implement Actions

7. Is Hearing Monitoring Required —No

Yes

Safety Professional

Ensure Media and Training is Available and Support Management with Preliminary Work.

2. Conduct General Noise Survey

Support With Training As Required

8. Organize Testing

Employees

9. Participate In Testing

Follow Instructions and Highlight Issues

Routinely Report on Noise Assessment Monitoring

Supporting Media Available

Example Media Available at practicalsafety.org

Management Systems Gap Analysis
Compliance Register
Job Safety Analysis Form
Job Person Analysis JPA® Form
Noise Map Guideline

Emergency Management Handbook

Appendix 10.1 Asbestos Risk Management Process

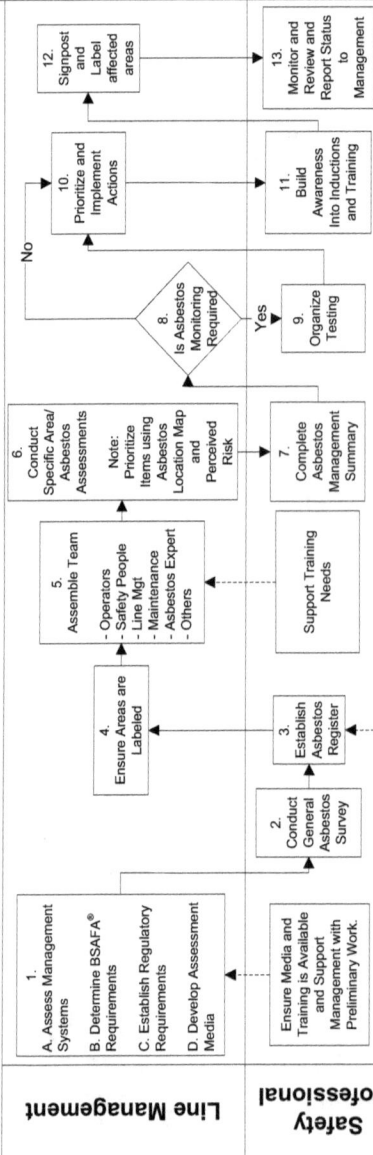

Line Management

1.
A. Assess Management Systems
B. Determine BSAFA® Requirements
C. Establish Regulatory Requirements
D. Develop Assessment Media

2. Conduct General Asbestos Survey

4. Ensure Areas are Labeled

5. Assemble Team
- Operators
- Safety People
- Line Mgt
- Maintenance
- Asbestos Expert
- Others

6. Conduct Specific Area/ Asbestos Assessments
Note: Prioritize Items using Asbestos Location Map and Perceived Risk

10. Prioritize and Implement Actions

12. Signpost and Label affected areas

13. Monitor and Review and Report Status to Management

8. Is Asbestos Monitoring Required?
No
Yes

9. Organize Testing

11. Build Awareness Into Inductions and Training

7. Complete Asbestos Management Summary

Safety Professional

Ensure Media and Training is Available and Support Management with Preliminary Work.

3. Establish Asbestos Register

Support Training Needs

Employees

Consult Asbestos Register as Part of Work Preparation Especially Maintenance

Supporting Media Available

Example Media Available at practicalsafety.org

Management Systems Gap Analysis
Compliance Register
Asbestos Material identification sheet
Asbestos Register
Asbestos material risk assessment and control summary
Asbestos signage and labelling
Asbestos material risk control review
Job Safety Analysis Form
Job Person Analysis JPA® Form
Emergency Management Handbook

Appendix 10.2 Working With Asbestos Management Process

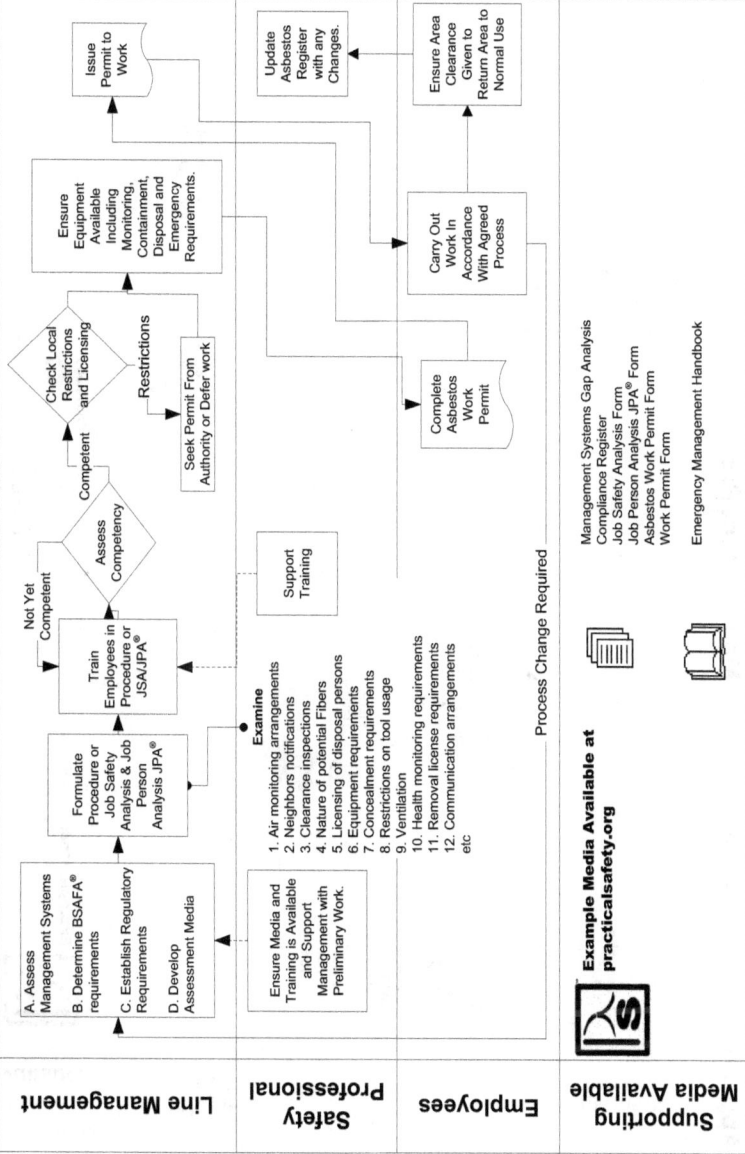

Line Management

A. Assess Management Systems

B. Determine BSAFA® requirements

C. Establish Regulatory Requirements

D. Develop Assessment Media

Formulate Procedure or Job Safety Analysis & Job Person Analysis JPA®

Train Employees in Procedure or JSA/JPA®

Not Yet Competent

Assess Competency

Competent

Check Local Restrictions and Licensing

Restrictions

Seek Permit From Authority or Defer work

Ensure Equipment Available Including Monitoring, Containment, Disposal and Emergency Requirements.

Issue Permit to Work

Update Asbestos Register with any Changes.

Safety Professional

Ensure Media and Training is Available and Support Management with Preliminary Work.

Examine

1. Air monitoring arrangements
2. Neighbors notifications
3. Clearance inspections
4. Nature of potential Fibers
5. Licensing of disposal persons
6. Equipment requirements
7. Concealment requirements
8. Restrictions on tool usage
9. Ventilation
10. Health monitoring requirements
11. Removal license requirements
12. Communication arrangements
etc

Employees

Support Training

Complete Asbestos Work Permit

Carry Out Work In Accordance With Agreed Process

Ensure Area Clearance Given to Return Area to Normal Use

Process Change Required

Supporting Media Available

Example Media Available at practicalsafety.org

Management Systems Gap Analysis
Compliance Register
Job Safety Analysis Form
Job Person Analysis JPA® Form
Asbestos Work Permit Form
Work Permit Form

Emergency Management Handbook

Appendix 11 Manual Handling Risk Management Process

	Line Management	Safety Professional	Employees	Supporting Media Available

1.
A. Assess Management Systems
B. Determine BSAFA® Requirements
C. Establish Regulatory Requirements
D. Develop Assessment Media

2. Conduct General Manual Handling Survey

Ensure Media and Training is Available and Support Management with Preliminary Work.

3. Establish Manual Handling Task Register

4. Ensure Items are Labelled Appropriately with Handling and Weight Information

5. Assemble Team
- Operators
- Safety People
- Line Mgt
- Maintenance
- Consider ergonomist
- Others

Support Training

6. Conduct Specific Area/Manual Handling Assessments

Note: Prioritize Items using Manual Handling Task Register and Perceived Risk

Build General Awareness Into Inductions and Training

Participate in Risk Assessments

7. Complete Manual Handling Management Summary

8. Prioritize and Implement Actions

9. Formulate Procedure or Job Safety Analysis & Job Person Analysis JPA®

Support Procedure Development

Participate in Procedure Writing

10. Train Employees in Procedure or JSA/JPA®

Support Training

11. Assess Competency

Not yet Competent

Competent

12. Observe Instructions and Highlight Issues

13. Monitor and Review

Process Change Required

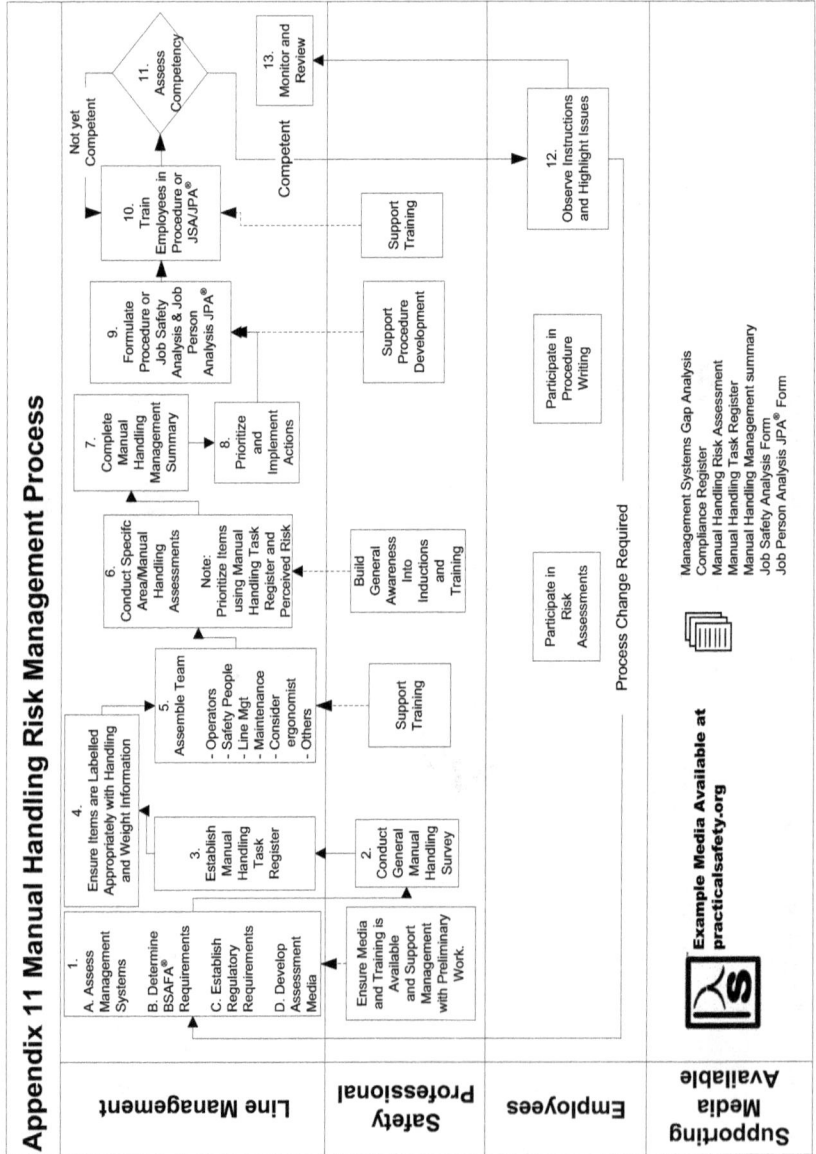

Example Media Available at practicalsafety.org

Management Systems Gap Analysis
Compliance Register
Manual Handling Risk Assessment
Manual Handling Task Register
Manual Handling Management summary
Job Safety Analysis Form
Job Person Analysis JPA® Form

Appendix 12 Ergonomics Risk Management Process

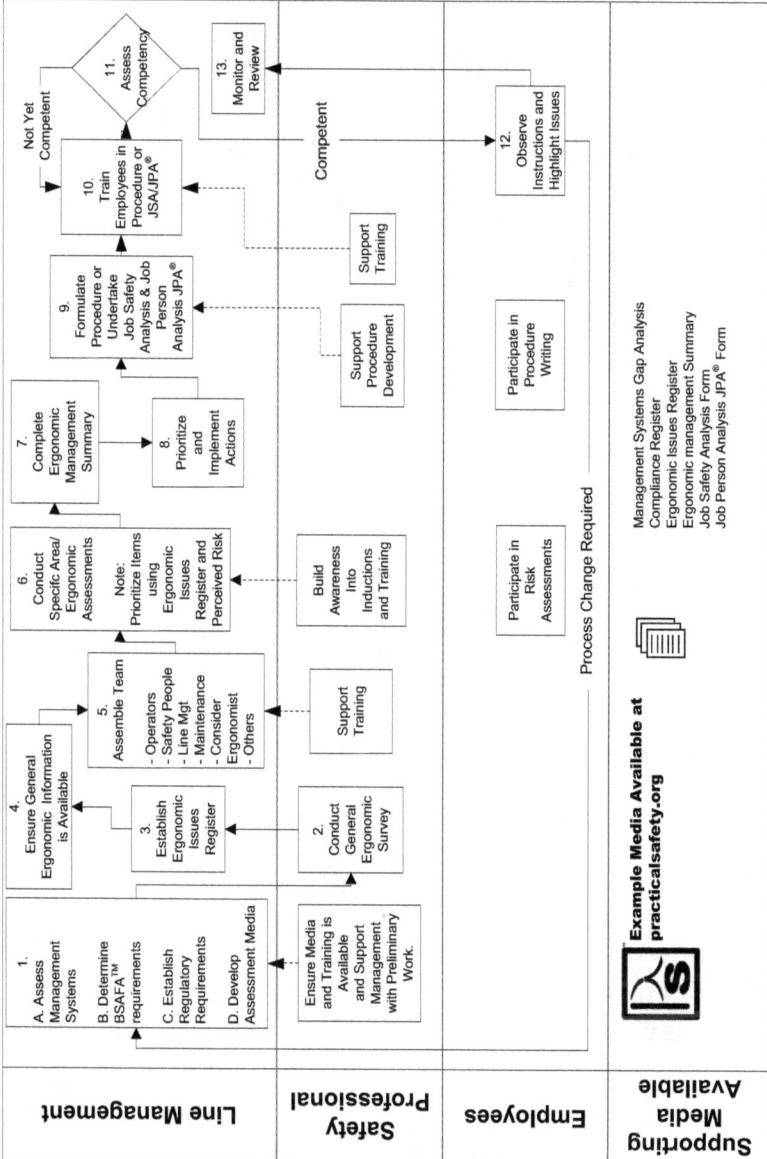

Line Management

A. Assess Management Systems
B. Determine BSAFA™ requirements
C. Establish Regulatory Requirements
D. Develop Assessment Media

4. Ensure General Ergonomic Information is Available

3. Establish Ergonomic Issues Register

6. Conduct Specific Area/ Ergonomic Assessments

Note: Prioritize Items using Ergonomic Issues Register and Perceived Risk

7. Complete Ergonomic Management Summary

8. Prioritize and Implement Actions

9. Formulate Procedure or Undertake Job Safety Analysis & Job Person Analysis JPA®

10. Train Employees in Procedure or JSA/JPA®

11. Assess Competency

Not Yet Competent

13. Monitor and Review

Safety Professional

Ensure Media and Training is Available and Support Management with Preliminary Work.

2. Conduct General Ergonomic Survey

5. Assemble Team
- Operators
- Safety People
- Line Mgt
- Maintenance
- Consider Ergonomist
- Others

Support Training

Build Awareness Into Inductions and Training

Support Procedure Development

Support Training

Process Change Required

Competent

Employees

Participate in Risk Assessments

Participate in Procedure Writing

12. Observe Instructions and Highlight Issues

Supporting Media Available

Example Media Available at practicalsafety.org

Management Systems Gap Analysis
Compliance Register
Ergonomic Issues Register
Ergonomic management Summary
Job Safety Analysis Form
Job Person Analysis JPA® Form

Appendix 13 Traffic Risk Management Process

Line Management

1.
A. Assess Management Systems
B. Determine BSAFA® Requirements
C. Establish Regulatory Requirements
D. Develop Assessment Media

4.
Ensure General Signage is in place

3.
Establish Traffic Issues Register

5.
Assemble Team
- Operators
- Safety People
- Line Mgt
- Maintenance
- Consider Truck and Courier Drivers
- Others

6.
Conduct Specific Area/Traffic Assessments

Note:
Prioritize Items using Traffic Issues Register and Perceived Risk

7.
Complete Traffic Management Summary

8.
Prioritize and Implement Actions

9.
Prepare Traffic Management Procedures Using JSA and JPA® Including:
1. Site Traffic Map
2. Truck loading unloading procedures
3. Site Demarcation Standards
4. Security Arrangements
5. Emergency Arrangements

10.
Train Employees in Procedure or JSA/JPA®

Not Yet Competent

11.
Assess Competency

Competent

13.
Monitor and Review

12.
Observe Instructions and Highlight Issues

Safety Professional

Ensure Media and Training is Available and Support Management with Preliminary Work.

2.
Conduct General Traffic Survey/Audit

Support Training

Build General Awareness Into Inductions and Training

Support Procedure Deevelopment

Support Training

Process Change Required

Employees

Participate in Risk Assessments

Participate in Procedure Writing

Supporting Media Available

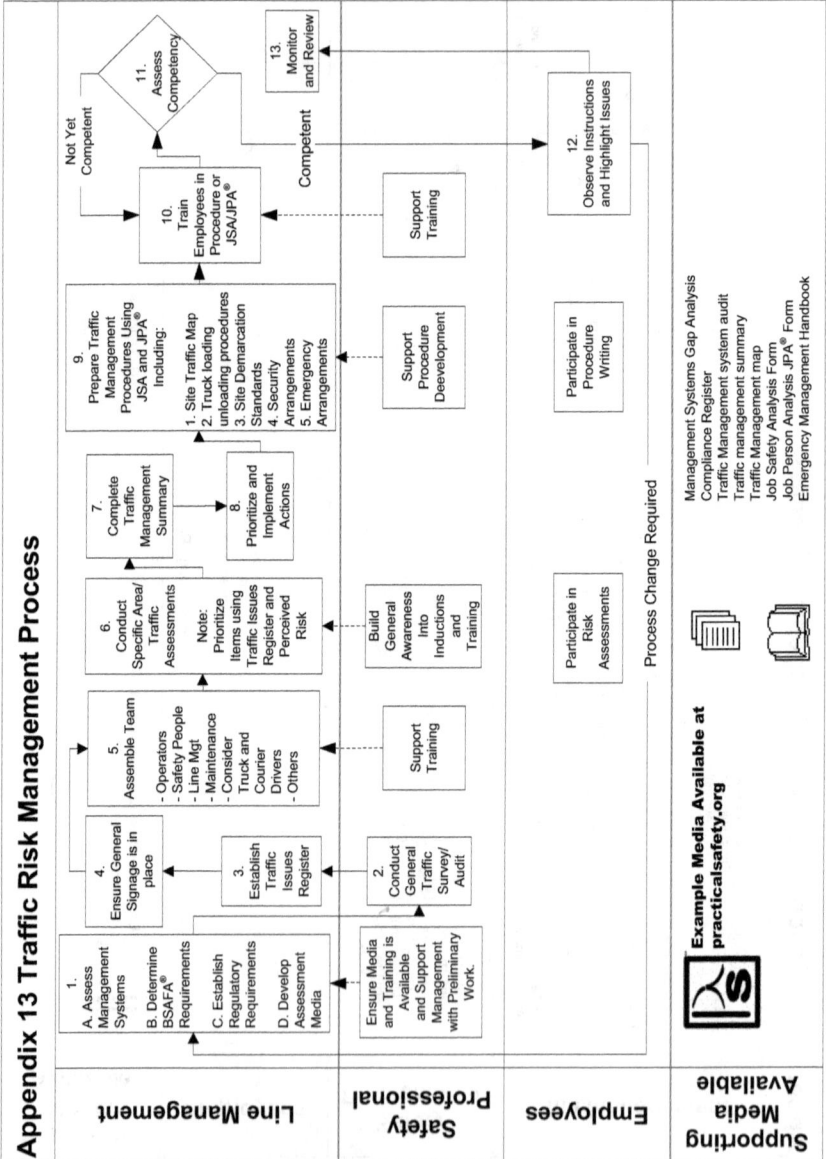

Example Media Available at practicalsafety.org

Management Systems Gap Analysis
Compliance Register
Traffic Management system audit
Traffic management summary
Traffic Management map
Job Safety Analysis Form
Job Person Analysis JPA® Form
Emergency Management Handbook

Appendix 14 Lead Risk Management Process

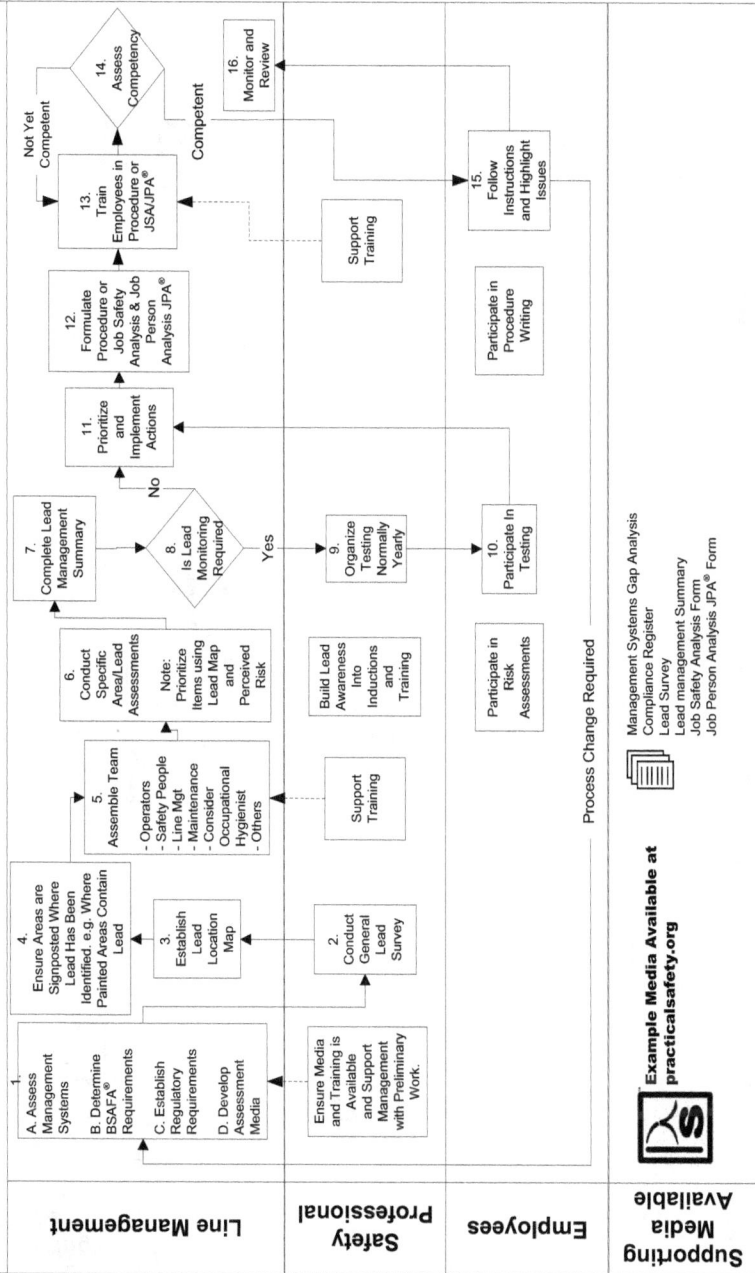

Line Management

1.
A. Assess Management Systems
B. Determine BSAFA® Requirements
C. Establish Regulatory Requirements
D. Develop Assessment Media

2. Conduct General Lead Survey

3. Establish Lead Location Map

4. Ensure Areas are Signposted Where Lead Has Been Identified. e.g. Where Painted Areas Contain Lead

5. Assemble Team
- Operators
- Safety People
- Line Mgt
- Maintenance
- Consider Occupational Hygienist
- Others

6. Conduct Specific Area/Lead Assessments

Note: Prioritize Items using Lead Map and Perceived Risk

7. Complete Lead Management Summary

8. Is Lead Monitoring Required

No → 11. Prioritize and Implement Actions

Yes → 9. Organize Testing Normally Yearly → 10. Participate In Testing

12. Formulate Procedure or Job Safety Analysis & Job Person Analysis JPA®

13. Train Employees in Procedure or JSA/JPA®

14. Assess Competency
Not Yet Competent → 13.
Competent → 16. Monitor and Review

15. Follow Instructions and Highlight Issues

16. Monitor and Review

Safety Professional

Ensure Media and Training is Available and Support Management with Preliminary Work.

Support Training

Build Lead Awareness Into Inductions and Training

Support Training

Employees

Participate in Risk Assessments

Participate In Testing

Participate in Procedure Writing

Follow Instructions and Highlight Issues

Process Change Required

Supporting Media Available

Management Systems Gap Analysis
Compliance Register
Lead Survey
Lead management Summary
Job Safety Analysis Form
Job Person Analysis JPA® Form

Example Media Available at practicalsafety.org

Appendix 15 Electromagnetic Radiation (EMR) Risk Management Process

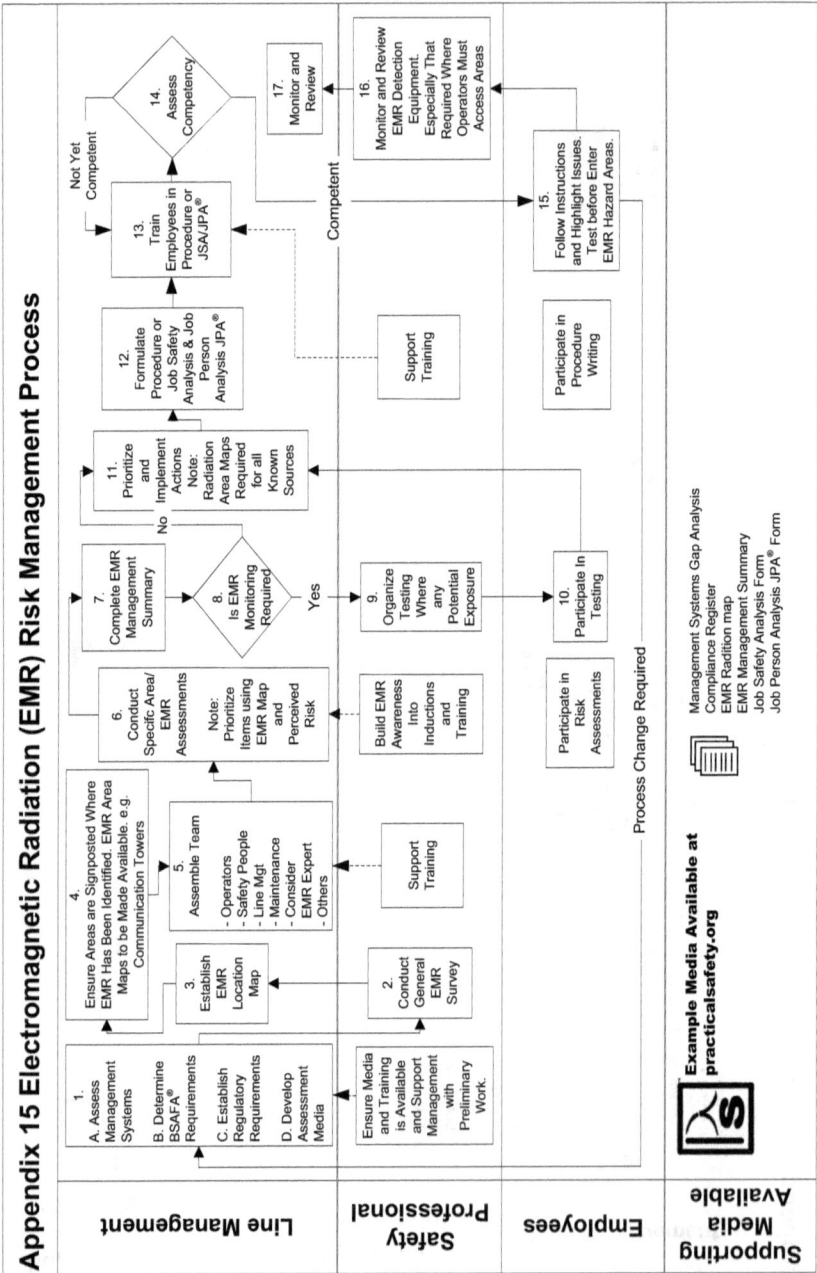

Line Management

1.
A. Assess Management Systems
B. Determine BSAFA® Requirements
C. Establish Regulatory Requirements
D. Develop Assessment Media

Ensure Media and Training is Available and Support Management with Preliminary Work.

2. Conduct General EMR Survey

3. Establish EMR Location Map

4. Ensure Areas are Signposted Where EMR Has Been Identified. EMR Area Maps to be Made Available. e.g. Communication Towers

5. Assemble Team
- Operators
- Safety People
- Line Mgt
- Maintenance
- Consider EMR Expert
- Others

6. Conduct Specific Area/EMR Assessments
Note: Prioritize Items using EMR Map and Perceived Risk

7. Complete EMR Management Summary

8. Is EMR Monitoring Required

11. Prioritize and Implement Actions
Note: Radiation Area Maps Required for all Known Sources

12. Formulate Procedure or Job Safety Analysis & Job Person Analysis JPA®

13. Train Employees in Procedure or JSA/JPA®

14. Assess Competency

Not Yet Competent

Competent

17. Monitor and Review

16. Monitor and Review EMR Detection Equipment, Especially That Required Where Operators Must Access Areas

15. Follow Instructions and Highlight Issues. Test before Enter EMR Hazard Areas.

Safety Professional

Support Training

Build EMR Awareness Into Inductions and Training

Support Training

Employees

Participate in Risk Assessments

9. Organize Testing Where any Potential Exposure

10. Participate In Testing

Yes

No

Participate in Procedure Writing

Process Change Required

Supporting Media Available

Example Media Available at practicalsafety.org

Management Systems Gap Analysis
Compliance Register
EMR Radtion map
EMR Management Summary
Job Safety Analysis Form
Job Person Analysis JPA® Form

Appendix 16.1 Emergency Management Process

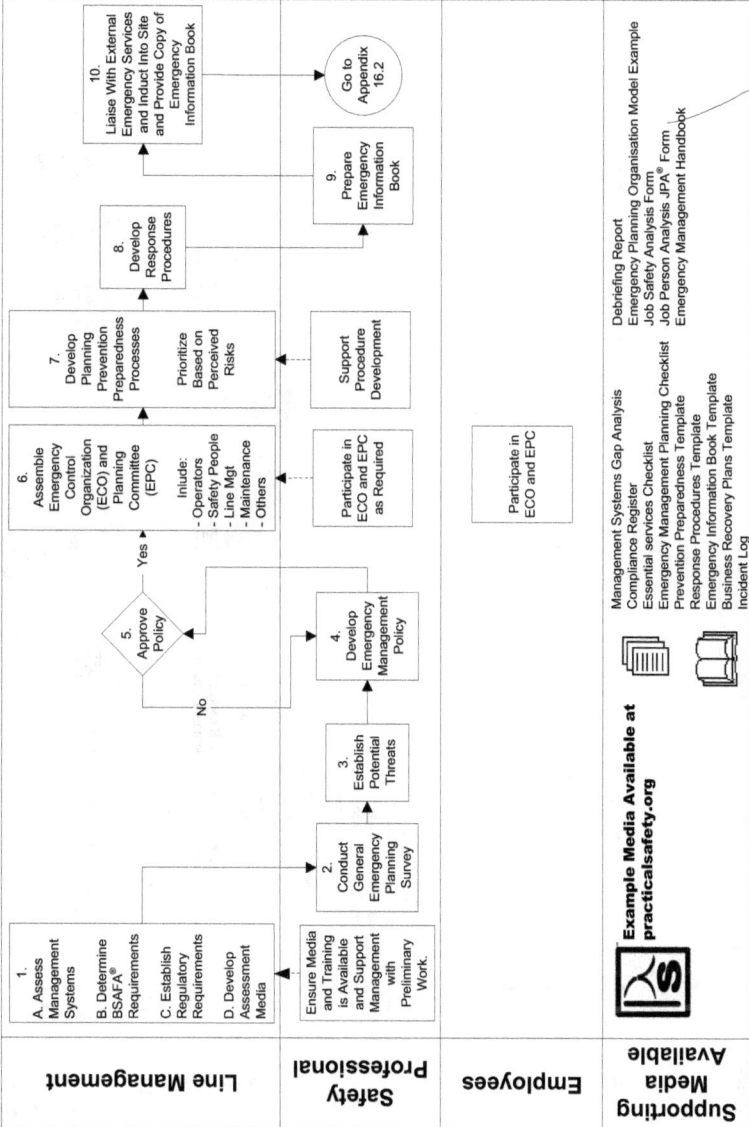

Line Management

1. A. Assess Management Systems
B. Determine BSAFA® Requirements
C. Establish Regulatory Requirements
D. Develop Assessment Media

2. Conduct General Emergency Planning Survey

3. Establish Potential Threats

4. Develop Emergency Management Policy

5. Approve Policy — No / Yes

6. Assemble Emergency Control Organization (ECO) and Planning Committee (EPC)
Inlude:
- Operators
- Safety People
- Line Mgt
- Maintenance
- Others

7. Develop Planning Prevention Preparedness Processes
Prioritize Based on Perceived Risks

8. Develop Response Procedures

9. Prepare Emergency Information Book

10. Liaise With External Emergency Services and Induct Into Site and Provide Copy of Emergency Information Book

Go to Appendix 16.2

Safety Professional

Ensure Media and Training is Available and Support Management with Preliminary Work.

Participate in ECO and EPC as Required

Support Procedure Development

Employees

Participate in ECO and EPC

Supporting Media Available

Example Media Available at practicalsafety.org

Management Systems Gap Analysis
Compliance Register
Essential services Checklist
Emergency Management Planning Checklist
Prevention Preparedness Template
Response Procedures Template
Emergency Information Book Template
Business Recovery Plans Template
Incident Log
Debriefing Report
Emergency Planning Organisation Model Example
Job Safety Analysis Form
Job Person Analysis JPA® Form
Emergency Management Handbook

Appendix 16.2 Emergency Management Process

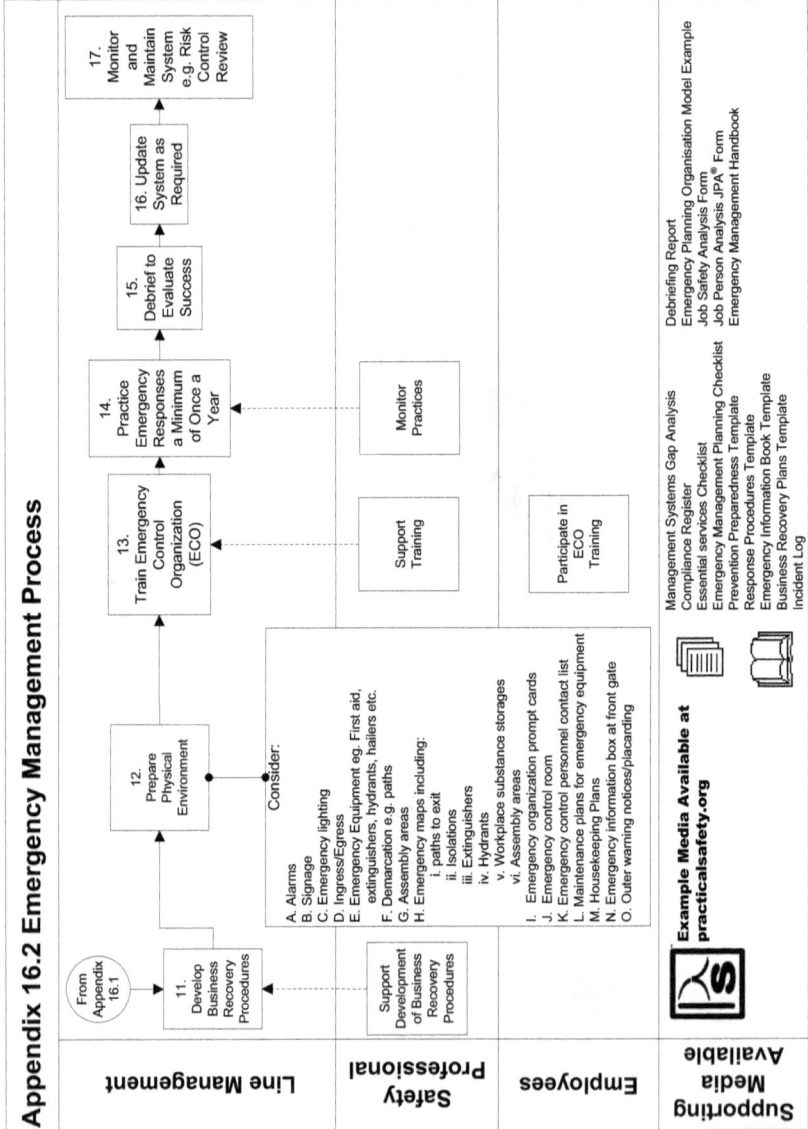

Line Management	From Appendix 16.1 → 11. Develop Business Recovery Procedures → 12. Prepare Physical Environment → 13. Train Emergency Control Organization (ECO) → 14. Practice Emergency Responses a Minimum of Once a Year → 15. Debrief to Evaluate Success → 16. Update System as Required → 17. Monitor and Maintain System e.g. Risk Control Review
Safety Professional	Support Development of Business Recovery Procedures · Support Training · Monitor Practices
Employees	Participate in ECO Training

Consider:

A. Alarms
B. Signage
C. Emergency lighting
D. Ingress/Egress
E. Emergency Equipment eg. First aid, extinguishers, hydrants, hailers etc.
F. Demarcation e.g. paths
G. Assembly areas
H. Emergency maps including:
  i. paths to exit
  ii. Isolations
  iii. Extinguishers
  iv. Hydrants
  v. Workplace substance storages
  vi. Assembly areas
I. Emergency organization prompt cards
J. Emergency control room
K. Emergency control personnel contact list
L. Maintenance plans for emergency equipment
M. Housekeeping Plans
N. Emergency information box at front gate
O. Outer warning notices/placarding

Supporting Media Available

Management Systems Gap Analysis
Compliance Register
Essential services Checklist
Emergency Management Planning Checklist
Prevention Preparedness Template
Response Procedures Template
Emergency Information Book Template
Business Recovery Plans Template
Incident Log

Debriefing Report
Emergency Planning Organisation Model Example
Job Safety Analysis Form
Job Person Analysis JPA® Form
Emergency Management Handbook

Example Media Available at practicalsafety.org

Appendix 17 Essential Services Management Process

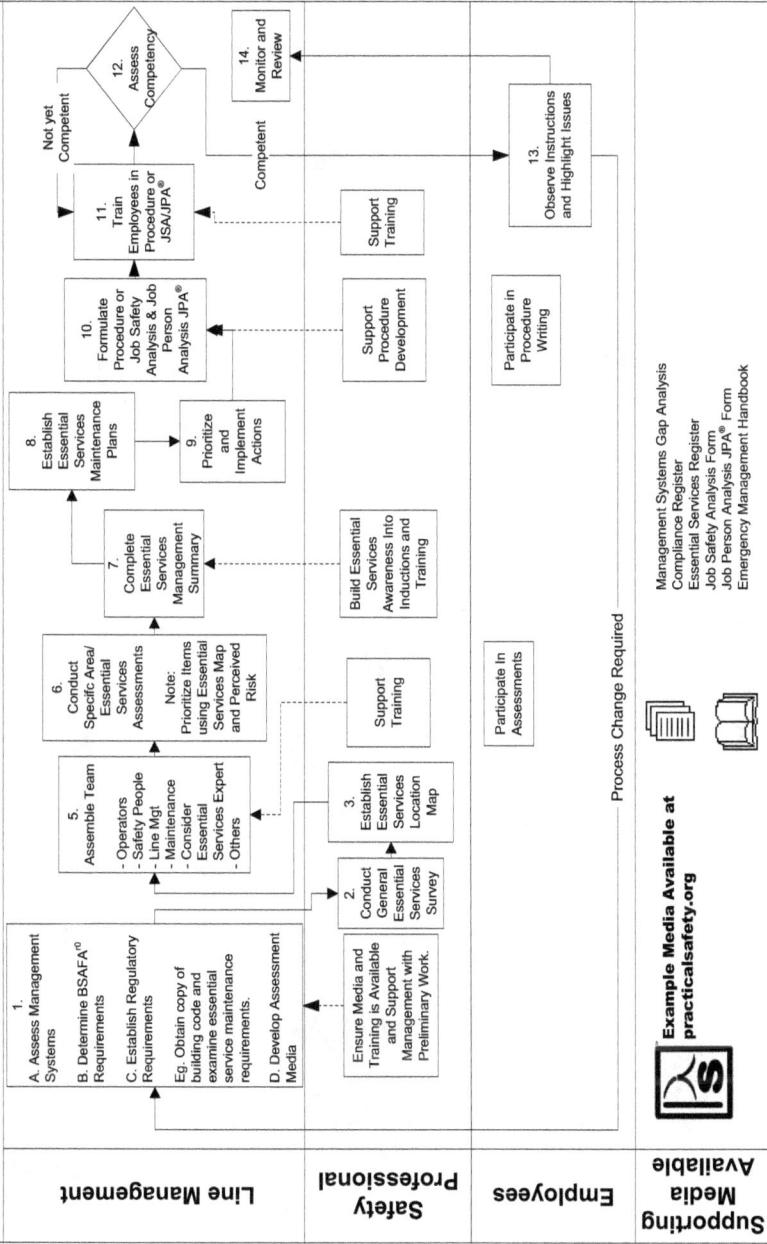

Line Management	

1.
A. Assess Management Systems

B. Determine BSAFA™ Requirements

C. Establish Regulatory Requirements

Eg. Obtain copy of building code and examine essential service maintenance requirements.

D. Develop Assessment Media

2.
Conduct General Essential Services Survey

5.
Assemble Team
- Operators
- Safety People
- Line Mgt
- Maintenance
- Consider Essential Services Expert
- Others

6.
Conduct Specific Area/ Essential Services Assessments

Note:
Prioritize Items using Essential Services Map and Perceived Risk

7.
Complete Essential Services Management Summary

8.
Establish Essential Services Maintenance Plans

9.
Prioritize and Implement Actions

10.
Formulate Procedure or Job Safety Analysis & Job Person Analysis JPA®

11.
Train Employees in Procedure or JSA/JPA®

12.
Assess Competency

Not yet Competent

Competent

14.
Monitor and Review

Safety Professional

Ensure Media and Training is Available and Support Management with Preliminary Work.

3.
Establish Essential Services Location Map

Support Training

Support Procedure Development

Support Training

Employees

Participate In Assessments

Build Essential Services Awareness Into Inductions and Training

Participate in Procedure Writing

13.
Observe Instructions and Highlight Issues

Process Change Required

Supporting Media Available

Example Media Available at practicalsafety.org

Management Systems Gap Analysis
Compliance Register
Essential Services Register
Job Safety Analysis Form
Job Person Analysis JPA® Form
Emergency Management Handbook

Appendix 18 First Aid Provision Management Process

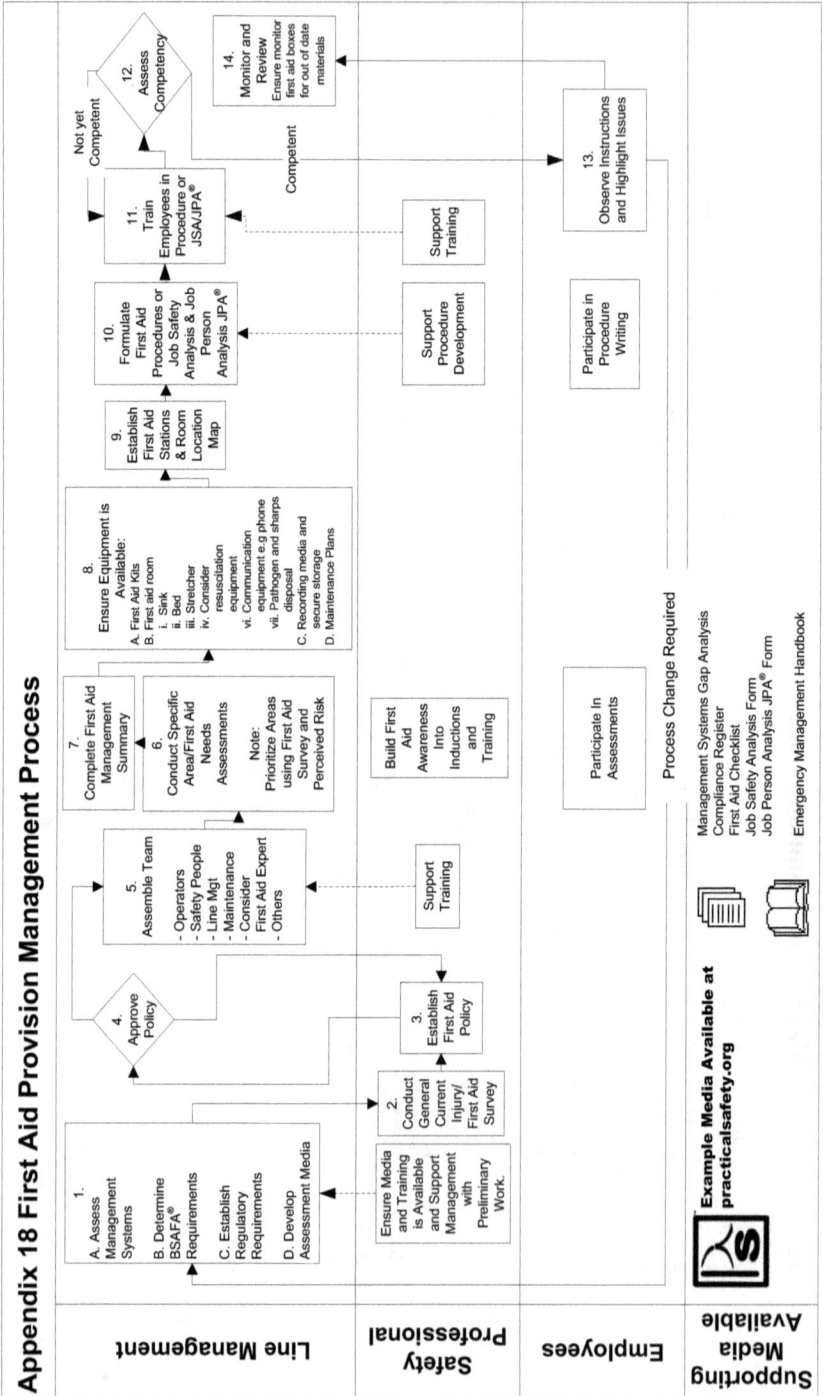

Line Management

1.
A. Assess Management Systems
B. Determine BSAFA® Requirements
C. Establish Regulatory Requirements
D. Develop Assessment Media

2.
Conduct General Current Injury/ First Aid Survey

3.
Establish First Aid Policy

4.
Approve Policy

5.
Assemble Team
- Operators
- Safety People
- Line Mgt
- Maintenance
- Consider First Aid Expert
- Others

6.
Conduct Specific Area/First Aid Needs Assessments

Note:
Prioritize Areas using First Aid Survey and Perceived Risk

7.
Complete First Aid Management Summary

8.
Ensure Equipment is Available:
A. First Aid Kits
B. First aid room
  i. Sink
  ii. Bed
  iii. Stretcher
  iv. Consider resuscitation equipment
  vi. Communication equipment e.g phone
  vii. Pathogen and sharps disposal
C. Recording media and secure storage
D. Maintenance Plans

9.
Establish First Aid Stations & Room Location Map

10.
Formulate First Aid Procedures or Job Safety Analysis & Job Person Analysis JPA®

11.
Train Employees in Procedure or JSA/JPA®

12.
Assess Competency

Not yet Competent

Competent

14.
Monitor and Review
Ensure monitor first aid boxes for out of date materials

Safety Professional

Ensure Media and Training is Available and Support Management with Preliminary Work.

Support Training

Build First Aid Awareness Into Inductions and Training

Support Procedure Development

Support Training

Employees

Participate In Assessments

Participate in Procedure Writing

13.
Observe Instructions and Highlight Issues

Process Change Required

Supporting Media Available

Example Media Available at practicalsafety.org

Management Systems Gap Analysis
Compliance Register
First Aid Checklist
Job Safety Analysis Form
Job Person Analysis JPA® Form

Emergency Management Handbook

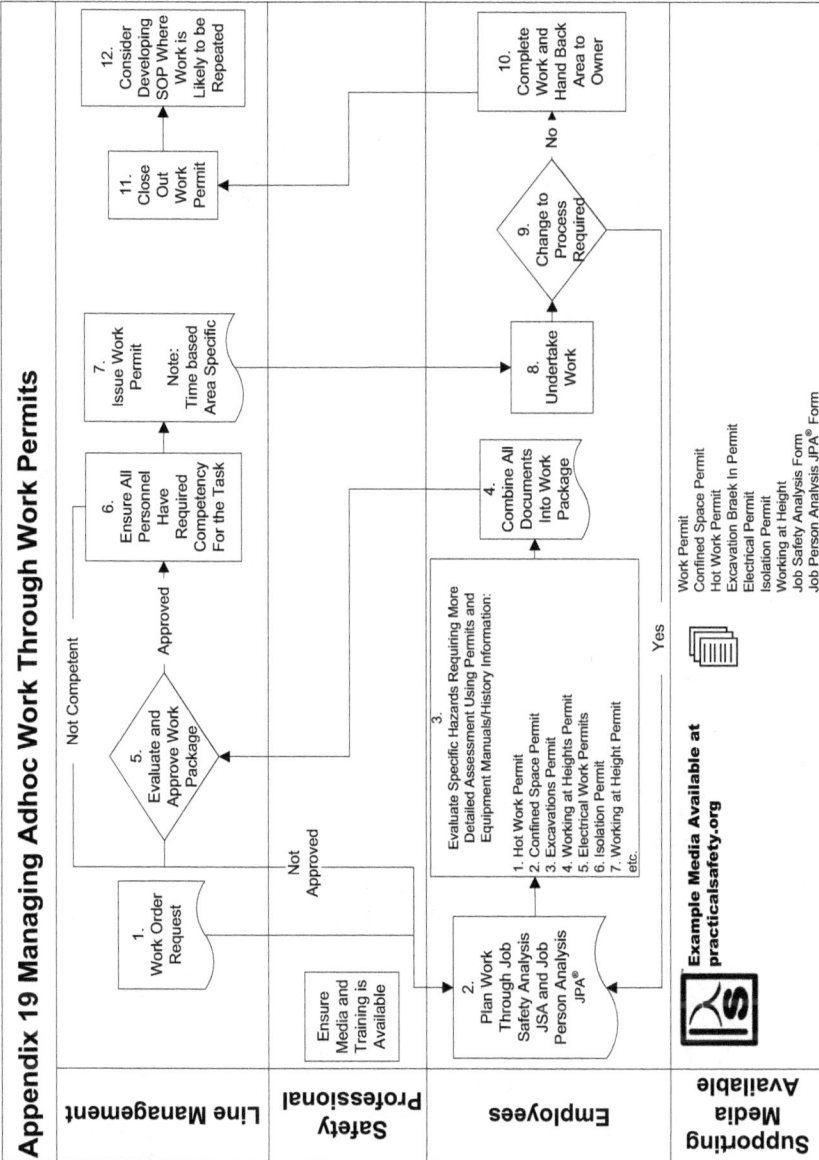

Appendix 19 Managing Adhoc Work Through Work Permits

Line Management

Safety Professional

Employees

Supporting Media Available

1. Work Order Request

Ensure Media and Training is Available

5. Evaluate and Approve Work Package

Not Competent

Approved

Not Approved

6. Ensure All Personnel Have Required Competency For the Task

7. Issue Work Permit

Note: Time based Area Specific

11. Close Out Work Permit

12. Consider Developing SOP Where Work is Likely to be Repeated

2. Plan Work Through Job Safety Analysis JSA and Job Person Analysis JPA®

3. Evaluate Specific Hazards Requiring More Detailed Assessment Using Permits and Equipment Manuals/History Information:
1. Hot Work Permit
2. Confined Space Permit
3. Excavations Permit
4. Working at Heights Permit
5. Electrical Work Permits
6. Isolation Permit
7. Working at Height Permit
etc.

4. Combine All Documents Into Work Package

8. Undertake Work

9. Change to Process Required

Yes

No

10. Complete Work and Hand Back Area to Owner

Example Media Available at practicalsafety.org

Work Permit
Confined Space Permit
Hot Work Permit
Excavation Break In Permit
Electrical Permit
Isolation Permit
Working at Height
Job Safety Analysis Form
Job Person Analysis JPA® Form

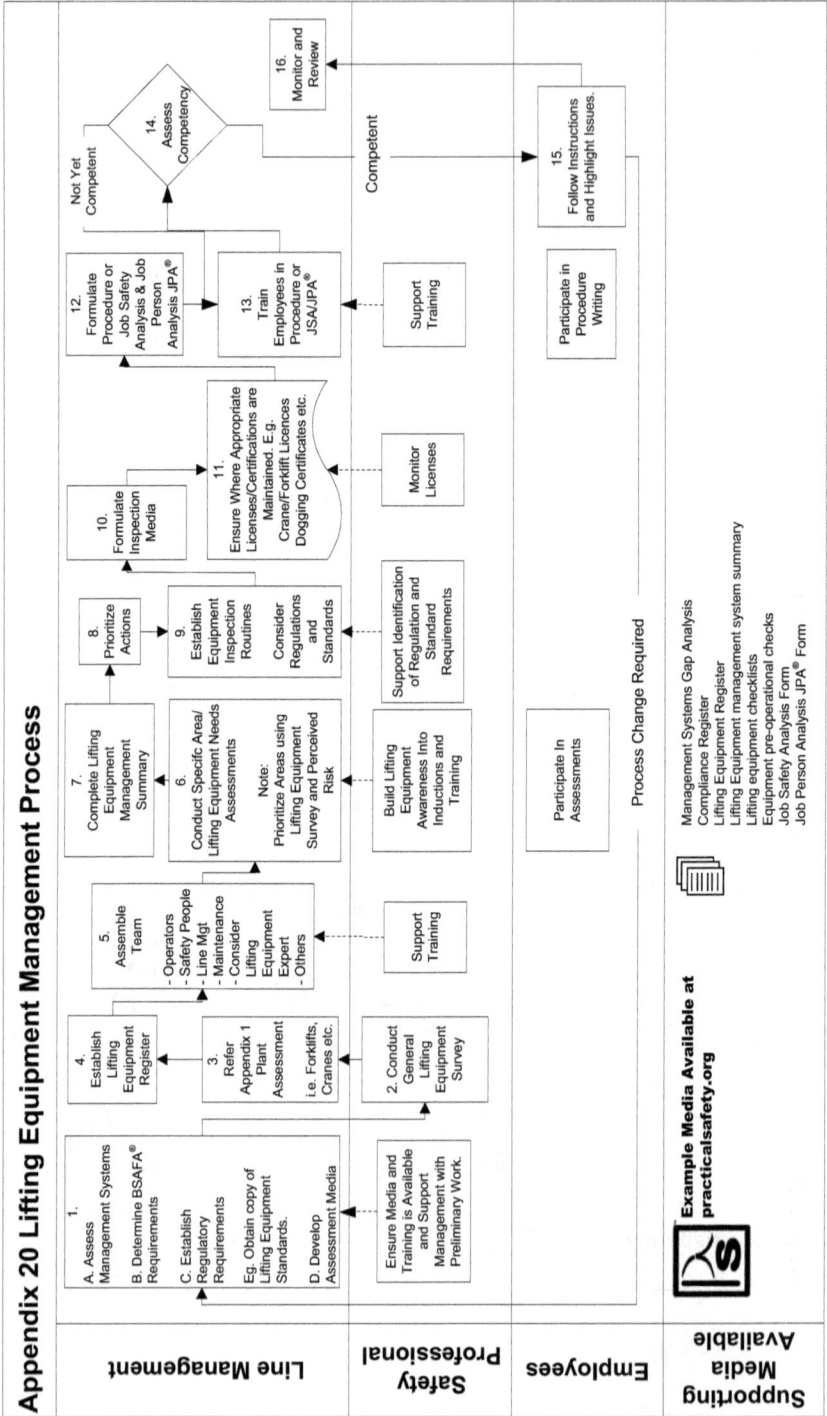

Appendix 20 Lifting Equipment Management Process

Line Management

1.
A. Assess Management Systems
B. Determine BSAFA® Requirements
C. Establish Regulatory Requirements
Eg. Obtain copy of Lifting Equipment Standards.
D. Develop Assessment Media

2. Conduct General Lifting Equipment Survey

3. Refer Appendix 1 Plant Assessment i.e. Forklifts, Cranes etc.

4. Establish Lifting Equipment Register

5. Assemble Team
- Operators
- Safety People
- Line Mgt
- Maintenance
- Consider Lifting Equipment Expert
- Others

6. Conduct Specific Area/ Lifting Equipment Needs Assessments
Note:
Prioritize Areas using Lifting Equipment Survey and Perceived Risk

7. Complete Lifting Equipment Management Summary

8. Prioritize Actions

9. Establish Equipment Inspection Routines
Consider Regulations and Standards

10. Formulate Inspection Media

11. Ensure Where Appropriate Licenses/Certifications are Maintained. E.g. Crane/Forklift Licences Dogging Certificates etc.

12. Formulate Procedure or Job Safety Analysis & Job Person Analysis JPA®

13. Train Employees in Procedure or JSA/JPA®

14. Assess Competency

Not Yet Competent

Competent

15. Follow Instructions and Highlight Issues.

16. Monitor and Review

Safety Professional

Ensure Media and Training is Available and Support Management with Preliminary Work.

Support Training

Build Lifting Equipment Awareness Into Inductions and Training

Support Identification of Regulation and Standard Requirements

Monitor Licenses

Support Training

Employees

Participate In Assessments

Participate in Procedure Writing

Process Change Required

Supporting Media Available

Example Media Available at practicalsafety.org

Management Systems Gap Analysis
Compliance Register
Lifting Equipment Register
Lifting Equipment management system summary
Lifting equipment checklists
Equipment pre-operational checks
Job Safety Analysis Form
Job Person Analysis JPA® Form

Appendix 21 Smoking, Drugs and Alcohol Management Process

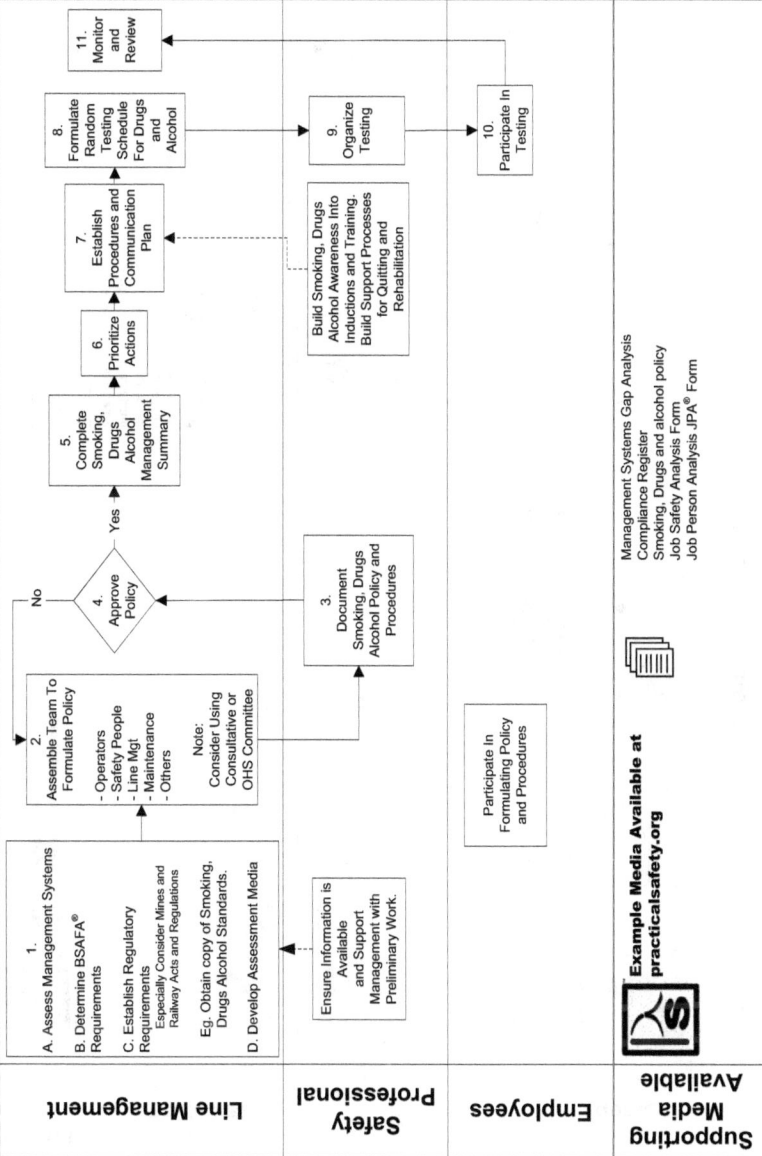

Line Management

1.
A. Assess Management Systems

B. Determine BSAFA® Requirements

C. Establish Regulatory Requirements
Especially Consider Mines and Railway Acts and Regulations

Eg. Obtain copy of Smoking, Drugs Alcohol Standards.

D. Develop Assessment Media

2.
Assemble Team To Formulate Policy
- Operators
- Safety People
- Line Mgt
- Maintenance
- Others

Note:
Consider Using Consultative or OHS Committee

4. Approve Policy — No / Yes

5. Complete Smoking, Drugs Alcohol Management Summary

6. Prioritize Actions

7. Establish Procedures and Communication Plan

8. Formulate Random Testing Schedule For Drugs and Alcohol

11. Monitor and Review

Safety Professional

Ensure Information is Available and Support Management with Preliminary Work.

3. Document Smoking, Drugs Alcohol Policy and Procedures

Build Smoking, Drugs Alcohol Awareness Into Inductions and Training. Build Support Processes for Quitting and Rehabilitation

9. Organize Testing

Employees

Participate In Formulating Policy and Procedures

10. Participate In Testing

Supporting Media Available

Example Media Available at practicalsafety.org

Management Systems Gap Analysis
Compliance Register
Smoking, Drugs and alcohol policy
Job Safety Analysis Form
Job Person Analysis JPA® Form

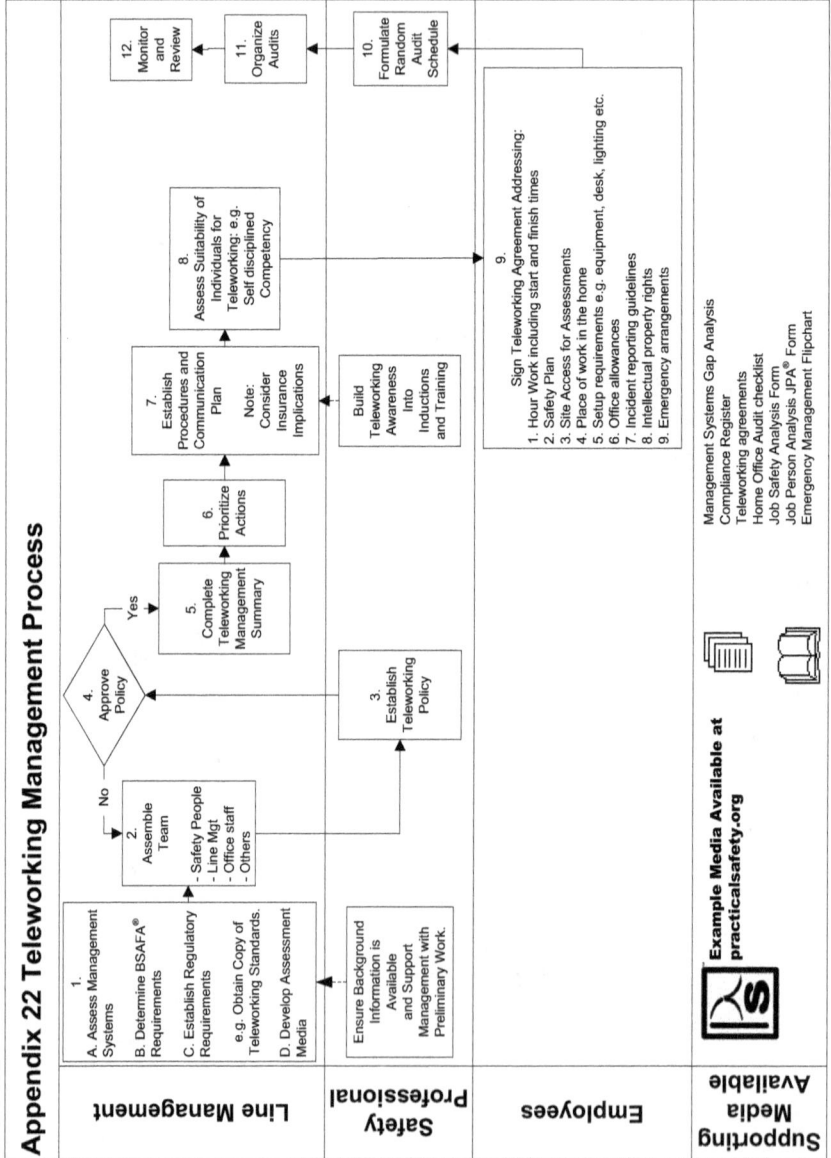

Appendix 22 Teleworking Management Process

Line Management

1.
A. Assess Management Systems
B. Determine BSAFA® Requirements
C. Establish Regulatory Requirements e.g. Obtain Copy of Teleworking Standards.
D. Develop Assessment Media

2. Assemble Team
- Safety People
- Line Mgt
- Office staff
- Others

4. Approve Policy — No / Yes

5. Complete Teleworking Management Summary

6. Prioritize Actions

7. Establish Procedures and Communication Plan
Note: Consider Insurance Implications

8. Assess Suitability of Individuals for Teleworking: e.g. Self disciplined Competency

10. Formulate Random Audit Schedule

11. Organize Audits

12. Monitor and Review

Safety Professional

Ensure Background Information is Available and Support Management with Preliminary Work.

3. Establish Teleworking Policy

Employees

Build Teleworking Awareness Into Inductions and Training

9. Sign Teleworking Agreement Addressing:
1. Hour Work including start and finish times
2. Safety Plan
3. Site Access for Assessments
4. Place of work in the home
5. Setup requirements e.g. equipment, desk, lighting etc.
6. Office allowances
7. Incident reporting guidelines
8. Intellectual property rights
9. Emergency arrangements

Supporting Media Available

Example Media Available at practicalsafety.org

Management Systems Gap Analysis
Compliance Register
Teleworking agreements
Home Office Audit checklist
Job Safety Analysis Form
Job Person Analysis JPA® Form
Emergency Management Flipchart

Appendix 23 Engineering Design Safety Management Process

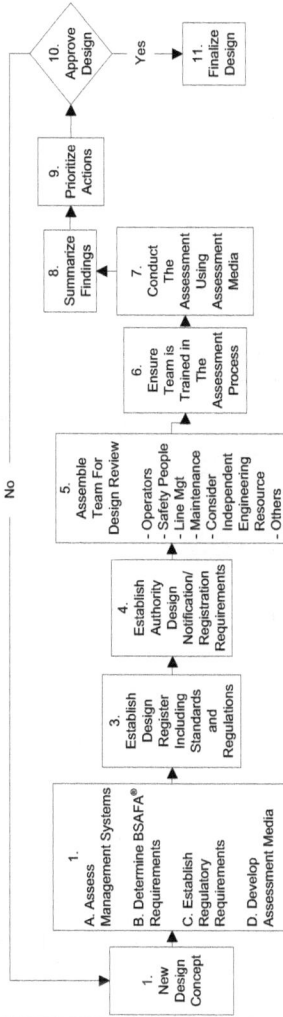

Line Management

1. New Design Concept

1.
A. Assess Management Systems
B. Determine BSAFA® Requirements
C. Establish Regulatory Requirements
D. Develop Assessment Media

3. Establish Design Register Including Standards and Regulations

4. Establish Authority Design Notification/ Registration Requirements

5. Assemble Team For Design Review
- Operators
- Safety People
- Line Mgt
- Maintenance
- Consider Independent Engineering Resource
- Others

6. Ensure Team is Trained in The Assessment Process

7. Conduct The Assessment Using Assessment Media

8. Summarize Findings

9. Prioritize Actions

10. Approve Design

No

Yes

11. Finalize Design

Safety Professional

Ensure Media and Training is Available and Support Management with Preliminary Work.

Support Identification of Standards and Regulations

Support Safety Design Review

Employees

Participate In Design Review

Note:
Further Design Reviews are Required as Part of Manufacture, Install/ Erect, Commissioning and Operation Start Up.

Supporting Media Available

Example Media Available at practicalsafety.org

Management Systems Gap Analysis
Compliance Register
Design Register
Notification Register
Standards Register
Job Safety Analysis Form
Job Person Analysis JPA® Form

Appendix 24 Contractor and Project Management Information Flowchart

Phase	Process	Records
Pre Tender	**Evaluate Proposal** 1. Identify Hazards 2. Assess Risks 3. Propose Controls	**Records** 1. Risk assessment results
Tender	**Document Tender** 1. Document Conceptual Risk Assessment Findings Including Hazards and Risks. 2. Identify Legislative Impacts 3. Identify Standards 4. Broad competency requirements	2. Tender Documents 3. Compliance Register 4. Standards Register 5. Competency Matrix
Mobilization	**Award Contract** 1. Award Contract 2. Establish confidentiality requirements 3. Determine issue resolution protocols 4. Determine Key Performance Indicators- Customer/Primary contractor and subcontractors 5. Determine Reporting Requirements 6. Establish Understanding of Project Milestones 7. Clarify use of subcontractors and how information will be transferred **Site Access** 1. Determine Access Control to site and areas on site 2. Passes (consider competency differentiation on passes) 3. Induction requirements 4. Determine workplace substance controls **Site Establishment** 1. Establish site amenities 2. Establish work areas 3. Chemical Storage areas 4. Lay down areas 5. Establish site safety committee 6. Establish toolbox meeting schedules 7. Incident notification requirements documented 8. Site observation and audit system established 9. Project execution plan in place 10. Establish People Requirements BSAFA® 11. Employee selection	6. Confidentiality agreements 7. Meeting minutes 8. KPI's 9. Site plan 10. Safety committee constitution 11. Meeting schedules 12. Project plan with milestones 13. Recruitment records 14. Medical Records 15. Job Person Analysis JPA® Records
Execution	**Execution** 1. Induct all personnel 2. Ensure competency and establish competency matrix 3. Issue Work Packages 4. Employees document hazards, risks and controls on a JSA and other supporting media. 5. Site Controller evaluates JSA and other required permits and issues Work Permit where controls are adequate. 6. All incidents reported and investigations carried out 7. Progress Meetings a Toolbox meetings held 8. Site safety committee responds to data	16. Induction, Skills and competency matrix 17. Employee personnel files 18. Work packages 19. Risk Assessments, JSA's, Permits records 20. Incident records 21. Toolbox minutes 22. Management Meeting Minutes 23. Site diary notes 23. Site safety committee minutes 24. Investigation records 25. Project plan progress 26. Variations and issue resolution records 27. Corrective action/verification records 28. Sub-Contractor Records 29. Observation and Audit records 30. Performance statistics Reactive & Proactive 31. Completion records 32. Test records
Handover	**Project Completion** 1. Hazard and risk assessments of the completed project documented 2. Competencies for operation outlined 3. Training requirements for operation outlined and/or provided 4. Maintenance information provided 5. Equipment documentation completed – manuals, guarantees 6. Lessons Learned	33. Hazard and Risk Assessments 34. Risk Control documentation 35. Competencies for operation 36. Commissioning records 37. Equipment documentation 38. Test records 39. Handover signoffs

12. REFERENCES

1. Standards Australia, "AS/NZS 4801:2001 Occupational Health and Safety Management Systems- Specifications With Guidance For Use", Sydney, 2001
2. British Standards Institution, "Occupational Health and Safety Management Systems Specification- OHSAS18001"London, 1999
3. Worksafe Victoria, "SafetyMap", Melbourne, 2002
4. Thomas R. Krause, " Leading with Safety", John Wiley and Sons, Inc, Hoboken, 2005
5. Thomas R. Krause, "The Behavior Based Safety Process: Managing Involvement for and Injury Free Culture, 2nd Edition", John Wiley and Sons, Inc, New York, 1997.
6. E.Scott Geller, "The Psychology of Safety Handbook", CRC Press LLC, Boca Raton 2001
7. John Ledwith, "Organizational Strategic Development Model", http://members.aol.com/jledwith/sm-mdl.htm, 1997
8. Paul Gustavson, Organization Planning and Design, Inc, "Organizational Systems Design Workbook", 1996
9. Robert Kaplan & David Norton, "The Balanced Scorecard," Harvard Business School Press, 1996
10. W Herbertson, "The Application of a Balanced Scorecard," QUALCOM, 2003
11. W Herbertson, "The Application of a Balanced Scorecard," QUALCOM, 2003
12. W Herbertson, "The Application of a Balanced Scorecard," QUALCOM, 2003
13. © jupiterimages 2008
14. International Organization for Standardization (ISO), "Quality Management Systems-Requirements ISO9000" 2000
15. Paul Gustavson, Organization Planning and Design, Inc, "Organizational Systems Design Workbook", 1996
16. © jupiterimages 2008
17. Standards Australia/Standards New Zealand, "AS/NZS 4801:2001 Occupational Health and Safety Management Systems – Specifications with guidance for use", Sydney, Australia 2001.
18. WorkSafe Victoria, "Plant Hazard Checklist", Melbourne, Australia, 2003. http://www.worksafe.vic.gov.au
19. © jupiterimages 2008
20. Standards Australia, "AS/NZS 4360: Risk Management" Sydney, Australia 2004
21. © jupiterimages 2008

22. E. Scott Geller, "Working safe: How to Help People Actively Care for Health and Safety, Second Edition", CRC Press LLC, Boca Raton 2001

23. Thomas R. Krause, "Leading with Safety", John Wiley and Sons, Inc, Hoboken, 2005

24. Thomas R. Krause, "The Behavior Based Safety Process: Managing Involvement for and Injury Free Culture, 2nd Edition", John Wiley and Sons, Inc, New York, 1997.

25. Reproduced with permission from Talsico International. Extracted from www.Talsico.com example Talsico ® Process Picture Maps™

26. Paul Gustavson, Organization Planning and Design, Inc, "Organizational Systems Design Workbook", 1996

27. Bird F E, *"Management guide to Loss Control"*, Institute Press, Atlanta, Georgia, USA, 1974.

28. E.I. du Pont de Nemours and Company, , "Managing Safety: Techniques that Work For Line Supervisors Edition 1", Wilmington, Delaware. 1995

29. Stewart Liff & P.A.Posey, "Seeing Is Believing: How the New Art of Visual Management Can Boost Performance Throughout Your Organization", AMACOM, A Division of the American Management Association, New York: 2004

30. Reproduced with permission from APEX Plastics Extrusions Pty Ltd, Melbourne 2008.

31. © Stockexpert 2008 – Iceberg image

13. SUBJECT INDEX

A

Aesthetics, 93

Alignment Choice Table, 20
Asbestos Risk Management Process, 176

Attributes, 17

Audit, 52

Audit Process, 131

Audit Reports, 130

Auditing, 128

Auditing Tool, 129
Authority, 52

B

Balanced Scorecard, 28

Balanced Scorecard Company, 31

Balanced Scorecard Division, 31

Balanced Scorecard Example, 30
Balanced Scorecard Individual Employee, 31

Behaviors, 17,42

Behaviors At Risk, 54

Behaviors Common, 81

Birds Triangle, 185

BSAFA® , 18, 20, 25, 61, 79

BSAFA® Desired, 21

BSAFA® Design Choice Table, 22

BSAFA® Identification Process, 80
BSAFA® in Change Management, 148

BSAFA® in Investigations, 142

BSAFA® in Observations, 132
Budget, 20, 52

C

Change Management, 36, 147
Change Management - Work Environment, 93

Change Management Process, 151

Commitment, 39, 45

Commitment and Involvement, 41, 46

Communication, 57
Communication - Physical Environment, 59

Competency, 111
Competency - Developing a Performance Model, 113

Compliance Register, 85

Compliance Assessment, 84
Confined Space Risk Management Process, 162

Confront - At Risk Behaviors, 132

Consequential Cost, 34

Consultation, 46, 56

Consultation Barriers, 57

Consultation Process, 56

Consultative committees, 56
Contractor and Project Management Information Flowchart, 192

Corrective action, 144

Corrective action form (ORA), 145

Costs, 34, 35

Costs Proactive, 34,35

Culture, 17, 42, 43, 51

Culture - Desired, 47

Culture - Mistrust, 58

Culture - Reporting Culture, 124
Customers, 28

D

Dangerous Goods and Hazardous
Substances Risk Management
Process, 165

Design Choice Table, 23, 27

Design Principles, 19
Desired Behaviors, 132

E

Electrical Risk Management Process,
171
Electromagnetic Radiation EMR Risk
Management Process, 182

Emergency Management Process, 183
Engineering Design Safety
Management Process, 191
Ergonomics Risk Management
Process, 179

Escalation Process, 138
Essential Services Management
Process, 185
Excavation Break In Risk
Management Process, 170

F

Falls Risk Management Process, 174

Feelings, 17

Financial, 28

Financial - Benefits, 34

Financial - Total Cost, 34
First Aid Provision Management
Process, 186
Fundamentals, 41

G

Gap Analysis Checklist –
Fundamentals, 63

Gap Analysis Checklist - Step 1, 78

Gap Analysis Checklist - Step 2, 83

Gap Analysis Checklist - Step 3, 87

Gap Analysis Checklist - Step 4, 95

Gap Analysis Checklist - Step 5, 106

Gap Analysis Checklist - Step 6, 122

Gap Analysis Checklist - Step 7, 155
Goals, 61

H

Hazard Definition, 64

Hazard Identification, 64
Hazard Identification and Risk
Assessment, 64
Hazard Identification and Risk
Assessment Management Process,
71
Hazardous Substances Assessments,
74

Hazards Types List, 65

Health Assessments, 136

Hierarchy of Controls, 102
Hot Work Risk Management Process,
169

I

Iceberg Principle, 124

Incident Causes, 142

Incident Investigation, 142

Inspection Checklist, 136

Inspections, 134

Intervention, 133

Investigations - Conducting, 143
Isolation Lock Out Tag Out Risk
Management Process, 172

J

Job Person Analysis JPA®, 79

Job Safety Analysis JSA, 100
Job Safety Analysis JSA Form, 102

L

Latent Measures, 124

Latent Measures Examples, 125

Lead Risk Management Process, 181

Leadership, 44

Leadership Transition, 44
Lifting Equipment Management
Process, 188

M

Management Behaviors, 43

Management Commitment, 43
Management Commitment Measure,
42

Management Involvement, 42
Managing Adhoc Work Through
Work Permits, 187
Manual Handling Risk Management
Process, 178

Material Safety Data Sheets, 74

Measurement, 30

Measuring and Reporting, 123

Mission, 23
Monitoring Processes, 123

N

Noise Risk Management Process, 175

O

Objectives, 30, 61

Observation, 43

Observation Analysis, 134

Observation Form, 134

Observation Intervention, 133

Observations, 52, 132

ORA Form, 38

Organizational Design, 11
Organizational Design External
Environment, 12

Organizational Framework, 11

Organizational Model, 24

Outcomes, 16, 21

Outcomes - Desired, 21, 22, 47

P

People, 17, 28, 17
Performance - Monitor and Review,
123

Performance Model, 112,116
Performance Model - Assessment,
116

Performance Model - Components,
116

Performance Model Process, 113

Planning, 93

Plant Hazard Checklist, 73

Plant Risk Management Process, 161

Practical Isolation Process, 173

Practical Safety Process Model®, 40

Practical Safety Process®, 39

Principles, 49

Proactive Measures, 124

Proactive Measures - examples, 126

Procedure Development Process, 101
Procedures - Standard Operating
Procedure Example, 104
Procedures - Writing Procedures, 100,
121, 122
Processes - Asbestos Risk
Management Process, 176

Processes - Audit, 131
Processes - BSAFA® Identification
Process, 80

Processes - Change Management, 151
Processes - Confined Space Risk
Management Process, 162
Processes - Contractor and Project
Management Information Flowchart,
192
Processes - Dangerous Goods and
Hazardous Substances Risk
Management Process, 165

Processes - Determining Safety Values and Principles, 50

Processes - Electrical Risk Management Process, 171

Processes - Electromagnetic Radiation EMR Risk Management Process, 182

Processes - Emergency Management Process, 183

Processes - Engineering Design Safety Management Process, 191

Processes - Ergonomics Risk Management Process, 179

Processes - Essential Services Management Process, 185

Processes - Excavation Break In Risk Management Process, 170

Processes - Falls Risk Management Process, 174

Processes - First Aid Provision Management Process, 186

Processes - Hazard Identification and Risk Assessment Management Process, 71

Processes - Hot Work Risk Management Process, 169

Processes - Isolation Lock Out Tag Out Risk Management Process, 172

Processes - Lead Risk Management Process, 181

Processes - Lifting Equipment Management Process, 188

Processes - Managing Adhoc Work Through Work Permits, 187

Processes - Manual Handling Risk Management Process, 178

Processes - Noise Risk Management Process, 175

Processes - Performance Model, 113

Processes - Plant Risk Management Process, 161

Processes - Practical Isolation Process, 173

Processes - Procedure Development, 101

Processes - Rehabilitation, 140

Processes - Safety Planning, 53

Processes - Safety Responsibility and Authority Process, 55

Processes - Smoking, Drugs Alcohol Management Process, 189

Processes - Teleworking Management Process, 190

Processes - Traffic Risk Management Process, 180

Processes - Vision, 48

Processes - Working With Asbestos Risk Management Process, 177

Processes- Safety Goals and Objectives, 62

Project Observations, 45

R

Recognition, 51, 146

Records - Management, 153

Records - Register, 153

Recruitment, 111

Rehabilitation, 137

Rehabilitation - Manipulation, 139

Rehabilitation - Process, 140

Responsibility, 52

Responsibility Chart, 54

Risk Assessment,64, 67

Risk Assessment Media, 72

Risk Standard, 67

Role Modelling, 58

S

Safe Systems of Work, 98

Safety, 30

Safety - Financial Benefits, 34

Safety - Goals and Objectives Process, 62

Safety - Induction, 58

Safety - Maturity, 44

Safety - Objectives, 30

Safety - Performance Ratios, 127

Safety - Planning, 51

Safety - Planning Process, 53

Safety - Processes (see processes)

Safety - Professional Qualities, 157
Safety - Responsibility and Authority
Process, 55

Safety - System Design, 21
Safety - Values and Principles
Process, 49

Skills, 17

Skills - Matrix, 120
Smoking, Drugs Alcohol
Management Process, 189

Standard, 39

Standard - Risk Standard, 67

Standards Checklists, 85

Statistics, 52
Step 1 - Identify Hazards and Assess
Risks, 41, 64
Step 2 - Identify Desired People
Requirements BSAFA® , 41, 79

Step 3 - Evaluate Compliance, 41, 84
Step 4 - Ensure Safe Physical Work
Environment, 41, 92
Step 5 - Develop Safe Systems of
Work, 41, 98

Step 6 - Assess Competency, 41, 111
Step 7 - Monitor and Review
Performance, 41, 123

Strategic Planning Calendar, 29

Strategic Planning Cycle, 28

Strategy, 28

Strategy - Alignment, 32

Strategy - Balanced Scorecard, 28

Strategy - Cascade, 33

Suggestion Schemes, 56

System Choices - Differentiating, 25
System Choices - Differentiating
System, 25
System Choices - People, 25
System Choices - Recognition, 26

System Choices - Renewal, 28
System Choices - Renewal System,
28

System Choices - Reward, 26
System Choices - Reward and
Recognition, 26

System Choices - Unifying, 23
System Choices - Unifying Choices,
23

System Design Choices, 21, 23
System Failures, 142

T

Target, 41

Task, 82

Technology, 93
Teleworking Management Process,
190

TFCS, 34

Toolbox, 56
Traffic Risk Management Process,
180

Transition, 36

V

Values, 49

Variance Chart, 114

Variance Control Table, 116
Variance Safety,Quality
Environmental, 115

Vision, 23

Vision Process, 48
Visual Factory, 135

W

Work Instruction, 105

Work Permit Process, 165
Workplace Substances, 73
Working With Asbestos Risk
Management Process, 177

VISIT OUR WEBSITE TO ACCESS PRACTICAL RESOURCES THAT WILL HELP YOU IMPLEMENT YOUR SAFETY SYSTEM

Go to…

www.practicalsafety.org

14. RESOURCE CENTRE

The following is a representation of resources that are available at **www.practicalsafety.org.** They are designed to fit within the Practical Safety 7 Step program. Our website provides valuable workplace information, training guides, model assessments, useful links and step by step procedures complete with the media required to enable the user to achieve the goal of Zero Harm.

Standard Operating Procedures

- Use of Observations, Recommendations & Actions (ORA), Summary of Hazard ID, Assessment of Risk and Risk Controls ☐
- Management of Change ☐
- Prevention of Hearing Loss from Noise in the Workplace ☐
- Induction and Assimilation
- Workplace Communication and Toolbox Meetings
- Contractor Selection
- Planning and Scheduling of Work
- Job Request, Registration & Authorisation ☐
- Use of Job Safety Analysis (JSA)
- Use of Job Person/People Analysis (JPA)®
- Lock out and Tagging of Plant
- Front End Loader Serviceability
- Excavator / Bobcat Serviceability
- Vehicle Serviceability
- Safe Forklift Operation
- Lifting, Slinging and Dogging
- Use and Handling of Static Straps
- Organisation Design
- Management of Hazardous Manual Handing Tasks ☐

- Guide for Installation / Restoration of Chemical Storage and Handling Facilities other than Flammable Liquids Class 3 ☐
- Flammable & Combustible Cat 1-5 Tanks ☐
- Incident / Near Miss Investigation and Reporting ☐
- Management of Plant Safety ☐
- Decommissioning, Dismantling and Disposal of Plant ☐
- Management of Workplace Substances ☐
- Transport of Dangerous Goods by Road ☐
- Diesel Handling (Class C1 Combustible) ☐
- Management of Confined Spaces ☐
- Prevention of Falls from Height ☐
- Managing Insitu Asbestos in the Workplace ☐
- Traffic Management Planning ☐
- Environmental Management ☐
- Issue Resolution ☐
- Rehabilitation ☐
- Drawing Standards and Requirements ☐
- Emergency Management Planning ☐
- Performance ☐

Training Manuals

- The Practical Safety Guide to Managing Workplace Substances ☐
- The Practical Safety Guide to Managing Plant Safety - Project Managers Manual ☐
- The Practical Safety Guide to Managing Plant Safety - Team Leaders Manual ☐
- The Practical Safety Guide to Emergency Management ☐

Flowcharts

- Safety Vision Process ☐
- Safety Values and Principles Process ☐
- Safety Goals and Objectives ☐
- Role of Observations, Recommendations and Actions ☐
- Management of Change ☐
- Contractor Selection ☐
- Lifting, Slinging and Dogging ☐
- Principles JSA & Work Instructions ☐
- Dangerous Goods / Hazardous Substances ☐
- Substances Purchasing ☐
- Confined Spaces ☐
- Managing Insitu Asbestos in the Workplace ☐
- Issue Resolution ☐
- Developing Performance Models and Assessing Competency ☐

- Safety Planning Process ☐
- Safety Responsibility and Authority Process ☐
- BSAFA® Identification Process ☐
- Workplace Communication and Toolbox Meetings ☐
- Induction and Assimilation ☐
- Engineering and Maintenance Control ☐
- Emergency Management ☐
- Management of Plant Safety - Project Mgr ☐
- Installed and Operating Plant - Employer ☐
- Manual Handling ☐
- Prevention of Falls ☐
- Traffic Management ☐
- Environmental Management ☐

Supporting Checklists and Resource Media

The Core Forms
- Observations Recommendations & Actions ☐
- Risk Ranking Guidelines ☐
- Hazard and Control Measure Summary ☐
- Risk Control Review ☐
- Job Safety Analysis (JSA) ☐
- Job Person/People Analysis (JPA)®

Organisational Design
- Safety Systems Element Comparisons ☐
- Determining BSAFA®'s ☐
- BSAFA® Alignment Choice Table ☐
- BSAFA® Design Choice Table ☐
- Design Choice Action Summary ☐
- Scorecards ☐
- Compliance Gap Analysis ☐
- Responsibility Chart ☐
- Variance Chart Excel Template ☐

Policies
- Health and Safety ☐
- Environmental ☐
- Emergency Management ☐
- Sexual Harassment ☐
- Drug and Alcohol ☐
- Rehabilitation ☐

Induction and Assimilation
- Induction Guide ☐
- Visitor Induction Guide ☐
- Questionnaire ☐
- Declaration of Induction ☐
- Employee Induction Register ☐
- Employee Training Registers ☐

Contractor Selection
- Expression of Interest / RFT Statement ☐
- Contractor Induction Register ☐
- Contractor Selection ☐
- Contractor Assessment Guide ☐
- Standard Letters - Contractor Selection ☐
- Contractor Management System Checklist ☐

Supporting Checklists and Resource Media

Health and Safety Committee Model
- Health and Safety Committee Constitution
- Health and Safety Committee Agenda
- Health and Safety Committee Minutes
- Meetings - A Guide to Effectiveness

Workplace Communication
- Workplace Communication and Meeting Record
- Workplace Attendance Record

Engineering and Maintenance Control
- Simple Job Request Register
- Work Order
- Job Safety Analysis (JSA) Form
- Job Person / People Analysis (JPA)® Form
- JSA Guidance Note and Examples
- Personal Tag / Out of Service Tag
- Isolation System Checklist
- Excavator Serviceability Checklists
- Front End Loader Serviceability Checklists
- Bobcat Serviceability Checklists
- Vehicle Serviceability Checklists
- Forklift Serviceability Checklists
- Crane Pre-operating Inspection Checklist
- Register of Lifting Slings
- Inspection Checklist Flat Synthetic Webbing Slings
- Inspection Checklists Chain Slings
- Inspection Checklist Wire Rope Slings
- Class 3 Tank Inspection Checklist
- Hot Work Permit

Emergency Management Planning
- Emergency Management Planning C'cklist
- Response Procedures Template
- Emergency Information Book Template
- Business Recovery Plans Template
- Memory Aids
- Evacuation Exercise & Scenario Example

Emergency Management Planning cont..
- Internal Incident / Near Miss Investigation Report
- Security Incident and Investigation Report
- Incident Log
- Debriefing Report
- Essential Services Checklist
- Threatening Communications - Telephone Checklist
- ECO Model Example
- Dangerous Goods Manifest Template

Incident Reporting and Recording
- Workplace Incident and Dangerous Occurrence Notification and Form
- Incident Report - Fire Authority
- Incident Log
- Security Incident & Investigation Report
- Internal Incident / Near Miss Investigation Report
- Incident Log
- Debriefing Report

Plant Safety
- Detailed Description of Duties and Obligations
- Plant Safety Management Systems Checklist

Project Manager
- Hazard and Risk Statement
- Expression of Interest General Statement
- Explanatory Letter - Plant and Equipment Suppliers
- Plant Identification and Safety Data
- Hazard Guidance Sheet
- Plant Register
- Regulations and Standards Register
- Plant Notification & Registration Record
- Schedule of Operator Competencies

Employer
- Plant Register
- Plant Notification & Registration Record
- Employee Certification Register
- Regulations and Standards Register

Supporting Checklists and Resource Media

Plant Safety - Employer cont..

- Hazard Guidance Sheet ☐
- Plant Hazard Checklist ☐
- Other Exposures - Operating Environment ☐
  - Scaffolding ☐
  - Decommissioning ☐
  - Plant Not in Use ☐
  - Powered Mobile Plant ☐

Dangerous Goods / Hazardous Substances

- Management Systems Checklist ☐
- Workplace Substances Worksheet ☐
- Workplace Substances Register ☐
- Dangerous Goods Register ☐
- Dangerous Goods Manifest ☐
- Internal Note ☐
- Standard Letter to Chemical Suppliers ☐
- Standard Labels ☐
- Verification Checklists against AS/NZS ☐
- MSDS Review ☐
- Workplace Assessment Sheet ☐
- Product Identification & Hazard
  Implication - Dangerous Goods ☐
- Purchasing Requests and Forms ☐
- Example Labels ☐

Manual Handling

- Manual Handling Task Register ☐
- Risk Assessment and Control Measure
  Form ☐

Confined Spaces

- Confined Space Register ☐
- Confined Space Identification Checklist ☐
- Confined Space Management Summary ☐
- Confined Space Assessment ☐
- Confined Space Entry Permit ☐
- Confined Space Entry / Exit Register ☐
- Confined Space Air Monitoring Record ☐

Inspection Checklists

- Site Condition Checklist ☐
- Essential Services Checklist ☐
- Housekeeping Checklist ☐
- First Aid Checklist ☐
- Signage Review ☐
- Electrical Hazards Checklists ☐
- Office Monitoring Checklist ☐
- Offsite Job Safety Checklist ☐

Asbestos

- Asbestos Containing Material ID Sheet ☐
- Asbestos Containing Material Risk
  Assessment and Control Summary ☐
- Asbestos Containing Material Register ☐
- Asbestos Containing Signage and labels ☐
- Asbestos Containing Material Risk Control
  Review ☐

Traffic Management

- Traffic Management Safety Overview ☐
- Traffic Management System Basic Audit ☐
- Typical Signage Checklist ☐
- Typical Truck Loading Safety Instruction ☐
- Typical Truck Management Drawing Legend ☐
- Example Observations, Recommendations
  and Actions ☐
- Typical Traffic Management Drawing ☐

Environmental Management

- Environmental Policy ☐
- Environmental Management Checklist ☐
- Environmental Management Verification
  summary ☐

Noise

- Noise Hazard Identification Checklist ☐

Prevention of Falls from Heights

- Guidance Checklist ☐
- Prevention of Falls Register ☐
- Fall Hazard Assessment and Risk Control
  Summary ☐
- Single Task Fall Hazard Assessment and
  Risk Control Summary ☐

QUICK ORDER FORM

Website orders: www.practicalsafety.org

Email orders: orders@practicalsafety.com.au

Fax orders: + 61 3 9793 2077. Send this form.

Postal orders:
Practical Safety International Pty Ltd
PO Box 414
Salamander Bay, NSW   2317, Australia
Please include Cheque/Money Order made out to
'Practical Safety International Pty Ltd'

Please send me _____ copies of **'The Practical Safety Guide to Zero Harm'**

@ \$A 27.50 incl GST   \$A
+ Postage & Handling   \$A _____
                                      \$A _____

Standard Postage Estimates

Std Australia - \$A 9.95 for first book and POA for additional books
Std International - \$A 15.95 for first book and POA for additional books
- Bulk discounts for shipping may apply

Note: Postage and Handling Charges are estimates only and are subject to change without notice

Name: _____

Company: _____

Address: _____

_____

_____ **Postcode:** _____

Telephone: _____

Email: _____

PLEASE CHARGE MY CREDIT CARD BELOW

Valid Until: ☐☐ / ☐☐   **Amount** \$A _____

Name on Card: _____

Signature: _____

Date: _____

Credit Card (x)   ☐ **MasterCard**   ☐ **Visa**

BECOME A LICENSEE TO SELL AND USE OUR METHODOLOGIES AND MATERIALS

PRACTICAL SAFETY INTERNATIONAL PTY LTD

CONSULTANT / LICENSEE INFORMATION

Go to...

www.practicalsafety.org

QUICK ORDER FORM

Website orders: www.practicalsafety.org

Email orders: orders@practicalsafety.com.au

Fax orders: + 61 3 9793 2077. Send this form.

Postal orders: Practical Safety International Pty Ltd
PO Box 414
Salamander Bay, NSW   2317, Australia
Please include Cheque/Money Order made out to
'Practical Safety International Pty Ltd'

Please send me _____ copies of **'The Practical Safety Guide to Zero Harm'**
@ $A27.50 incl GST $A
+ Postage & Handling $A _____
                                             $A _____

Standard Postage Estimates

Std Australia   - $A 9.95 for first book and POA for additional books
Std International   - $A 15.95 for first book and POA for additional books
                           - Bulk discounts for shipping may apply

Note: Postage and Handling Charges are estimates only and are subject to change without notice

Name: _____
Company: _____
Address: _____
_____
_____   **Postcode:** _____
Telephone: _____
Email: _____

PLEASE CHARGE MY CREDIT CARD BELOW

Valid Until: ☐☐ / ☐☐   **Amount** $A

Name on Card: _____

Signature: _____

Date: _____

Credit Card (x)   ☐ **MasterCard**   ☐ **Visa**

QUICK ORDER FORM

Website orders: www.practicalsafety.org

Email orders: orders@practicalsafety.com.au

Fax orders: + 61 3 9793 2077. Send this form.

Postal orders:
Practical Safety International Pty Ltd
PO Box 414
Salamander Bay, NSW   2317, Australia
Please include Cheque/Money Order made out to
'Practical Safety International Pty Ltd'

Please send me _____ copies of **'The Practical Safety Guide to Zero Harm Chinese'**

@ $A27.50 incl GST $A

+ Postage & Handling $A_____

$A_____

Standard Postage Estimates

Std Australia   - $A 9.95 for first book and POA for additional books
Std International   - $A 15.95 for first book and POA for additional books
- Bulk discounts for shipping may apply

Note: Postage and Handling Charges are estimates only and are subject to change without notice

Name: _____

Company: _____

Address: _____

_____

_____   **Postcode:** _____

Telephone: _____

Email: _____

PLEASE CHARGE MY CREDIT CARD BELOW

Valid Until: [ ] [ ] / [ ] [ ]   **Amount** $A_____

Name on Card: _____

Signature: _____

Date: _____

Credit Card (x)   [ ] **MasterCard**   [ ] **Visa**

This book comes out of a desire to make a difference. It's a passion driven out of a personal loss. I want to share what knowledge I've learnt after working 20 years in Manufacturing , Mining, and Refinery businesses in the hope that you not only read the information, but you apply it in your workplaces. I know what it is like to deal with the day to day issues. You will find that this is not just a safety book, as safety cannot be tackled that way. It's a whole of business approach that is essential to driving towards Zero Harm. What you get in this book is what's worked for me. My hope is that it adds value to your business by helping you to achieve Zero Harm.

Wayne Herbertson

Wayne Herbertson has a varied educational background holding a Master of Applied Science Metallurgy, a Bachelor of Science Multidiscipline, a Diploma in Safety and an Associate Diploma in Theology. This combined with broad industry experience with companies including, Bradken, BHP, Tubemakers, Siemens, Johnson Matthey, Comalco, Peko Wallsend and you have someone with a rich breadth of knowledge. He has produced various articles on topics as varied as quality management systems , business scorecards, the environment, safety and spirituality in leadership. He is currently General Manager Human Resources at Bradken Resources Pty Ltd and Director of Practical Safety International.

"Love your neighbor as yourself,
Love does no harm to its neighbor"

Rom 13:9-10 NIV 1985